BULLEN'S VOYAGES

BULLEN'S VOYAGES
THE LIFE OF FRANK T BULLEN

Sailor, Whaler, Author

Alston Kennerley

Seaforth
PUBLISHING

For Janet

Copyright © Alston Kennerley 2022

First published in Great Britain in 2022 by
Seaforth Publishing,
A division of Pen & Sword Books Ltd,
47 Church Street,
Barnsley S70 2AS

www.seaforthpublishing.com
British Library Cataloguing in Publication Data
A catalogue record for this book is available from the British Library

ISBN 978 1 3990 7427 8 (HARDBACK)
ISBN 978 1 3990 7428 5 (EPUB)
ISBN 978 1 3990 7429 2 (KINDLE)

Pen & Sword Books Limited incorporates the imprints of Atlas,
Archaeology, Aviation, Discovery, Family History, Fiction, History, Maritime, Military,
Military Classics, Politics, Select, Transport, True Crime, Air World, Frontline Publishing,
Leo Cooper, Remember When, Seaforth Publishing, The Praetorian Press, Wharncliffe
Local History, Wharncliffe Transport, Wharncliffe True Crime and White Owl

Typeset by Mac Style
Printed and bound in Great Britain by CPI Group (UK) Ltd, Croydon, CR0 4YY

Contents

List of Illustrations

Introduction and Acknowledgements

From the mid 1890s until his death at the age of fifty-seven in 1915, Frank Thomas Bullen produced a stream of magazine and newspaper articles, wrote thirty-seven books and delivered innumerable public lantern slide lectures. All this was substantially based on his experiences in merchant seafaring and shipping, and in the physical wonders of the oceans, which he keenly observed at every opportunity. His life was a rags to relative riches story, starting with a broken home, and followed with very limited schooling, becoming an uncared-for orphan, and then sea service, often in the dregs of merchant shipping. Innate ability, curiosity and self-education carried him forward intellectually to maritime qualifications, through a decade and more of humdrum shore employment into the 1890s, when his realisation of his ability to write (emerging since 1887) could sustain him without other paid employment. In the final phase of his life, and a self-employed author and lecturer, he not only maintained an enormous literary output, but was also embraced by London's literati, while as an evangelical, he was welcomed in religious circles. His principal works were lauded by the critics, in Britain, the British colonies, and the United States, taking him all over Britain and leading to overseas tours.

Many of his short pieces relate to episodes of Bullen's sea life, some of which are accessible in seven volumes of his collected essays. But he also narrated his experience in five fuller autobiographical volumes: *Cruise of the Cachalot, Log of a Sea Waif, With Christ at Sea, Confessions of a Tradesman* and *Recollections*. A century after his death, a set of these volumes can be difficult to pull together through the second-hand book trade. Yet interest remains, especially in his output on whaling, and there is a place for a single-volume biography. This is attempted with this volume. These books, and many of his separate essays, are effectively Bullen's own notes about his life and constitute the primary source here. Because his sea life is so important to his literary output and because the voyage records of almost all his ships can be traced through state-generated British maritime records, this biography concentrates on Bullen's time at sea, elaborating, explaining, and sometimes correcting his detail. Bullen's own input colours every page.

Bullen was born in the same year (some six months ahead) as Joseph Conrad, and as both became maritime writers, there is an obvious comparison to be made between the two. Conrad's life and literature fills many fathoms of library shelves with literary criticism and biographical examination. Bullen attracts no such adulation, and this volume may well be a first chronological contribution.

I first encountered Bullen in the early 1990s, when Roger Morriss, then on the staff of the National Maritime Museum, Greenwich, recommended me to the editors of *The Dictionary of National Biography* to draft the entry for Bullen in a proposed new DNB volume. The NMM provided images of Bullen's certificates of competency and his applications to prime my research. Since then I have been helped by generations of archivists and curators from the archives named in the Bibliography, enabling me to accumulate images of many of the maritime documents on which Bullen's name appears. Their help is gratefully acknowledged.

'Voyage' is used in this work to define Bullen's periods away from the United Kingdom, while 'passage' describes movement between one port and the next.

1

From Infant to Street Urchin

5 April 1857 to 23 March 1870

For the first nine years of his life Frank Thomas Bullen, apparently known throughout his childhood as Tommy, was based in the small part of London where he was born, less than a mile northwest of the Paddington railway station. This was a finger of densely housed land, developed in the 1860s, between the Great Western Railway tracks to the south and the Grand Union Canal to the north, which was bisected by the Harrow Road, a main thoroughfare trending there northwest and southeast.[1] Northwards, this road crossed the canal, beyond which was the Lock Hospital adjacent to the Paddington Workhouse. Regular attendance at the chapel of the Lock Hospital, increasingly functioning as an Anglican district church, would become a feature of Bullen's early life.[2] The Bullen home he remembered was in 15 Desborough Terrace, the fifth side street from the canal, branching off Harrow Road on its southwest side. A row of some twenty terraced houses ran down to the main railway line between Paddington and the West Country to which Bullen, as a toddler, was from time to time taken to watch the trains passing. At the railway track, Desborough Terrace turns sharp right and parallel to the railway, to accommodate a further dozen terraced properties. Bullen recalls meeting a waiter in Quebec, Canada, probably during his Canadian tour in 1908, in which he identifies 'a little turning off Jonson Place, Harrow Road, called Alfred Road', as his birthplace, next door to where the waiter originated. Alfred Road was the second turning from the canal and Jonson Mews a court nearby. The birth certificate names 40 Alfred Road, on 5 April 1857, as Frank Thomas Bullen's birthplace, his father as Frank Bullen, a journeyman stonemason, and mother as Margaret Bullen, formerly Brown.[3]

By 1861, the extended Bullen family was in Desborough Terrace, about halfway between Harrow Road and the railway tracks.[4] This had been renamed Torquay Street by the 1890s, possibly because there was a Desborough Street close by, northeast of Harrow Road.[5] On 28 June 1863 Tommy was baptised, along with a cousin, at Holy Trinity Church, Bishop's Road, Paddington, a quarter of a mile from the station, when the address given was 23 Alfred Road.[6] Frequent changes of addresses when renting houses or rooms were very common, though the possibility remains that, as Tommy's baptism was an addition to arrangements made for his cousin's baptism, the cousin's address was recorded against his name. Certainly, Bullen's narratives of his early years in *With Christ at Sea* (1900) and *Recollections* (1914) give the impression that, until the break-up of the household in about 1866, he was being cared for at 15 Desborough Terrace.[7] In *Recollections* he deals immediately with the disappearance of his mother:[8]

For before even I, precocious as I undoubtedly was, grew old enough to know intelligently, or say at eighteen months old, my father and mother quarrelled, the weaker vessel was thrown out, and myself, as well as an elder sister of whom I know nothing except that she did exist, were consigned to the care of a maiden aunt by my father, with a promise, never redeemed, to pay something towards the expense of keeping us. That shadowy sister very wisely took the earliest opportunity of becoming a shade, so I remember nothing of her but what I have been told ... [Since then] once and once only I had seen my mother. A heap of old clothing like a pile of autumn leaves was shown me, and I was told that *that* was my mother who had come to see me but had been taken ill. I was frightened, and ran to hide myself. I never saw her again.

His elder sister is possibly the birth in Paddington registered in the fourth quarter of 1855 as Mary Anne Bullen, and born to a mother whose maiden name was Brown.[9] Further, two deaths of a Mary Ann Bullen, born in 1855 in Paddington are recorded in 1857 and 1859.[10] Infant mortality was considerable in the nineteenth century, and could account for the infant's disappearance.

It was his maiden aunt, aged forty at the time of the 1861 census, who made herself his mother substitute. Curiously, Bullen does not name her, and this census entry gives only her initials, M A (Matilda Ann), and the Bullen surname. Certainly, Frank Thomas Bullen was the product of a broken home. His father, Frank Robert Bullen (twenty-five in 1861), seems to have taken little interest in him. Bullen implies that he was fond of gambling and of drink. As a journeyman stonemason, at a time when London was growing rapidly, he was presumably readily employable, but this was peripatetic work and there may well have been times when he had to seek accommodation away from the Desborough Terrace household, headed in 1861 by 61-year-old John Bullen (father of Frank Robert and grandfather of Frank Thomas), a doorkeeper. Also resident on that census night in addition to Aunt Matilda Ann, a dressmaker, were another aunt, Kathy Bullen, aged thirty, also a dressmaker, and an uncle Edwin Bullen, aged twenty-seven, a dairyman. Frank Thomas was listed as four years old. He remembers quizzing his Aunt Matilda about family members who lived or visited the home in Desborough Terrace:[11]

'Auntie, you used to have quite a lot of people to dinner. I can remember Grandfather, Uncle John, Uncle George, Uncle Tom, Uncle Ted and Aunt Kitty.'

'Ah,' she replied, 'yes, but you never knew that my poor fingers were working for them all, except Aunt Kitty – she always worked hard enough for her keep.'

Possibly young Tommy mixed up Uncle John with Grandfather John, and Uncle Ted may be Uncle Edwin. Uncles named Tom and George were not present on census night 1861.[12] The former has not been identified, but George was the shipmaster who would reluctantly take Tommy to sea when he was a little older.

From an exploration of the family background in earlier census returns, there was a concentration of Bullen family members born in country locations near Yeovil in Somerset. This was close to the border with Dorset, and birth locations in Dorset also appear. In 1841 a family best matching the grouping in 1861 was that of John and Mary Bullen, both born in Somerset in 1801, resident on the outskirts of Bristol, where John's occupation was a butcher. The eldest child was daughter Matilda, aged twenty. Sons George and Henry were aged fifteen, and may well have been twins, Edwin Bullen was nine and son Frank Robert was aged five.[13] By 1851 this family appears to have moved to London, Paddington, and were housed in 15 Jonson's Place, off Alfred Road, and only a few minutes walk from Desborough Terrace, the family residence in 1861. In 1851 John Bullen was a cow keeper/dairyman, as were his sons Edwin and Frank Robert. Pursuing the Henry Bullen, close in age to Captain George Bullen, the 1871 census shows him living at 15 Jonson's Place and practising as a cheesemonger. By 1881, his family is in Hackney, where Henry continued his calling until retirement. This is not far from the residence of George, in St Pancras, the address he gives on the Agreement and Account of Crew of the barque *Caroline*, Frank Thomas's first ship.

Bullen's introduction to religion was a training his aunt delivered from an early age, teaching him to say his prayers each night by his bed and on his knees. As an untutored evangelical, his aunt emphasised formal religious behaviours, including learning prayers by heart and attendance on Sundays at the Lock Chapel. Sunday may well have been taken up with the morning service, Sunday school in the afternoon, and when old enough, the evening service. Meals at home were probably started with saying 'Grace', and possibly ended with a 'thanksgiving'. He found himself in the Lock Chapel choir when it was formed, at 'a ludicrously early age', when he learned favourite hymns of the day, and would later find himself called upon to sing in the fo'c'sles of several of his ships. He remembered well, and with great affection, the Sunday School superintendent, Miss Emily Hensley, with whom he seems to have had contact later in life after leaving the sea. *Cruise of the Cachalot* is dedicated to her. It is well established that the Sunday School movement delivered much more than religion to the less advantaged members of congregations, of which literacy was perhaps the most important. Bullen places the Sunday School a little way along the canal from the Lock Chapel, above the 'Westbourne Park Railway Station'.

His aunt's fear of the dirt of the streets meant that at home Bullen was corralled within the Desborough Terrace house and its wall-enclosed garden. There is no further mention of the sister also placed in his aunt's care. His description is of a child making his own amusement, and reading the few books the household contained. He recollects the family Bible and a copy of Milton's *Paradise Lost*. The former he disliked, perhaps because of the reading and recitation of passages in church and Sunday School, but he loved the latter, despite it really being too advanced a text for a child of his age. He had no recollection of learning to read and write, being a natural reader, and was probably well ahead of other children of his age. Such reading as he had, meant that his vocabulary was enlarged beyond that of his contemporaries, with perhaps more misuse of words he little understood than normal.

Living next door to a 'Dame School' kept by three maiden ladies, his aunt must have found the money to pay the fees for the basic education they were able to offer, when he was about five, and at seven to attend a day school, possibly an elementary school promoted by the National School Society, the Anglican educational charity of 1811. The nearest 'national' school to Desborough Terrace was probably St Stephen's National School in Westbourne Park Road, across the railway tracks from the western end of Desborough Terrace, which were easily crossed by a footbridge and footpaths offering quite a short walk to school. This elementary school had been established in 1859 in temporary premises. Being under local Church of England management, the school was recognised and supported by the National School Society, which was charged with the distribution of government education grants. School attendance was not yet compulsory or free, so reduced fees remained payable, known as school pence, one or two pennies per day. In 1851 the National Society was supporting 17,015 church schools with 955,865 pupils.[14] Tommy Bullen, with his religious training rooted in the Lock Chapel, and his intelligence, would surely have been welcome at St Stephen's National School. Bullen is generous about Aunt Matilda's contribution to his early upbringing, being:

> ... entirely due to the good influence of my poor aunt, who, amidst all her worries, always kept a cosy corner for me. My education was her chief care ... A worse preparation for a rough-and-tumble with the world could hardly be imagined, but my poor auntie did her best, the best she knew for me, and kept me, as far as in her lay, unspotted from the world.[15]

The break-up of the Desborough Terrace household in 1866, according to *Recollections*, appears to have been triggered by the removal of three of the regular occupants through marriage and death. Bullen, without naming them, says that an uncle died, then his grandfather, John. Soon after Tommy had had that final glimpse of his mother, he says his Auntie Matilda passed away, but that most significant death, as far as the care of Bullen was concerned, must be incorrect as census returns show Aunt Matilda alive in 1891, in the household of a nephew, Andrew Smith.[16] The uncle, a gentlemen's groom according to Bullen, may have been Edwin Bullen, named in the 1861 and 1871 censuses with Aunt Matilda. If so, he had become an invalid, suffering from some disease of the throat. Bullen gives his occupation as gentleman's groom, but the census entries are dairyman and pork butcher respectively. He attended Dr Sieveking at St Mary's Hospital, close to Paddington Station, and took Tommy with him when making his outpatient's visits.[17] Talk of death was avoided in Tommy's hearing, but when the sufferer died and was lying in a coffin in the house, after bedtime Tommy sneaked out into the room and took a look at the face of his uncle in the moonlight, with his jaw strapped up with a rag, thus scaring himself back to his bed. However, both Uncle

Edwin and Aunt Matilda, alive in 1871, were living in lodgings in 9 Stalham Street, a few minutes' walk from Desborough Terrace. Further, Bullen's assertion that he was on his own from 1866 is surely undermined by his name appearing on the same census form in 1871.[18] His age is given as fourteen and occupation as billiard marker. This was during his time ashore between his first and second round voyages. A more cheerful event was the marriage of Tommy's Aunt Kathy, when she became Kate Allpress, after which she moved to Brighton, Sussex. Before marriage, she was a member of the Desborough Terrace household in 1861.

With the removal of grandfather John, an unclearly identified uncle and Aunt Kathy from 15 Desborough Terrace, probably went financial stability, and likely the ownership of the tenancy of the property. It is from the break-up of the household that Bullen dates his period as a 'street Arab', the term in use in the nineteenth century for the homeless children who somehow survived foraging and begging on London's streets, and sleeping wherever they could find a hole with some shelter. He sets the event in 1866 when he was 'barely nine years old', which implies late spring or early summer that year. There can be no doubt that young Tommy felt the abrupt change of circumstances intensely. He mentions none of his relatives in connection with this next phase of his life. In such situations orphaned children, if not taken in by an orphanage, might be taken to the local workhouse, in this case the Paddington Workhouse adjacent to the Lock Chapel. However, the needy poor had great fear of workhouses with their prison-like enclosure and labour tasks. They were to be avoided at all costs. Certainly, there seems to have been no thought of continuing Tommy's education, as someone must have arranged for him to be taken in by a local laundry in the immediate area, then becoming known as Kensal New Town, where a dozen coarse, crudely-spoken women were employed. There he was promptly put to work:[19]

to turn the mangle and wringing-machine, to scrub the dirtiest of dusters ... to go long dreary journeys with parcels such as I could carry, to do all to a running accompaniment of blows and abuse and shortness of food. My hours were from six in the morning until eleven at night, except on Sundays, when I sat, like Cinderella, after the dinner things had been washed up and put away, by the ashes of the kitchen fire, with no other company than the black-beetles and crickets.

In *Confessions of a Tradesman*, Bullen tells us that he lived at that time with a laundress, working for her between his often short-lived periods of employment, who must also have kept him fed. When he had employment, he was expected to pay the laundress as a lodger.[20] It seems unlikely that his catalogue of different employers was related in chronological sequence, but his errand boy and dogsbody periods of paid employment with small shopkeepers gave him quite varied experiences. An early job was with a newly opened 'oil shop', trading in paint, soap, paraffin, glue, dog biscuit, size, chopped wood, and so on. One delivery he had to make was of seven bundles of firewood (threepence worth) to an upmarket house. His employer kept him fully occupied in the shop or on errands, and his hours were 7am to 10pm. Given the fare to take the recently opened Metropolitan Railway, from nearby Westbourne Park station to Moorgate Street, to collect an order for some treacle from a dealer in Shoreditch, the salesman produced a drum which he could not lift. Tommy resorted to rolling the drum back to Moorgate station, where the guard helped him board, and alight at Westbourne Park. The inconsiderate shopkeeper moaned about the time all that had taken. Another delivery was of a box of bars of soap, using the shop's ill-suited hand truck. Inevitably, the box slid off in a very muddy road, and burst open to shoot blocks of soap into the mud. Having attempted to clean them, Tommy reached the customer who, of course, rejected the soap. Back at the shop the bars were scraped clean, but Tommy promptly had half his week's wage docked. One further disaster, fetching a box of candles which he had dropped when he tripped in the street, resulting in a box of broken candles, led to his dismissal by that shopkeeper.

Tommy's next job was as an errand boy for a boot shop in Archer Street, Notting Hill at 3s 6d per week plus tea. The wage only just covered his lodging, so he resorted to a fiddle by adding a few pennies to the repair fee for shoes he was delivering. Of course, he was discovered and promptly dismissed. He was then taken on by a trunk-maker in Edgware Road, whose products he had to drag outside the shop each day for display, and recover them in the evening.

Waste paper for linings occasionally included boy's magazines and he was able to satisfy his thirst for reading matter with material more suited to his age. After some months, his employer sent him, thoughtlessly, to Hoxton, to fetch a portmanteau from a home worker who had made it. He was not given any money for transport, and it was too large and heavy for him. So he dragged it in the drizzle the considerable distance back to Edgware Road, a success at the cost of considerable damage to the trunk, and he was dismissed on the spot. But his luck was in, as he was almost immediately taken on by a milk-delivery business which ran sixteen delivery vans, each served by a milkman and boy. This paid him six shillings weekly, but demanded an early morning start, finishing at 9pm. His milkman must have had a kindly streak as he was bought a drink and a cake each morning, and in the afternoon during the second delivery round. The evening was taken up with washing all the utensils ready for the morning. Bullen's description of the work is a contribution to the social history of the milk trade.[21]

Tommy was suddenly dismissed from the milk round, but he never knew the reason why. Then a kindly, elderly cobbler took a fancy to him and took him in at two shillings a week plus board and clothing. Other employments included a paper pattern maker in Westbourne Grove, for which he was dressed up as a walking advertisement, and a large chemist's where, on a delivery run, he splashed some soda water into his mouth, and suffered the ill effects. After other episodes, he had to go. By this time he had fallen in with other waifs, and was living rough and resorting to pilferage when sustenance called. Then he was taken on by a billiard marker as his assistant scorekeeper during games in a billiard hall. Within a few days he was master of the task and trusted. This was evening work, but afternoons were mostly devoted to cleaning and preparations for the evening. Then one day there was a jewellery robbery for which Tommy was at first accused, though a known shark or swindler had been hanging around that afternoon. The man was arrested and Tommy cleared with apologies, but a change of ownership of the business soon put him out of work. After another period on the streets, he was engaged on a building site first as a timekeeper, at which he was initially too assiduous, then as an assistant to a moulder of house external ornamentation, dirty but interesting work. This lasted until that housing development was finished, during which he was being paid eight shillings per week, and the working day six to six, with breaks for meals.

Having been put out of a stable home in 1866, perhaps by then the year was 1869, and Tommy was becoming fed up with the instability and insecurity. At some stage he conceived the idea that foreign-going sea employment, in which food and accommodation was provided for whole voyages, offered a kind of solution. Little did he realise that he would not be successful until March 1870. Unresolved is Tommy's removal from the care of Aunt Matilda from 1866, and his obvious awareness of where she was living when he returned to London in 1871 following his first voyage. Also unanswered is the apparent failure of his father to step in if Aunt Matilda was no longer able to care for Tommy. Certainly, by 1871 Frank Robert Bullen had secured stable employment as the stationary engine driver to the Wickham Court estate in Bromley, Kent, and, his first wife Margaret having died in 1870, he was married to Jane, who worked as a laundress on that estate.[22]

2

First Voyage in Four Ships

24 March 1870 to 13 February 1871

A t this distance of time it is hard to realise that Tommy Bullen
was probably just twelve years of age when he decided to try to
get away to sea, through pestering an uncle to take him in the ship
which he commanded.[1] He explains that belonging to 'the ignoble
company of the unwanted', he was well aware of the hardships to
be expected; however, the prospect of regular food and shelter, so
uncertain and hard-fought for over the past three years, outweighed
other considerations.[2] How did he know what conditions could be
like in a merchant sailing ship? It is not too difficult to surmise that
before the break-up of the Bullen family, Tommy encountered his
uncle visiting the home in Desborough Terrace between voyages and
had overheard chat about the progress of the most recent voyage.
But his wanderings as a 'street Arab' would have brought him into
contact with the vast numbers of 'the street folk', many homeless,
amongst whom would be aged and down-and-out former seafarers,
and those who were down and out between service in ships.[3]
Bullen's wanderings throughout what is now central London would
eventually have taken him eastwards and into the 'sailortown'
district, with its concentration of maritime businesses mixed up
with seafarers' lodging houses, pubs frequented by seafarers, and
the concentration of shipping in the enclosed docks and those
crowding at the tiers on the tidal river.

It is in *Confessions of a Tradesman* that we find his description of
the period when he haunted the dives west and east of the Tower,
and where a contact advised hanging around 'a certain public-
house in Thames Street [close west of the Tower] whither coasting

skippers used to resort for their crews.'[4] Named the King's Head (or Arms) this was opposite Custom House steps, where a man, known as Sam, acted as go-between. This person was probably a species of 'crimp', men who preyed on seafarers in various ways, fleecing them of their pay-off if homeward bound, by providing accommodation, food, drink and female company.[5] Men outward bound and short of funds were also prey through crimps' involvement in crew supply, and the practice of paying a month's advance of wages on signing on a ship, by means of a post-dated note to the ship's owners. The advance note was commandeered by the crimps, and the values heavily discounted to their advantage. This was the world into which young Thomas Bullen was taking himself, at a particular disadvantage owing to his age and flimsy stature. Getting noticed in the boozy, crowded pubs where ships' masters and other seafarers congregated must have been a tall order, and it could have been days or weeks without success, while getting something to eat remained a priority. Fortunately, as Bullen relates, close upriver was Fresh Wharf, where Mediterranean steamers berthed to discharge their cargoes of fruit and nuts, and where there was a good deal of breakage. If he had managed to accumulate a few coppers, a cookshop opposite Billingsgate market sold pea soup at a penny for a half basin, generously measured. The broth grew thicker as the week progressed and made a good meal with a ha'penny hunk of bread. It seems likely that he continued to sleep rough in various hiding-holes he had used previously. For occasional amusement he managed to tour the Tower of London either by sneaking past the guards or tagging onto a tour party, listening repeatedly to the patter of the 'beef-eaters', and spending the night in a corner on one occasion when he had become locked in.

Failing in his efforts to get himself away to sea, he was told by Sam that he needed to grow a bit or to stow away. Street gossip had warned him that stowaways could be very badly treated, and he did not fancy taking that risk. However, longing for a home of some kind, he thought of the possibility of locating his shipmaster uncle, whom he eventually found, and who with ill grace agreed to take him at five shillings per month. How he found this uncle remains undisclosed, and thus part of the mystery of how Tommy Bullen came to be thrown out on the streets when his aunt died, rather than being taken under the wing of other relatives who had passed through her house. It seems unlikely that he knew the name of the ship his uncle currently commanded, as from masters' naming in *Lloyd's Register of Shipping* for 1869 George Bullen, his uncle, was only appointed to his current ship that year. Then there was the problem that such ships, trading across the Atlantic Ocean, even if they were regular traders to certain ports and regions, were absent from London for lengthy periods which could stretch to a year or more. Bullen clearly knew his uncle's name and could possibly recognise him, so a chance meeting in the port district could not be ruled out. If Uncle George had a fixed home in London, his nephew might have known where that was. The shipping newspapers, such as *Lloyd's List* and *Shipping and Mercantile Gazette*, listed reports of merchant ships worldwide and in port; however, knowing of that and how to interpret the abbreviated entries was probably beyond young Tommy Bullen. But, speculating that this uncle was a brother to his father, searching for ships having masters named Bullen, together with checking these ships in *Lloyd's Register of Shipping*, allowed the conclusion that the ship's name was *Caroline*. Of several *Caroline*s, only one was commanded by G Bullen, whose name was bracketed from 2 March 1870 with the *Caroline* of 358 tons lying in West India Dock (import) north side.[6] That was where Tommy Bullen joined his first ship.

Nowhere in his writing does *Caroline* appear as the name of Bullen's first ship. Instead he names her as 'Arabella', a practice he was to adopt when describing any of his ships of whose personnel he wished to be critical, so we shall meet the practice again. Because Bullen chooses alternative names having loose connections with a real name, we can speculate that perhaps 'Arabella' stands for little 'street Arab', that term in vogue for the waif and stray children known to roam the streets scratching a poor existence. So what does he have to say about this uncle who condescended to rescue him by taking him as a cabin boy? '[A] stubborn, surly, but thoroughly capable old seaman. Soured by misfortune and cross-grained by nature, it was no wonder that he had no friends, not even the sterling quality of his character, or his high ability, being sufficient to counter-balance the drawback of this atrocious temper.'[7] However, it seems likely the G Bullen who passed the examination for master ordinary (the alternative was extra) in London in 1855, and was issued with his certificate of competency, no 4912, was Uncle George.[8] This has been confirmed from the Agreement and Account of Crew of the *Caroline*, official number 908, for the voyage from London commencing 26 March 1870 terminating at Cork on 11 February 1871, which names the master as George Bullen, aged forty-five, born Somerset, certificate 4912, resident at 47 Clarendon Square, St Pancras, London.[9]

Bullen says he first saw *Caroline* on a bleak, snowy January day in a corner of West India Docks. A barque, she was 'a survival of a bygone day', malformed, ill-rigged and leaky as a basket, and a candidate for joining the ranks of missing vessels. But she was taking in cargo for Demerara, British Guyana, and riggers were aloft in the rigging. Clearly, Bullen had had to find his own way east from the area near the Tower, but his uncle was not aboard and there was no welcome from the ship's mate, who silently led him to the saloon area aft where he was to toil as maid-of-all-work.

How long Bullen was aboard before *Caroline* finally sailed is unrecorded, but the original crew of thirteen, including Captain Bullen and Thomas Bullen, were engaged on 24 March 1874. We therefore cannot be certain whether Bullen was allowed to live aboard the ship, or for how long, before the crew was formally engaged a day or two before the date of leaving London. Normally, only one or two crew were paid a daily rate to stand by a ship in a home port such as London. This was often the first mate who would supervise discharge of cargo, routine ship maintenance, taking in stores and water, and loading the outward cargo. But eventually the day came for the crew to sign on, and the ship's mate took Bullen ashore from the West India Docks to the government shipping office in East India Dock Road, occupying the former Green's Sailors' Home building. This was the nearest shipping office to where the *Caroline* lay. There was another shipping office in Well Street adjacent to the original Sailors' Home and close to St Katherine's and London Docks nearer to the Tower of London. Shipping offices were where the Marine Department of the Board of Trade administered the numerous requirements of the Merchant Shipping Acts concerning the safety of merchant ships and their manning. Before the start of each voyage all the crew of a foreign-going ship were required to attend the shipping office to sign the Agreement and Account [list] of Crew, which commenced with a clerk reading out the terms of the contract of employment for the proposed voyage. After this, starting with the master and officers, each member of the crew gave his name, rating, age, name of last ship, learned his monthly rate of pay, had the option of claiming an immediate cash advance (actually a promissory note), could make provision for an allotment (regular payment) to a relative, and was formally told the location of the ship and when to be aboard. As each member of the crew then signed (or made his mark) the two copies of the agreement (one printed in red ink to be retained by the shipping office and the other in black to go with the ship), the ceremony was known as 'signing on'. On the ship's return to the United Kingdom, the crew would attend the shipping office to 'sign off', receive the balance of pay and the certificate of discharge. This gave the basic ship data, the dates of the seafarers' service and the master's grading of character and ability. There was nearly always some turnover of crews at overseas ports for which the master was, with the seamen concerned, required to attend a local shipping office or the local British consul, who would oversee the appropriate entries being made on the ship's copy of the agreement. This first experience of signing on must have been quite frightening for young Bullen, though being literate he was certainly able to sign his name. The mate no doubt kept an eye on him in the engagement room crowded with the crews of other ships, and the clerks shouting out the terms of agreements and ships' names.

At the end of the voyage, perhaps after two or even three years, the black ship's copy of the agreement, often referred to as the 'ship's articles', on completion of signing off was retained by the superintendent of the shipping office for future reference. Large numbers of them have survived and many of those for Bullen's voyages or passages have been located, and will throw light on his sea career. The term 'voyage' is here used in the definition implicit in each agreement. That is, commencing in a port in the United Kingdom, and perhaps after numerous 'passages' from one port to another overseas, ending with the termination of the voyage in the United Kingdom. There will be several occasions when Bullen took passages in different ships, as indicated in the chapter heads here, before finally arriving at a United Kingdom port. His name was on *Caroline*'s agreement, and should then be on that of *Investigator* and finally *Sea Gem*, but perhaps not *Potosi*, which rescued him from a reef in Caribbean waters. She was a French vessel, where different state rules from those in British ships may have applied.

On *Caroline*'s sailing day, some of the deckhands failed to reach the ship before she was towed from her berth by a paddle tug, all having taken an advance of wages, which paid for a final 'carouse' ashore. They turned up at the locks into the river in various states of inebriation shepherded by crimps, and were dragged aboard, according to Bullen, by the master and the pilot.[10] Another tug towed the ship down the River Thames, while the decks were cleared of clutter by the mates, the deckhands being too far gone to be of use. During this, Bullen received his initiation into the language of the sea with an order to fetch a marline spike from the fo'c'sle, both of which needed explanation. At anchor off Gravesend to change pilots and make final contact with the shore, his uncle recited to him his duties as kitchen- and housemaid to the officers, but gave no instruction as to how he was to feed and sleep. His next lesson came with weighing anchor, helping to lay out the anchor chain in its locker, and during which he learned to 'surge' a rope while the anchor was 'catted'. After some clearing up of ropes scattered while getting under sail, the whole crew was called aft for the selection of hands for the sea watches, the mate and second mate taking it in turn to pick a man for his watch, port for first mate, starboard for second mate. This ceremony was followed by the order to pump ship, which took so long that the crew feared *Caroline* was a leaky ship. Then Bullen succumbed to seasickness for several days until he found his sea legs, stretched out on deck under the longboat, with no one paying any attention to him except a young black shipmate from the West Indies who befriended him, and tried to keep him fed.

Returning to his duties, Tommy Bullen noticed the behaviour of *Caroline*'s master to his officers even at meals, standing aloof from them, holding no conversation, and not even allowing them to participate in the navigation of the ship. The food they shared was as appalling as that served to the deckhands: 'of so unspeakably vile a quality that it was hardly fit to give to well-reared pigs.' There was no reading material aboard ship, and Bullen's natural inquisitiveness was completely discouraged. However, he found an outlet in taking an interest in the sea itself, and the abounding marine life that he was able to witness – this an early practice which would ultimately find its outlet in his stories about the maritime world. But he soon discovered that no one on board had any knowledge or interest in the marine world around the ship. This wall of silence was exacerbated by his uncle's injunction against him entering the crew's fo'c'sle. Tommy Bullen found the Sargasso Sea, with its mass of floating seaweed packed with marine creatures, extremely fascinating, but everyone else moaned about the prevailing near-calm conditions and the ship's slow progress. Allied to the daily, lengthy bouts of bilge pumping, and the appalling condition of the sails and rigging, this was food for extensive speculation among the deckhands that the *Caroline* ('Arabella' in *Log of a Sea Waif*) was a coffin ship not intended to survive the voyage. As Bullen expressed it:[11]

The rigging was dropping to pieces; so that a man never knew, when he went aloft, whether he would come crashing down by the run, from the parting of a rotten footrope or a perished seizing.

The sails were but rags, worn almost to the thinness of muslin, every flap threatening to strip them from the yards. There was no material for repairs, no new rope, canvass or 'seizing stuff;' half a barrel of Stockholm tar, and a few pieces of old 'junk' for sennit and spunyarn, representing all the boatswain's stores on board.

The Agreement and Account of Crew (AAC) for Tommy's first sea voyage in *Caroline*, of course, has nothing to say about the condition of the ship, being confined to personal details about all members of the crew, their position on board, dates of service, wages and final pay-off at the end of the voyage. The terms of the agreement covered, amongst other details, the maximum duration of the voyage, the parts of the world to which the vessel might go, and the minimum diet which the ship supplied. Bullen was twelfth on the list of men originally engaged in the shipping office in the Green's Home building. His date of engagement was 24 March 1870 and his age was entered as thirteen, though he would not achieve that age for a week or two. London is correctly given as his birthplace, as is his rating as 'boy'. His wage is given as five shillings per month. In the 'last ship' column are the words 'Not been to Sea', words which confirm 1870 as the year he went to sea, not 1869 when he may have started searching for a berth in a ship. The entries in the discharge section of his entry on the AAC show that he was 'sent home in a ship' on 20 September 1870 from Sant' Ana in Mexico and his uncle's justification as 'useless' for conduct and for ability is given in the official log for the voyage, in the section naming all the crew and giving the master's gradings for those characteristics. Tommy's pay off without deductions would have been £1 10s 0d, but £0 0s 0d is the entry. Bullen mentions his uncle's ill-treatment in several places in his text, and Captain Bullen's misuse of what were legal documents stands out in his documented handling of his nephew. Captain Bullen failed to handle the discharge entry on the AAC correctly by having Tommy sign the 'release' in front of the first mate. Instead, he writes his name in the release column and labels it 'X his mark', the device used with entries for illiterate seamen.

Thomas Bullen would have been very offended had he known of this entry. A final omission is that his discharge of his nephew is not recorded in the official log, where all crew changes during the voyage had to be recorded, in addition to entries on the crew agreement. Captain Bullen surely knew this, given his recording of crew arrivals before leaving West India Dock.

Merchant shipping law required all foreign-going ships of one hundred tons burden or more to be commanded by a certificated master and to carry one other officer holding at least a certificate as first mate or second mate. Apart from Captain Bullen, the first mate and the carpenter, none of the original crew completed the voyage back to the United Kingdom. The first mate, aged twenty-six, held a certificate of competency no 81952, probably not as master; though giving his name as Henry Thompson, his birth country was Norway. Tommy Bullen names the mate as Svensen, and credits the carpenter, Frederick William Young, aged twenty-five, with also acting as second mate.[12] The remainder of the crew comprised a cook/steward, Charles Clark, aged fifty-three, eight able seamen, two ordinary seamen and Thomas himself. The young seaman who gave him some care while he was sea sick was probably Jamaica-born William Ritchie, aged twenty. There was an exceptional level of turnover during *Caroline*'s voyage from the River Thames and eventually back to end the voyage in Queenstown (Cork), with only the master, first mate, carpenter/second mate and AB, Charles Hablett, eighteen, from Brixham in Devon surviving from the original fifteen.

Bored with the 'deadly' atmosphere 'down aft', Tommy Bullen increasingly disobeyed his uncle's injunction not to fraternise with the crew in the fo'c'sle, becoming something of a spoilt favourite among the men. One of the men 'Joe, the big Yorkshireman' approached the master requesting a bit of canvas to make Tommy some clothing, he having come on board only with what he stood up in. This, together with the discovery of Tommy's disobedience, sent George Bullen into a rage in which he banished his nephew from the saloon to live among the crew forward and adding to the physical punishment he had inflicted the day before.

Despite his 'private navigation', George Bullen managed to make a satisfactory landfall, bringing the ship to anchor in the approaches to Demerara river near the light ship to await a pilot. The main sign of nearing land had been the change in colour of the water, becoming increasingly fresh and muddy as river water mingled with seawater. Despite the use in England of the name of the river as *Caroline*'s first destination, the destination port was really Georgetown, the capital of Guyana, a British colony. With a pilot on board, the anchor was weighed, causing Bullen and a seaman named as Jem to become covered in foul river mud while they stowed lengths of chain cable in the chain locker. The ship was sailed up river to the main anchorage opposite Georgetown. This was crowded with ships, but Bullen is full of praise for the local pilot who anchored the ship with the tricky manoeuvre of a flying (or running) moor, with two anchors widely separated to restrict the ship's swing as the tide turned every twelve hours or so.

Caroline having sailed from Gravesend according to the newspapers on 29 March 1870, and arriving at Georgetown, Demerara, on 11 May 1870, the passage had taken about six weeks. The great joy for the crew was the local boats (bumboats) loaded with fruit, vegetables and other foodstuffs which they purchased for a glorious feast of the fresh stock. As the only literate person in the fo'c'sle, young Bullen found himself appointed bookkeeper, making the record of the joint expenditure. Discharging the outward 'general' cargo started without delay after the crew had rigged suitable cargo handling gear. The local labour went to work with a will, aided by the vocals of their 'chantey man' co-ordinating the heaving on the purchases.[13] It was common in the sail era for no leave to be granted to ships' crews at all, or perhaps one Saturday or Sunday only to be given. Tommy Bullen was taken ashore by the mate who, entering a grog shop, allowed him to wander around the town. He chanced upon the home of a white family, who invited him in to tea. Staying beyond the time set to return to the ship, the father accompanied him aboard and interviewed his uncle about his treatment. The outcome was that he was never allowed ashore again from the *Caroline*.

With the outward cargo discharged, and there being no cargo on offer on the Demerara river, *Caroline* was ballasted for the coming passage. The crew were granted a liberty day and a small amount of pocket money, the port watch going first and returning inebriated, though they avoided ending up in jail, as often happened. The starboard watch's turn followed, to be due back on the morning of sailing. Returning late, bearing supplies of rum, and quarrelsome, they refused to turn to for the process of unmooring the ship.[14] Something of a battle broke out, but it was the crew themselves who hoisted the red ensign upside down as a signal to shore that urgent assistance was needed. The master was ashore at the time, presumably clearing the ship for departure. A police canoe with a white sergeant answered the call. The mutineers, who were to be arrested, managed to get the local police high with drink, and a further signal for aid brought on board a stronger force, bringing also the master, who vented his fury. The miscreants were rapidly rounded up, manacled and run ashore into prison. The incident delayed the ship that day, while the master sought a replacement crew. The following morning, unmooring finally took place and *Caroline* sailed for the Gulf of Mexico. Stealing some biscuits from the galley for a former naval sailor who had ruptured himself, Tommy received another severe beating from his uncle on being found out.

After a relatively short passage of a week or two, *Caroline* found her way to Tupilco, a port of call for orders to some obscure location from which tropical hardwood was to be loaded in an open, unsheltered roadstead. Four days at anchor passed before a launch with a crowd of mixed-race labourers arrived, who were to handle the loading at a location along the coast named Sant' Ana. These locations were in the Gulf of Campeche on the east coast of Mexico, west of the Yucatan peninsula.[15] At 'Sant' Ana' (Bullen's spelling), *Caroline* joined a surprising number of vessels lying in the open anchorage. She was subject to a heavy landward swell which made the ships roll and pitch unpleasantly, and the handling of the heavy logs, which were floated out to be loaded, a very dangerous operation.

Bullen gives an informed description of the preparations aboard *Caroline* for loading, and the assembly of the logs in the nearby river for towing out to the ships. The log handlers were surprisingly good at their task, and commanded very high wages. One or two had to 'dance' on the log raft alongside, releasing one by one each log and slinging it to be lifted aboard. Once in the air, the ship's unsteady movements made it potentially a lethal weapon, liable to slither in unexpected directions due to the slime on it that had accumulated during its long passage downriver from the country's interior. When half-loaded, the supply of logs dried up. Meanwhile, two of *Caroline*'s crew, having stolen the ship's longboat, deserted to an American ship where high wages were on offer. Other ships had crew troubles. The master of a Liverpool barque, *Panuco* (Bullen misspells it 'Panuca') came aboard to relate his tale that his crew had refused duty and deserted ashore, only to return apparently regretful of their action. But after a couple of nights, and a disturbance aboard, the crew took the ship's whaleboat after raiding the master's cabin while he was ashore, and presented this booty to the local commandant who had primed that fiddle. *Caroline*'s crew suffered from the outbreak of a malady which caused the feet and legs to swell, and led to wounds which were slow to heal. The ruptured invalid, after a long decline, finally died. Meanwhile, Bullen remained unaffected, and managed to pick up sufficient Spanish to hold a conversation. Then, out of the blue, his uncle sent for him, explaining, kindly for once, that the loading season being late, with dangerous northerly winds expected, and the risk of her never reaching Britain, he had decided to send him over to a friend's ship named *Investigator*, which was about to sail. The reason for that decision sounds genuine enough, but given Tommy's unwelcome treatment throughout his association with his uncle in *Caroline*, it could also have been a device for George Bullen to rid himself of a boy he never really wanted to have on board.

Before dealing with Thomas Bullen's experiences aboard *Investigator*, it is necessary to note that in *The Log of a Sea Waif* (p53) he conceals his new ship by giving it the name 'Discoverer', and to clear up his assertion that the ship had been built as an Arctic exploration ship. There was such a ship, HMS *Investigator*, used in two Franklin relief expeditions in 1849 to 1851, but that ship was abandoned and sank, remaining lost for 150 years. Systematic searching of digital sources has established that there was another *Investigator*, built in 1849 by the well-known London shipbuilders and owners, R & H Green.[16] This was ship-rigged and the tonnage in 1849 was 570. She was operated initially in the Indian and China trades. In 1856 the ownership passed to J Rogers of London, and by 1863 the owner was Skelton, also of London. At about that date *Investigator* was cut down to a barque rig, and the tonnage became 503. There is no doubt that it was one of Green's well-built ships, but it seems unlikely that there was any strengthening for Arctic conditions. We know that the name was *Investigator*, from the Agreement and Account of Crew for *Sea Gem*, where it is named as Bullen's last ship. Bullen's name does not appear on the AAC for the voyage of the *Investigator*, and it seems unlikely that there was any entry in its official log, though that was lost in the subsequent shipwreck.

Though larger than *Caroline*, *Investigator* was manned with a similar-sized crew, seventeen including the master. Only Captain Robert Cameron, aged forty-eight from Leith, and Thomas Dobbin, twenty-six, from Cheshire, held Board of Trade certificates of competency. Of the total, nine were born in Britain and eight in north European countries. *Caroline* had ended her voyage with similar proportions of overseas-born crew, but leaving London carried only four from overseas.

It was on 20 September 1870 that Bullen, now aged thirteen, joined *Investigator*. In *Caroline* he had nothing to pack, and owing to the crew change following the mutiny, he left without saying farewell to anyone.[17] He was delighted to have the opportunity to leave, and was even more delighted and surprised at the warm welcome he received on boarding his new ship. He was immediately shown where he was to berth (with the steward), and he found that he had a free run of the ship, now homeward bound for Falmouth for orders with its mahogany log cargo. But getting under way there was a most unseamanlike and highly dangerous incident which delayed the ship another day. The anchor had been hove up hanging above the waves, the ship under canvas making headway, when the master, described by Bullen as a 'confirmed drunkard', came forward and let slip the hawser bearing the weight of the anchor. This ran out drawing its full 120 fathoms of chain, and abruptly re-anchored the ship, which was still in shallow water. The fast action of the crew, and their careful handling by the mate, rescued the situation while the master was kept out of sight.

Unlike in *Caroline*, the food was of good quality and ample. For about a week in balmy weather the crew carried out their duties in a slack manner, the master offering no example or taking any lead in his drunken state. Bullen himself had no particular duties. Then *Investigator*, on a clear starlit night with a gentle breeze, ran aground on one of the numerous reefs, Cayo Arenas, in Banco de Campeche, a shallow area of the Gulf of Mexico off the west coast of the Yucatan peninsula.[18] Clearly, the gross neglect of navigation and lookout, as Bullen tells it, was a major factor in the grounding and total loss of *Investigator*, but in the prevailing light winds, the effect of unknown currents could have been a factor.[19] The reef is now marked with a light and radio beacon, but in 1870 was probably unmarked. After fifteen days since leaving Sant' Ana, the ship had made very slow progress on her voyage. All hands landed safely on the barren islet, and were able to salvage ample supplies of food and water. The deckhands themselves insisted on dumping all the alcohol aboard, while the sails and cordage enabled tents to be constructed for shelter. Bullen was in his element observing the marine life around the reef. He draws on this experience for his short story 'A Waking Nightmare'.[20] In this he imagines himself marooned alone on the reef, with marine life for company, but terrified by the antics of a skate. *Investigator*'s pinnace had been rescued, and was fitted up for a sea voyage to the shore, no more than a hundred miles away. These well-constructed preparations were rounded off by setting up a flagstaff to attract the attention of passing ships. It worked very well, as after ten days a French barque, *Potosi* of Bordeaux, bound for Havana in Cuba, stopped to pick up *Investigator*'s crew. To the amazement of the French crew, *Investigator*'s master, mate and four deckhands declined to be rescued, putting their faith in the pinnace, and eventually reaching the shore.

Compared with *Caroline* and even *Investigator*, *Potosi* fed extremely well, leading Bullen to discuss the limitations of the diet in British ships feeding to the basic scale attributed to Board of Trade regulation. Bullen describes a pleasant passage to Havana. The barque was 'wonderfully handy', with very good equipment, while the discipline was quite naval in character. That might have been due to the requirement for seafarers in French merchant ships to be naval reservists. *Investigator*'s crew residue were rescued about 6 October 1870, and, after a run of about five hundred nautical miles, landed at Havana, Cuba, on 10 October. Cuba was then a Spanish colony, so it became the responsibility of the British consul in Havana to provide food and accommodation for the shipwrecked crew, and pay for clothing if needed, while taking steps to find them a berth in another ship or to ship them as distressed British seamen (DBS) in a United Kingdom-bound British ship.

An ample meal, though over-seasoned with garlic, was arranged for them at an eating house, and then they were taken to a shed behind the building having an earth floor but no furniture, where they had to bed down for the night.[21] In this far from comfortable situation and total darkness, a gang of robbers invaded, the crew waking up in time to flee the building and away into the street, returning in the morning to the eating house. A visit to the consulate followed, with a lecture as to their behaviour, and then at a clothes shop they were rigged out with fresh clothes. Bullen seemed to be treated more generously than his shipmates, receiving a new suit, good underclothes, patent leather shoes and a Panama hat. But this just turned out to be an example of kindness shown by local people, including traders, to a youngster who had had a hard time. A British naval officer gave him a couple of dollars, and trying to spend money on fruit and other foods in shops led to gifts of what he had selected and small gifts of cash. Indeed, he obtained enough to share among his shipmates. Well used to wandering the streets in London, Tommy soon found himself an 'occupation' he had learned during his 'street Arab' days, that of a billiard marker. Wandering into the Hotel St Isabel, which had three billiard tables, he started helping the one-armed resident marker (scorekeeper). The room was frequented by British and American shipmasters, to whom, with his ability in Spanish, he became doubly useful. Of course, he was fed by the hotel and tipped by the players, but he shared his income with his shipmates, whose numbers were dwindling as they found berths in ships.

About this time there was a major outbreak of yellow fever in Havana. The great bell of the cathedral tolled repeatedly, and waggons rumbled through the streets night and day collecting the dead. Shipping in the harbour was denuded of its crews as the sick were taken to hospital. Meanwhile, the healthy inhabitants kept up appearances of normality. Bullen says several weeks passed away but, as shall be seen, data on his next ship calls that into question. Down in the harbour one day, Bullen noticed a peculiar glow in the sky topped by a huge cloud. Suddenly, the storm burst out around him as Havana was hit by a hurricane.[22] Jammed in a corner and drenched, Bullen could do no more than hold tight until the worst passed over. Enormous devastation was wreaked among the shipping in port. Returning to the hotel, he found it had not been much damaged, and business revived. The storm seemed to have swept away the yellow fever as well. Soon after, he was apprehended by the British vice consul and taken aboard a large barque to see the master and sign on the *Sea Gem*, 566 tons, registered in St Andrews, Nova Scotia.[23]

The original Agreement and Account of Crew was lost while at the office of Havana's harbour master, so the British consul's office had to fill out a new form drawing on data from the ship's official log, which was held with other ship's papers on board. This tells a sorry story about the period while the yellow fever epidemic was rife. *Sea Gem* had arrived at Havana on 29 or 30 August 1870. On 8 September George Gordon, AB, died of yellow fever, followed on 12 September by William Lougham, AB. On 15 September Arthur Hall, boy, died of cholera, as did John Owens, master, on 19 September. The mate, Thomas Rees died of yellow fever on 3 October, and on October John James, AB, from the same cause. These details came from medical certificates, and the bodies were buried in Havana's cemetery. From this catalogue, it is clear that these diseases were rampant in Havana before Bullen and his shipmates arrived in *Potosi*. The survivors from the original crew were the second mate, the carpenter, the cook, three ABs and an ordinary seaman. Bullen was among nine crew members signed on 27 October 1870. The consul did not return the agreement until 3 November, possibly a day or so before *Sea Gem* actually sailed from Havana. She was bound across the Gulf of Mexico to Mobile in Texas to load cotton for the United Kingdom. Thomas Bullen is the signature on the agreement.

But Tommy Bullen was not yet finished with Havana. Having signed on at the consular office and being admonished with the others to join immediately, he slipped away, returning to the hotel with the billiard tables. However, there was a new billiard marker, and it was made clear that he was no longer welcome. Perhaps the consular staff had warned them off. Rambling the town once again, he teamed up with an American youth who had just been paid off, and for a couple of days they enjoyed themselves rambling into the countryside, and sleeping rough. With money running out, they parted company. Having a coffee in a cafe, he was accosted by a drunk who turned out to be the newly appointed mate of the *Sea Gem*, named Alexander Todd. This man begged him to take him aboard *Sea Gem*. Having hauled the mate aboard in a bowline, the second mate prevented Tommy from slipping away in the boat he had hired, and sent him to Captain John James Pearse, the new master.

Captain Pearse had come out of retirement to fill the urgent vacancy, and events approaching Mobile were trying enough for him to resign his command there. A sudden squall, blowing out all the sails and causing the stone ballast to shift, had laid the ship on her beam ends, though she was able to limp into the anchorage off the port. There a gale raised an ugly sea and links of the anchor cable jumped off the windlass drum. Just in time, the other anchor was dropped and veered out to its full extent, thus holding the ship. After this, a tug towed the ship to a berth and loading commenced. Within a few days a new master was appointed, Griffith Jones. On joining, he interviewed all the crew and threatened to be tough on them if they were not up to scratch. Tommy Bullen was appointed cabin boy, and was ordered to call the mate. Then the pair settled down to drink themselves into stupidity. Captain Jones sobered up after a couple of days, but though capable as master made no attempt to censure the mate. Nearing the end of loading, and the port shut down for Christmas, the master went ashore to return with live turkeys, geese and pigs, and piles of fresh beef, vegetables, and alcoholic drink. All this he offered for sale to the masters of other ships lying in port. Making a comfortable profit, he was generous to his own crew with a share in those Christmas supplies. The ship had arrived on 22 November 1870, and would leave for Liverpool on 3 January 1871.[24]

The Atlantic passage proved to be one of a succession of gales generating very rough seas. In such conditions, sail had often to be reduced at short notice, and with the wind direction being mainly westerly, only the most able helmsmen could be trusted with steering. Bullen suffered greatly from two causes, lack of appropriate clothing and footwear, and the bullying treatment of the mate, who seemed to delight in striking him. Tommy stole a pair of the master's socks, his own having worn through, only to be found out and chastised by the master. The mate's treatment culminated in Tommy being knocked senseless with internal injury, following which Tommy turned on the mate reminding him that he was 'the Consul's passenger', that is a DBS, and he would report the mate for his treatment. That turned out to be sufficient a threat. Meanwhile, the weather conditions meant that the master was increasingly uncertain of his position, when in fog they caught a glimpse of the *Coningbeg* light ship off County Wexford in Ireland, and at the entrance to St George's Channel between Ireland and England. Immediately after, breakers were sighted, and there ensued a desperate struggle to claw the ship away from the Irish coast. Then it was not long before *Sea Gem* was off Lynas Point (Anglesey) and picking up a pilot and a tug, which towed her into the River Mersey and a short anchorage off Brunswick Dock waiting for the tide to rise for entering its lock. Brunswick Dock was a location in Liverpool which was to become very familiar to young Tommy, who was still not yet aged fourteen.

3

A Voyage in Three Ships

4 June 1871 to 9 October 1871

Despite his accumulated street wisdom, Tommy Bullen, still a teenager of thirteen in modern thinking, would have been at a loss as to what to do with himself once *Sea Gem* had berthed in Brunswick Dock in Liverpool. All the other crew members had deserted the ship immediately on arrival, and an elderly ship keeper had boarded and was ensconced in the galley where the stove offered some warmth.[1] Outside it had snowed. On the following day, Tommy had scavenged a pair of boots and augmented his meagre apparel with discarded rags. He was ready to venture ashore. He knew something about the ship being paid off a day or two later, but as a DBS had no expectation of receiving much money. He had noticed a small shop labelled Brunswick Dock Eating House, knocked on the door and asked to lodge until he could be paid off. No doubt the mistress of the eating house, admitting him, thought she spotted an income-making opportunity, even a meagre one, as all seafarers arriving in a home port and freed from the ship were like blank or post-dated cheques: they would be in funds if they could be supported until pay-off. For the moment he would be fed by the eating house and would be given a bed. Returning briefly to the ship, its cook had returned and told him when and where the pay-off would take place.

The pay-off was probably at the Liverpool Sailors' Home, where the Local Marine Board rented accommodation for the shipping office, examiners and surveyors, about twenty minutes walk from Brunswick Dock. In an act of collective generosity typical of merchant seafarers, each crew member gave Tommy a small tip from their balance of wages amounting, all told, to twenty-two shillings. When his own turn came, Captain Jones gave him £2 10s 0d, representing a pound per month pay. Having been led to believe he was a DBS and unpaid, he would have been surprised had he been able to study the Agreement and Account of Crew, to see that he had been properly signed on as a 'boy' with a monthly wage of $5.00 (currency uncertain), which the superintendent of the shipping office would have insisted be paid. Back at the Brunswick Dock Eating House the landlady effectively commandeered the money, which she would look after on his behalf, suggesting also that he treat her and a friend to a little drop of 'Donovons' (cheap gin).

To no avail, Bullen tried for a berth in outward-bound ships in Liverpool. For a few weeks he fell on his feet as a temporary trainee with a figurehead carver who had a workshop adjacent to the eating house. This young, energetic man of great skill not only taught him the art of sharpening tools and carving, but also paid Tommy a wage which covered his board and lodging. He proved his worth to 'Mr R', the carver, but fell foul of the jealousy of Mr R's brother, a much less able man, who was also employed in the workshop.[2] Tommy becoming the subject of much argument and even violence, Mr R regretfully had to discontinue his employment, advising him to return to the greater familiarity of London, and giving him the fare. Following that advice Tommy secured a half-fare (as a child?), leaving him with little money over. His sojourn in Liverpool had lasted six weeks, as on census night, 2 April 1871, he is listed staying once again with Aunt Matilda, then in Stalham Street, a few minutes' walk from Desborough Terrace, which he remembered so well. This is clear evidence that he knew where to find the closest of his relatives if he chose. In the two months before joining his next ship and then aged fourteen, he may well have picked up one or two of the errand boy jobs of which he wrote in telling of his phase as a 'street Arab'. Certainly, his time as a billiard marker, cited in the census, would seem to belong in this period ashore rather than before he went to sea.

Towards the end of this period ashore, he tells of haunting the familiar environment of Thames Street, the King's Head and the cookshop with pea soup simmering in its window. For accommodation, he avoided trying the Sailors' Home (the original one in London, Well and Dock Street) as it only catered (so he thought) for those who had the ability to pay in full.[3] So he tried his approach which had worked so well in Liverpool, going to West India Dock Road and knocking on the door of the first seamen's boarding house he came across. Run by an old boatswain and his mother, Tommy was taken in and a few days later was found a ship. This was the barque *Brinkburn* (named 'Bonanza' by Bullen), bound to Falmouth, Jamaica, with a general cargo. He was duly signed on at Green's Home as a boy at twenty shillings a month. His age was entered as fifteen, though he had only turned fourteen in April 1871. A month's advance paid the boarding-house keeper his due, who also provided a 'straw bed' (or donkey's breakfast), hook-pot, pannikin, plate, knife and a suit of oilskins, as well as some old clothing. Bullen comments: 'So he didn't rob me to any extent'.[4]

Brinkburn's manning was much like that of *Sea Gem,* there being eighteen leaving the River Thames, including the master and Thomas Bullen, as he continued to sign his name. Almost unusually for this class of vessel, only two of the crew were not British-born, the carpenter George Evers from Lübeck in Germany, and James Lawson, the cook, from Jamaica. The ship also carried a certificated second mate, W H H Sutherland, in addition to the first mate, David Williams, from Swansea and the master, Edward C Jenkins from Bristol. Seven ABs, three OS's and two boys completed the manning. The other boy was 17-year-old William Alder, recently discharged from the 'Endeavour' sea training unit of the Feltham Industrial School in Middlesex. He was to be paid only ten shillings a month, subject to a note that if he proved competent there would be a bonus of ten shillings a month. This precaution on the part of Captain Jenkins reflects the wariness of merchant seafarers about boys fresh out from sea training schools (over twenty of them), because the training they had received was thoroughly Royal Naval in character and in the manning levels of that service.

The saga of the departure of the *Caroline* was repeated as the *Brinkburn* set off. The hands were all on board at the planned time of departure of 5pm. But they took advantage of an unexplained lengthy delay to run ashore for an additional carouse, and they could not be found at 10pm when the ship was finally ready to go. *Brinkburn* was moved into the Shadwell Basin and the men trickled back. Still two short, the master decided to go, and a tug helped *Brinkburn* through the locks and into the river for the tow to Gravesend. Bullen had turned fourteen by sailing date on 4 June 1871, and he found he was shipmates with a 17-year-old first tripper who had come from 'the Marine Society's training ship *Warspite*', in Bullen's words. Unfortunately, they soon found that that sea training was of little use for life in a merchant vessel. At anchor off Gravesend, while the hands slept off their debauch, the master went ashore to recruit two replacement hands, returning, luckily, with two who proved sober and good seamen. Raising the anchor by hand at midnight with just the weakened manpower proved a tortuous business. Once again, the boys found themselves flaking out the sections of chain as they came aboard. The tug slipped its tow off North Foreland. Being sent aloft to loosen the sails, he overheard the mate comment, 'That's a smart little boy', which did much for Tommy's self-esteem, but the ineptitude of the *Endeavour* boy, whom he calls Ben, was exposed, and he took his frustration out on Bullen. In fact, all the hands had the idea that the boys were born slaves and Tommy led a wretched life. A compensation was the provisioning of the ship by the master, making the ship a good feeder.

Twenty-eight days after leaving London, *Brinkburn* reached Falmouth, Jamaica. The weather had been fine throughout and the master had taken the opportunity to overhaul much of the ship's rigging, most of the crew being kept on day work and allowed to sleep the night through, unless hands were called to handle sail.

As a minor port, perhaps the arrival of the largest vessel to call at the port was sufficient novelty for an ad hoc festival, as so many people came down to the port to see the ship anchored among four smaller vessels. There were ample supplies of fruit and other foods, together with bottles of rum, for the crew to purchase. Reminding him of the welcome at Demerara, Bullen comments the locals were a jovial, musical and carefree lot, despite the poverty in which they existed.

Not long after arrival Tommy Bullen fell ill and was sufficiently unwell to be sent ashore to hospital. The place was presided over by a young black dispenser, who doled out medicine unsystematically. Food must have been supplied and the time in hospital must have been paid for by the ship. Whatever the malady, Bullen soon recovered, and enjoyed himself playing on the nearby beach with a crowd of youngsters, which included an impromptu game of cricket. Caught out by a visit from *Brinkburn*'s master, he was ordered back on board and had to resume his previous life. His shipmates thought of him as skulking while ashore and thus putting extra work on, particularly, the *Endeavour* boy.[5] A day after that was sailing day, the ship having discharged her outward cargo and loaded a cargo for London.

One of the fellowship practices between sailing ships anchored together was to send over boats and men to help the vessel about to depart to heave up her anchor and get under way. In Falmouth, as well as the effort of heaving up the anchor, there was the effort of getting her away between the reefs outside the harbour. Without that support, the ship would have had to resort to laying out the kedge anchor and warping (hauling) the ship up to it, repeating that process until sail could take over. It was important to get the ship out during the short, early-morning calm, before the sea breeze set in blowing all day, blocking the ship in the harbour. About two miles out, these boats cast off from *Brinkburn*. But this left the ship in a calm and at the mercy of local currents or tidal streams. Waiting for wind, this 'under tow' was sweeping the vessel towards a sandbank. Despite being warned by the mate, who advised preparing the anchors, the master seemed to freeze and gave no orders. The seabed could now clearly be seen and soon the ship grounded. Now the hard work began to lay out anchors in deeper water and to try to haul the ship off. The sea breeze set in, making the sea rougher, with hauling off becoming impossible. With the wind increasing to gale force and rolling seas pounding her, *Brinkburn* became a total loss.

The ship's plight was visible to those ashore, and *Brinkburn* was surrounded by boats carrying people now more interested in salving what they could of her cargo. All her three hatches were opened, and boat after boat left with its haul. But the ship was left open to the waves. The crew grabbed such possessions as they could, then taking to any of the boats nearby. Bullen grabbed an old hat containing five newborn kittens, and was followed closely by their mother. The raids on the cargo continued overnight until the ship broke up.

The people of Falmouth, Jamaica, were most welcoming, and took them to the town's only hotel. Tommy Bullen found himself the centre of attention, as the people were most taken by his rescue of the kittens.[6] They were taken over by the hotel manager's daughter. Arrangements were made for *Brinkburn*'s crew to occupy a vacant house, with meals provided at the hotel, which was too small for such numbers. Many of the population came to visit them bringing gifts. Near the wreck site, cargo was floating out of the ship's broken hull. Bullen lists puncheons of rum, bundles of walking sticks, cakes of beeswax and innumerable coconuts, all of which someone or other claimed. Calling at the hotel, the manager's daughter showed him the kittens and mother cat, who had settled in as though they owned the place. Noticing Tommy was limping, though after months of bare feet his soles were very tough, the girl washed and explored his feet, locating with a needle a large bunch of tiny eggs. Finding two other nests and cleaning them out, she made a compound of tobacco ash and kerosene, rubbing it into the wounds, which was extremely painful. For a week after Tommy was a cripple in the accommodation house.

With so much liquor most of the crew were tipsy of an evening. It got about that Tommy could sing, and one night he was carried over to entertain the officers of the garrison. The ample tips he received had perforce to be shared among the rest of the crew, so he did not benefit very much.

About three weeks after the wreck, and some kind of inquiry into the loss of the vessel which acquitted the master, it was decided to send *Brinkburn*'s crew to Kingston. There was a custom house at Falmouth, but only a limited shipping administration, while at Kingston, a capital of a British colony, there would be a shipping office and shipping master. News of the wreck had probably reached Kingston by that time, and it might have been possible that the shipping master suggested the move to enable repatriation. It seems that the arrangements were not thought through, and that the master and mate did not accompany the rest of the crew. One of the curiosities of British shipping law was that ships' masters were not defined as seamen, and therefore did not qualify, when shipwrecked, as distressed British seamen. They were not granted support at the state's expense. With Falmouth on Jamaica's north coast, towards the west end of the island, and Kingston on the south coast towards the eastern end, a sea passage was probably the quickest and easiest way of making the journey. So a small schooner with a crew of three was chartered. The most basic of provisions for three days was put aboard. Calms and light airs prevailed, progress was very slow and, predictably, food ran out after three days. *Brinkburn*'s deckhands were effectively passengers, and had little to do except gossip and reminisce. If there was any shelter below decks it was probably very crowded. Further, the authority which had existed under the Agreement and Account of Crew, such as it was, had expired on the date of the shipwreck. Chat came round to the ill-luck that the ship and its crew had experienced and someone asserted that there was a Jonah aboard. This was an old superstition amongst seafarers and amongst such ideas that lingered on in their collective mind, such as no whistling except for a wind in a calm. Combining this superstition with the hands' earlier habit of bullying the ship's boys, the lot fell upon Tommy, who being literate was a bit different from most of the men, and he had seemingly managed to dodge work aboard ship for much of their time in Falmouth. Now thoroughly worked up, they decided that the schooner would never reach Kingston unless Tommy was thrown overboard. The three Jamaican crew members were aghast at the turn of events when Tommy's hands were tied up and he was told to prepare himself. They rushed their passengers to rescue him but in the melee were repelled with the threat of similar treatment. However, relief came from the bosun, who had perhaps not realised how far things had gone, but had some residual authority. He stood over Tommy, drove the mob back and berated them for taking matters so far. It was enough to break the 'mob' effect. It helped that a breeze had sprung up, and was enough to carry the schooner into the harbour of Savannah Le Mar. This was on Jamaica's south coast, towards the western end, and about a third of the distance from Falmouth to Kingston, and where they obtained supplies of food and water. The schooner reached Kingston about two days later.

There was a sailors' home at Kingston, so they expected to be lodged there, owing to their DBS status. But they found that the home had received no instructions about them, and unless they paid in advance at the going rate, they could not be admitted. Clearly, the crew had had no instructions about going to the shipping office first. Taking that step next, the shipping master asserted that they had no business with him and ordered them away. Tommy, who had a letter of introduction to someone in Kingston, and who provided the necessary introduction, was admitted to the Sailors' Home. Among the rest of the crew common sense prevailed, and they deputised the bosun and one other man to approach the naval authorities, Kingston being a naval base in the West Indies. This presence was maintained aboard a naval guard ship HMS *Aboukir*, an aged man-of-war. The two borrowed a canoe and paddled across the harbour to this ship. The senior officer on duty listened to their story, ordered them something to eat, and the second lieutenant to accompany them ashore to the shipping office. There the shipping master had not a leg to stand on, and was told in no uncertain terms to attend to their needs and find them a ship home as soon as possible. The superintendent of the Sailors' Home was sent instructions to admit them. A parallel appeal had meanwhile been sent to the governor of Jamaica about ten miles out of town, which had the same effect. No doubt the shipping master was not allowed to forget his mistake for a very long time.

Tommy Bullen, his basic needs cared for, now set about having as good a holiday as possible. This included moonlight fishing excursions in canoes and rambles in the countryside, accompanied by local men and boys. He was avoiding any association with his former shipmates. A favourite pastime of the locals was dressing up, and gathering in large number on an old pier, singing shanties, hymns, and anything else with a rousing chorus, all of which was 'bread and butter' to Tommy. At one of these meetings, singing 'Marching through Georgia' and swaying with the music, the pier began to collapse. No one was hurt and great fun was had as the bedraggled singers emerged from the water. The thought of leaving disappeared from his mind. But then he received a note, from the contact to whom he had been referred, to go aboard a large steamer, where arrangements had been made for Tommy to work his passage home.

The steamer, not named by Bullen, might have been SS *Cuban* of the West Indies and Pacific Steam Ship Company under Captain Sandkey, as the dates seem to fit.[7] This Liverpool company was running a scheduled mail service between selected West Indies ports and Liverpool. On his reporting aboard, the steamer's captain sent him to the chief steward who, short of hands, welcomed the extra help, though he quizzed Tommy about his experience. The work amounted to endless dishwashing, silver-cleaning, floor-scrubbing and metal-polishing. The second steward, rejoicing in the nickname of Hadji, and an excellent worker, seems to have been the example Tommy followed. Imagine his surprise on sailing day when the rest of the *Brinkburn*'s crew were marched aboard as DBS, with no duties but messing with the crew. He would not be free of them until they reached Liverpool. Fortunately, Tommy and that crew were at different ends of the ship from each other. Nevertheless, Tommy tried collecting waste food and smuggling it to his former shipmates, only to be caught by the chief steward and banned from making that gesture.

The passage home of the SS *Cuban* from Kingston Jamaica was via Port-au-Prince, Haiti, to Liverpool. But none of the DBS seafarers are named in the SS *Cuban's* Agreement and Account of Crew, so that without additional evidence we cannot be certain of the steamer's identity. The outline of the crew here offers a close approximation of a similar steamer's manning.[8] Both *Cuban's* master, Captain Samuel Slater Sandrey, aged fifty-three, born in Devon, and First Mate Robert Omerond, aged twenty-seven, a Liverpool man, held ordinary master's certificates of competency, and both the second mate and third mate held lower-grade certificates as first mate or second mate. The deck crew included a carpenter and carpenter's mate, bosun, thirteen ABs and an ordinary seaman. In the engine propulsion department there were three engineers, qualified with first-class and second-class engineer's certificates, a storekeeper, three firemen and three trimmers. Because *Cuban* carried passengers as well as crew, provision for them included a purser, first and second stewards, two junior stewards, a stewardess, two cooks and a surgeon. There was very little crew turnover during her voyage. Two seamen failed to join in Liverpool, and two deserted in Colon. Two replacements were signed on in Kingston, Jamaica. Two crew members, towards the end of her voyage, died from diseases probably picked up in the West Indies, where yellow fever and cholera were widespread. A third seaman died soon after arrival in Liverpool, but there is no record of the cause. If Thomas Bullen was aboard, his experience of death at sea in his first round voyage was certainly continued, as he describes in his section on the steamer passage in *The Log of a Sea Waif.*

Cuban, like the steamer Bullen describes, was, as noted above, bound from Kingston to Port-au-Prince in Haiti and then on to

Liverpool. Tommy was told that there might be some 'fun' at Port-au-Prince. Haiti was in the throes of what became a successful revolution against the sovereignty of Spain and France. This led eventually to the separate states of Haiti and St Domingo. Port-au-Prince was supposedly blockaded, but the steamer paid no attention to that, or to the two warships with steam up in the approaches. She berthed as usual alongside the company's hulk, which bore a small amount of cargo. One other steamer in port was flying the American flag. Ashore, there was no knowing who had authority and there was considerable damage to buildings. Either in an error of judgement or taking unofficial leave of absence, a group of Bullen's steamer's crew managed a run ashore, probably drank too much and managed to fall foul of some or other ragtag military group, who threw them into a lock-up for not showing enough respect. This was an ancient cow shed in a pond of sewage, and they were left there overnight. Let out and back on board, their clothing had to be dumped overboard, and the ship's doctor examined them with growing anxiety.

Before the ship was finished with the port, a mysterious passenger came alongside from a canoe, with several weighty chests which he kept close sight of. He disappeared below and was rarely seen thereafter. Steam up, and at full pressure, all hands were called for stations ready for departure. At about the same time the American steamer, labelled a filibuster by Bullen, left her berth and came alongside Bullen's steamer. A figure stepped from her bridge on board, greeted the captain and had a private conversation in the chart room, after which the stranger returned to his own ship. As they steamed away, the two vessels kept close together. Immediately after leaving a berth at any time, while maintaining stations, there is not much to do on a steamer as she makes her departure. So everyone on board Bullen's steamer took in these curious developments with interest. Soon the two steamers were abreast the two warships, after which the American showed a turn of speed, shouted thanks, and soon disappeared ahead. The warships let off a couple of salvoes and began to chase, giving it up as the American got out of range.

Then, in Bullen's story, something much more serious claimed everyone's attention. The doctor reported yellow fever had broken out on board. It was common knowledge that yellow fever outbreaks were occurring in many West Indies locations, including Kingston and Port-au-Prince. The first who died was one of the men who had been ashore. The outbreak aboard the ship was serious, though Bullen says that none of the passengers were afflicted, but newspaper death notices in Liverpool attest to two passenger deaths. Of the crew, Bullen says, 'but of the ship's company, officer, engineers, firemen, sailors, and stewards all gave tythe to death.' The disease was terribly swift in its progress. Feeling unwell was quickly followed by delirium, then death. One of the crew ran amok with an axe and in his madness murdered a man named Carney. Following each death came rapid preparations for a sea burial, and a very short committal. The loss of regular crew was filled from *Brinkburn's* DBS group, for whom the money was welcome, but duty as firemen unwelcome. Tommy Bullen was not immune – he writes:[9]

One morning at five o'clock, when, as usual, I was called to begin my day's work, I lifted my head to rise, but it fell again like a piece of lead. A feeling of utter helplessness had seized my whole body, although I could not say I felt ill. But not even the awe in which I stood of the Chief Steward could overcome my want of strength, and I humbly said, 'I'm not able to get up, sir'. Instantly alarmed, the Steward fetched the doctor, who, after feeling my pulse, etc, pulled me out of the bunk and set me on my trembling legs, telling the steward to put me to some work that did not require any running about, but on no account to allow me to sit down His orders were strictly obeyed, but how I got through that dreadful day I cannot tell. I felt as though I would gladly have given the whole world to be allowed to lie down for a while and several times my legs doubled up under me letting me sink in a heap on the pantry deck, but there was no respite allowed me. This stern treatment was completely successful, for

41

by supper-time I felt quite strong again, and I was troubled no more by any recurrence of those alarming symptoms.

The deaths continued to mount, with the doctor paying most attention to those individuals who survived the initial onslaught of the disease. Nursing them back to fitness, beef tea with brandy was his chief remedy, administered in small doses as a reviver.

Another casualty due to age and overwork were the ship's boilers, which sprang a serious leak, leaving the ship stopped in the water. A not uncommon occurrence, the engineers and firemen had to work inside the still-roasting boilers to locate the leak, decide on how to treat the symptom, and do the mend. After a day and a night, the patch was completed and served to get the ship to port, though at reduced speed. Eventually, the doctor was able to announce that the epidemic was over, and no more deaths were expected. According to Bullen the death toll was thirty. Arriving in Liverpool on 7 October 1871, the ship was cleared without being put in quarantine, and continued normally with the discharge of all personnel and unloading her cargo. Despite the number of deaths, no report appeared in the newspapers, except the two death notices. The absence of publicity no doubt suited the shipowners, as such adverse news might put off prospective passengers. The mysterious man with chests re-emerged just before arrival, only to go berserk when he asked for the chests and neither the mate nor the master could remember their existence. He had to be locked in a cabin. It came out after arrival that in the new government in Haiti he had been in charge of the treasury and had taken his chance to run off with some of the funds. But he got nowhere with the British authorities with his complaint of his loss.

That there was disease aboard SS *Cuban* that voyage is confirmed by the two deaths recorded in the crew agreement. No evidence has been found concerning the passengers the ship was carrying, so there could have been more deaths among them, except that passenger deaths should have been recorded in the official log, as well as crew deaths. DBS crew ought also to have been recorded in both the AAC and the OL, but do not appear. So Bullen's thirty deaths might be down to hype, or the master was negligent in making the correct entries, or SS *Cuban* was not the correct ship. After another spell ashore in Liverpool, Tommy Bullen shipped out again on 13 November 1871.

4

A Voyage Without a Change of Vessel

13 November 1871 to 23 November 1872

Once again Bullen was faced with being cut adrift in Liverpool, for the moment penniless, once he set foot ashore. Perhaps he could work by the steamer he had arrived in (SS *Cuban*?) for a small wage until he had earned enough for accommodation.[1] But the chief steward appeared and told him he was not wanted and to get ashore at once. However, Hadji, the Chinese second steward, pressed half a crown into his hand and wished him luck. Ashore he walked the docks trying for a berth to no avail. Finding a heap of hay at Coburg Dock he bedded down, to resume his fruitless search the following day. Reaching Brunswick Dock, he found the figurehead carver had gone and he did not fancy trying the adjacent eating house again. Back at the Sailors' Home, and still with only his half crown, that institution refused to take him in. So a few days on, after contemplating the workhouse on Brownlow Hill, he plucked up courage to try the mistress of the Brunswick Dock Eating House once again, who, after many appeals, took him in. For a few weeks he was worked hard and really earned his keep but, trade dropping off, he was once again ordered away. Then came success: he was taken on as a cabin boy on a German ship, *Greif* of Rostock. Here he was to be known as Dan, the name of his predecessor in the job. He was really the servant of the master's wife and daughter, who, lacking English, struggled to make themselves understood. The ship had a crew aboard and when cabin duties had been done the mate, another man inclined to strike a youngster, found jobs around the deck for him to do. Chopping firewood for the cook, the axe he was given slipped, making a mark on the deck. Tommy

44

was knocked senseless by the mate, sending the rest of the crew into uproar for that unmerited action. Before the crew got out of hand, the master appeared, the crew dispersed and Tommy was ordered out of the ship.

For once Tommy now had a bit of luck. By a nearby vessel, he was musing aloud about a spar on the dockside fitted with three sheaves. While pondering where it fitted into the rigging of a sailing ship, he was overheard by a gentleman, the ship's master, who explained that it was his ship's 'foreto-gallanmast' with the third sheave for the 'skys'le-halliards'. After listening to Tommy's story, he took him aboard the *Jorawur* of London and paid him twelve shillings a week, feeding himself until the ship sailed. He had to leave then as she did not carry boys. When *Jorawur* sailed she would carry thirty-two ABs and six petty officers. Tommy was to be found jobs to do by the ship keeper. At knock-off time, the shore workers such as riggers disappeared, and the ship keeper soon left him in charge while he went for a run ashore. For food Tommy raided the pantry and found some arrowroot and biscuits, which served as his meal. Being helpful, he was on good terms with the ship keeper, though a job that man found for him to do was to clean out the ship's fresh-water tanks, mainly because he could get through the manhole in each tank. Some tanks had leftover water in them and this made him desperately cold. After removing rust and the residues of water, he had to coat the tanks with limewash: all that meant that he became coated in the filth. Another wheeze Tommy devised to save spending money on food was to supply the ship's tea to a team of painters working in the accommodation, who in return shared their lunches with him. The ship loaded a cargo of salt for Calcutta and just before sailing day its master took him to the Liverpool Sailors' Home, where he paid a fortnight's board and hoped they would find a ship for Tommy.

At the Sailor's Home, Tommy was allotted one of the six feet by eight feet cabins by a steward, who promised to find him a supply of clothing. Outside was a row of washbasins in which Tommy had a good wash. A gong rang, which he realised was for dinner, and he joined the throng of men emerging from their rooms. He had not yet learned the dining rules, and that each floor of cabins (called flats), dined at lettered tables. To him flats were Liverpool barges, and his confusion caused much merriment, until he found his table. The food was liberal and washed down by large cans of ale; the meal was over within half an hour. Exploring, Tommy found a sign to the library, and soon a room well stocked with books and only three people in it. Making the library his daytime home, he devoured its reading stock, between meals virtually hiding himself away. Moving around the home he took to dodging out of sight of the officials who might disturb his comfort by finding him a ship. Of course, it had to come to an end. The doorkeeper caught him and walked him into the shipping office, where he was signed on the *Western Belle* at twenty-five shillings a month. Altogether he had three weeks in residence in the building, and had to pay for the third week out of his month's advance of wages.

The majority of the crew of *Western Belle* had signed-on on 10 November 1871, to join the ship on the 14th.[2] Tommy, signing-on on the 13th, was amongst the last few hands. Including the master, the ship sailed with a crew of twenty-six: master, first mate, second mate, carpenter, bosun, sailmaker, steward, cook, fourteen ABs (including a man unusually labelled painter), an ordinary seaman and three boys. Of these, two of the ABs failed to join. *Western Belle* was owned in Greenock, so it was no surprise that there were eight Scots aboard. There were nine seafarers from England and Wales, two each from Denmark and parts of British North America, and one each from Ireland, Italy, Sweden, Belgium and the USA. Tommy's age is shown as sixteen, which may have been a bit of embroidery on his part, as he was still only fourteen. Including the master, nine of the crew gave *Western Belle* as their last ship, an indicator that that they were content with life under that master. This voyage she was bound initially for Bombay.

On joining day the crew members, with their belongings and accompanied by one of the Sailor's Home staff, crossed the River Mersey by ferry to Seacombe, and made their way to the Alfred

Dock, where *Western Belle* lay just inside the lock gates to the Birkenhead group of docks. The Alfred Dock was quite new, having been remodelled from a smaller facility in 1866. Tommy was rather better equipped than when joining previous ships, having from his hoarded funds been able to purchase oilskins, straw bed, hookpot, pannikin (small metal cup) and plate, soap, matches and knife. The crew were joining 'an old American-built soft-wood ship, with a deck house for the crew instead of the villainous den beneath the top-gallant-forecastle far in the forepart of the ship which is the lair of seamen in most English ships.' Tommy Bullen was allocated a berth in the petty officers' part of the deckhouse.

Possibly *Western Belle* had earlier been moved from a loading berth further in the Birkenhead dock system ready for sailing, because they had barely arrived when she started to move to the lock gates, where a Liverpool tug, the *Constitution*, passed her a hawser for the tow downriver. The crew's immediate, tricky, job was to rig out the jibboom in a rising wind and an increasingly heavy sea. This bowsprit extension had to be housed for the manoeuvres in the docks, shortening the length the ship took up, but weakening the interconnected arrangement of stays supporting the masts. It had a jumble of standing rigging attached, which hung loose until it had been launched ahead and secured in position and the rigging stretched. The danger and difficulty was increased by the weather conditions and the speed of the tow. This 'head gear' was essential for the setting of jibs, which were used as much for balancing the steering as for propulsion. Seas began breaking over the bowsprit and fo'c'sle head. A shout of 'man overboard', and the tug immediately stopped while a lifebuoy had been thrown and reached by the unfortunate AB. In the entanglement he drowned before he was picked up by the tug's boat. Peter Hill was his name, a 39-year-old Liverpool man who left a widow and two children. The tug took him ashore once the tow reached the Tuskar Rock, south coast of Ireland, when it let go and *Western Belle* set her sails. With the jibboom properly shipped, presumably, and perhaps owing to the shock of the accident, the crew had rushed to their accommodation, intent on dividing the poor man's belongings. True, it was customary for masters to auction deceased seamen's belongings among the crew, and normally for them to pay over the top for very ordinary items, to boost the amount of cash that would, at the end of the voyage, be due to the dead man's relatives. This greedy behaviour seems atypical, and was perhaps before a proper cohesion among the crew had become established. Somehow, making the entry in the official log, the master entered a list of twenty-five items, almost all selling for a shilling or two, which, with £1 in cash, amounted to £2 17s 7d.

That other outward-bound ritual now took place, the choosing of the watches. Now it became obvious that the ship was badly undermanned. It was already short of three men from the crew originally signed on. Further, the ship was 'parish rigged' according to Bullen, meaning that her gear, the rigging, was of the cheapest quality and short of the proper purchases which assisted labour, though there were two capstans. Bullen recorded his recollections of the crew and his opinions, which can be compared with the names on the Agreement and Account of Crew. Here he is less reliable. The elderly Yankee answering to 'Nat' 'one of the best seamen on board', would seem to be Nathan Martin Tyrrell, forty-five, AB, born in Folkestone. There was only one Irishman aboard, not two: George Fagan, aged fifteen, a boy, with previous sea experience. Jean Baptiste is not on the list, though there is a man hailing from Dunkirk, aged forty-one, William (?) Prees (?), AB. The taciturn Dane might be Henry Burgess from Elsinore aged twenty-nine, AB, or John Knight, who signed with an 'X', forty-five, AB from Denmark. John Bradley must be Edward Bradley, twenty-seven, AB, from Prince Edward Island, who would die later in the voyage. Peter Burn from Liverpool might be the unfortunate Peter Hill, AB, while the lad Julius Caesar was probably John Cadogan, seventeen, OS, from New York. The Yarmouth man was William Barber, painter and AB, aged twenty-five. Bullen says he was paid extra for his skill, but the Agreement has him receiving £2 10s 0d, the same as the other ABs. The cook was not Maltese, but Adolpho Burly

48

(?), twenty-seven, from Trieste. There was an apprentice on board, William Smith, whose name appears in the official logbook, and would be in the section of the Agreement for apprentices. He had been in the *Warspite*, training ship, and was now in his third year as an apprentice, and a first-class seaman. Frederick Charles Carter, aged fourteen, a boy, was a first tripper from Woolton in Liverpool. The master, Captain Thomas Smith, fifty (not sixty, as Bullen says), from Fife, was jolly, good-tempered, easy-going and not a worrier, and had his wife and daughter (about twenty-two) with him. They shared the master's qualities. The first mate Andrew Edny, forty-three (not thirty-five as Bullen has it), from Kirkcaldy was a 'splendid specimen of manhood', had coal-black hair and eyes, and was extremely hirsute. William Cottam, thirty-nine, second mate, from Hyde near Manchester, was the bane of Tommy's existence, but a prime seaman.

Tommy Bullen, despite the negatives discussed above, must have been pleased to be aboard his largest ship so far, with the prospect of a twelve-month voyage, and crossing the equator four times, which would mark him as a man of the sea who had sailed to the 'suthard'.[3] He found himself in the second mate's watch. The latter turned out to be something of a tyrant, sparing nobody. The apprentice, Smith, in the same watch, became an enduring friend and a helping hand when Tommy was struggling. Take out the helmsman and lookout and there were only six hands to man the watch. The ship was a very heavy-working vessel, and the food so bad that he was reminded of *Caroline*. The ship was not a good sailer, would not easily turn to windward and made a great deal of leeway. In the notorious Bay of Biscay and with an endless series of gales and high seas, working the ship was made extremely difficult. Tommy was swamped by a big sea carrying him over the side while he hung onto a rope, and was washed back aboard again in the next sea. Below decks there were signs of movement and the cargo of coal was generating dangerous gases which could not be ventilated away. In the fore hold, food stocks of salt beef and pork had mixed with the content of barrels of Stockholm tar. The food had to be rescued, scraped clean, and freshly pickled in brine. Yet it was eaten. One of the elderly ABs, named as Peter Burn by Bullen, but probably John Mains, aged fifty-eight, from Gourock, developed very ulcerated legs, and died on 4 March 1872.[4] The ship's progress was unusually slow, and Tommy continued to suffer the sharp tongue of the second mate, who never failed to find jobs for him to do. In the half deck shared with the petty officers, those men cheated the two boys from their fair share of the food, despite its doubtful quality. The apprentice, Tommy's roommate, eventually put up a fight, and portions became more even-handed. Whatever Tommy did seemed to end in trouble. When he usurped the mate's fishing tackle at the end of the jibboom, he succeeded in catching a bonito, but struggled to contain its resistance, almost losing his leg-hold and bedraggling the sails and deck with blood. Once cooked, that food was appreciated in the half deck as a welcome change of diet. Soon he was up before the first mate for soiling the decks and sails.

Reaching the doldrums, the downpours of rain were a welcome opportunity for everyone to bathe on deck and wash their clothing.[5] The ship's water tanks were refilled, a relief as such ships rarely had sufficient tank space for water to last a whole passage. The calms and dry periods continuing, the master commenced a pet project, to fashion new, heavier, topsail yards from balks of timber lashed to the decks. A saw pit was created to saw the spars lengthwise, and the more capable crew started the job of trimming the spars to shape and size. Metal fittings were forged to size and fitted towards the end of the eight weeks in the doldrums, with the job then finished. Meanwhile, John Mains was reaching his final moments and finally passed away. The sailmaker made a shroud, which was weighted, and all assembled for the burial service to be read by the master, and the committal. The master would then have written the entry in the official logbook and had it witnessed by the first mate. A breeze sprang up and *Western Belle* gathered headway, resuming her slow progress to her destination.

In the drawn-out duration of the passage, some of the crew developed scurvy in mild form, a painful and weakening condition.

Bullen says that William Barber, painter/AB, became quite useless through illness and never recovered sufficiently for the rest of the voyage. But there are no entries for him in the official log, and he signed off in London. The passage continued around the Cape of Good Hope into the Indian Ocean. In fair, steady weather the deck watch became somewhat slack and the second mate failed to recognise the black cloud gathering on the horizon which augured a serious squall, before which all sail should have been taken in. Suddenly, all was flat aback amid the howl of the wind and torrents of rain. The sails split in fragments, while the ship was being driven astern. Everything was let go. Fortunately, a sea helped the ship to turn into the wind and the crew were able to get topsails set and drawing.

The next worry were the cyclones to which at certain seasons of the year, and in certain areas, the Indian Ocean was prone. Tommy knew about these from his experiences in the West Indies.[6] However, the balmy weather continued, and they saw no other ships. In the Arabian Sea nearing Bombay, a dhow came alongside, from which a man jumped aboard *Western Belle*, and bowing to the master, and in perfect English, solicited the ship chandlery custom of the ship. But the master, an old Bombay hand, always employed the same 'dubash', or general purveyor. Now many local craft were encountered and Bullen was amazed at the number of deep-sea vessels anchored off the port. A white pilot boarded to take *Western Belle* to its anchorage in a stiffening breeze. The second mate ordered Bullen aloft to climb with the end of a flag halliard to reeve it through the mast cap which ended the truck of the mast. On all sailing ships there was no ratline ladder to help the climb up this last, almost bare, section of mast. On American-built ships like *Western Belle* these were extra-long, perhaps sixteen feet according to Bullen, who writes:[7]

I started aloft boldly enough; but when I reached the base of the pole, and saw to what height its bareness towered above me, while the staggering ship lurched to leeward, and the foaming sea roared a hundred and twenty feet below, my heart failed me, my head swam, and all my scanty stock of strength left me. For some time, I sat with my legs clutched round the pole just clinging, without power to move. Then I heard the voice of the Second Mate pealing up from the deck. 'Hurry up there with those halliards!' Strange as it might appear, although I felt I was going to certain death, my fear of him was so great I made the attempt. Trembling in every nerve, but fighting against my benumbing weakness, I actually struggled to the top ... Opening my eyes I thrust at the opening of the sheave with the end of the line; but it was knotted, and would not go through. I had tried and failed, and with my last flash of energy I grasped the pole with both hands, and slid down on to the eyes of the royal rigging ... I descended to the deck, walked up to Mr Cottam, and said, 'I have tried, and I can't do it, sir – not if you kill me.'

It must be remembered that climbing aloft with the end of a rope means dragging while climbing an increasing length and weight of rope. Once at the truck, two hands are needed to thread the end of the halliard through the sheave, and once achieved, climbing down means pulling the threaded end downwards against the weight of the rope going up the mast. Putting one's legs around the mast and resting one's whole weight on the grip demands exceptional strength. The second mate was at fault for not having had the job done earlier in the calm weather during the passage, for not choosing a much stronger and taller crew member, and for not ensuring that the end of the halliard was clear of knots and seized with twine, to make the threading as easy as possible. The apprentice Bill Smith soon carried out the job.

After making a 'flying moor' (running moor) with port and starboard anchors, the crew soon noticed a large ship nearby, recognising it as the ship that had passed them as they left the lock gates from Birkenhead docks. It was the *Stornoway* which was then homeward bound, which had completed another outward passage, and was now heaving up her anchors for her next homeward passage, while *Western Belle* had taken seven months on her own outward passage. Unloading *Western Belle*'s cargo of coal into lighters was by the primitive method of filling chains of small baskets with coal and passing it from hand to hand until it could be tipped in to lighters, there being a return chain of empty baskets. A very large number of local workers, known as 'coolies', was employed, some in the holds filling the baskets and the rest in the chains, men, women and children. The basketfuls could not have been very heavy, yet rhythm was achieved in passing the baskets through a monotonous chant. So the lighters gradually filled. Meanwhile, the crew had a light time of it, despite the coal dust, with plenty of fresh meat and vegetables provided by the ship. Bumboats offered fruit, eggs and so on, and Tommy once again found himself bookkeeper and in receipt of what he wanted from them. On Sundays, it seemed the whole of the trading population came afloat and filled ships' decks with large quantities of trade goods. Crew members, innocents as to values, were easily cheated into paying more for items which were much cheaper back in London. The ship also cheated them, charging an exchange rate of 2s 4d per rupee, which was publicly quoted at 1s 8d.

As unloading neared completion, stone ballast began to be taken in partly to stiffen the vessel as empty sailing ships became unstable, and partly because the homeward cargo had been booked at two ports on the southeast coast of India, Bimlipatam and Coconada. That meant a sea passage round Ceylon (Sri Lanka) into the Bay of Bengal. But before leaving Bombay, the concession to the crew of twenty-four hours' liberty ashore was observed. Bullen says each of the port watch (the mate's watch) was issued with twenty rupees, its value of course deducted from wages. All returned the following morning except the AB Edward Bradley. Predictably, the others returned in a miserable condition and aboard began to fight among themselves. As a result, the starboard (second mate's) watch could not be allowed their turn that day, causing a serious row with the officers. However, the petty officers could have their turn, and Bill Smith and Tommy were allowed to go with them. Bill and Tommy separated from the group and Bill took him shopping in the Bombay bazaars. Bill being an apprentice was not waged, but had earned a little doing chores for others on board. He gave Tommy a real lesson in bartering. Selecting a stall, he piled up a heap of clothes and other goods, and then invited the trader to name a price. This excessive sum he topped by offering ten rupees. The trader demanded to see his cash, and Bill ostentatiously counted out his ten rupees. The trader was appalled at Bill's offer, but forty-five rupees became a final offer of thirty. Bill and Tommy walked away, but after going some distance, the trader chased after them and accepted the ten rupees Bill had offered.

Bill went off on his own. Tommy eventually wandered back to the harbour, hiring a canoe which, after a short trip up the harbour, delivered him back aboard. The starboard watch had its trip ashore returning in much the same condition as the port watch. Meanwhile, there had been a robbery in the crew's accommodation. Bradley had crept aboard unseen and rifled through their chests. He finally had the cheek to return aboard, taking immediately to his bunk with the assertion he was ill. Sailing in fair weather, the ship proved to be tender, having taken insufficient ballast. Bradley really was ill and helpless, with suppurating pimples which burst out. He was moved to a shaded spot on deck and Tommy was ordered to attend to him and to bathe him during his, Tommy's, watch below. Arriving at Bimlipatam anchorage, Bradley died, and was taken ashore for burial without any ceremony.

The anchorage was off a surf-beaten beach, the rollers making *Western Belle* pitch and roll unpleasantly.[8] Cargo came off for loading from that beach in local sturdy boats. The mixed cargo included jaggery (black palm sugar), buffalo horns and hides, caster oil in cases, bags of myrobolams (dye-nut), and much else in small quantities. All this had to be stowed by the crew. Leaving Bimlipatam, a few hours' sail down the coast brought the ship to Coconada and an anchorage a long way from the town. The cargo included cotton, linseed and myrobolams, again stowed by the crew, until the holds were full up. As the ship was about to sail, an experienced AB raised the issue of obtaining more crew. The master listened courteously and explained the dearth of seafarers ashore, and the need to get out of the Bay of Bengal before the southwest monsoon set in. Bullen makes no mention of the two ABs, Alfred Gilbert from Germany, and James Furling from Wexford in Ireland, whom the master had engaged at Bombay.[9] The master did acquire a large number of fowls, and two goats, in addition to the twenty or so pigs, dogs, monkeys, parrots and cats already aboard. This menagerie was a mixed blessing: there was no housing for them, and many of the fowls were lost in the first spell of bad weather after sailing. Also the decks were fouled. Bullen explores the issue of animals aboard ship using a vessel he names as *Belle* as one of his examples. This is surely the case of the *Western Belle*.[10]

The homeward voyage to London was blessed with favourable weather across the Indian Ocean and up the South Atlantic to St Helena to have the ship reported, without stopping.[11] The second mate continued to be the bane of their lives for the starboard watch, this time having the painted areas of the ship sand and canvassed as a cleaner. Otherwise, the master did not push his short-handed crew. In the Atlantic Ocean, however, he busied the whole crew cleaning and decorating the ship, and overhauling the rigging ready for the eyes of the ship's husband on arrival in London. This meant 'field days' for both watches, which involved putting in two to three hours' work during their daylight watch below. Approaching St Helena, the ship was allowed to get too close to the cliffs and in the violent manoeuvre to get clear, split the mizzen topmast. Four days later Ascension Island was sighted and signalled. The second mate, Bullen comments, was in his element with the deck work to be done, as usual working as hard himself as the men in his watch. But he seemed doomed to be a junior officer, although he had somehow passed the examination for his Certificate of Competency as Second Mate. He could not pass the navigation examination, as he could not do the calculations without making stupid mistakes.

Further north, the weather became more uncertain, and the master more and more anxious as the ship entered the Western

Approaches to the Channel. He shortened sail and several ships going in the same direction overhauled *Western Belle*. A thick fog set in and the ship was hove-to for some six hours, hearing fog signals all around. A cruising pilot offered his services and was accepted. A Trinity House pilot eventually turned up near Dungeness and, further on, protracted negotiations with a tug for the tow fee were conducted. At Gravesend there was a short pause to take the river pilot and it was not too long before they were tied up in the basin to East India Dock. A hoard of boarding-house and tailors' runners swarmed aboard, persuading crew members to go with them to their establishments. So the crew rapidly dispersed. Tommy was invited to stay with the ship for the time being, at fourteen shillings a week, paying for his own keep. Signing off at Green's Home on 23 November 1872, Tommy says he received nine sovereigns. The Agreement and Account of Crew records £8 17s 3d. His fifteenth birthday had passed in April, and no doubt his stature had developed.

5

Sea Time in Coastal Steamers

26 January 1873 to 6 November 1874

L eaving the shipping office at Green's Home, Tommy Bullen could easily have been set upon by one of the crimps who hovered around the building, hoping to latch onto the men who had just received their money.[1] Having almost £9 in cash did worry him. He could have deposited it with the Seamen's Saving Bank at the Shipping Office, or if he had gone to the Sailors' Home in Well Street/Dock Street, he could have left it with their deposit facilities, and they were used to seafarers drawing small sums while residing there. Perhaps a little thoughtlessly, he determined to spend it on an outfit of clothing and took himself to the emporium of Moses and Sons, who eyed him suspiciously as the number of items piled up, until he flashed some of his cash before them. Of course, he was taken in and supplied with low-quality garments. Still, he had a complete stock, including a chest, bedding, oilskins and sea boots, and was cheeky enough to demand they be delivered to *Western Belle*. A fortnight on, his comfortable arrangement of standing by *Western Belle* came to an end, all the work needed having been done aboard that ship. Fortunately, he had retained some of his pay-off, enough to fund a week at his old boarding house in West India Dock Road. Also, he demanded he be found a ship. The boarding-house master was less pleased when he discovered that Tommy had been paid off with a much larger sum. He was found a berth in an American ship, *Pharos* of Boston, lying at South West India Dock and loading a general cargo for Melbourne. He was allowed to live and work aboard while loading was completed.

As an American ship, *Pharos* was not subject to the engagement regulations which covered British ships. No official crew list or logbook is known, so little of the detail of her voyage to Melbourne can be found excepting the movement notices in newspapers. However, a web search produced some information from the history of the town in Massachusetts, USA, to which she belonged, Cohassett.[2] The master of *Pharos* was Captain James Collier, born 1813, a very experienced mariner and owner or part-owner of the ship. The crew, a miscellaneous lot, signed on in a tailor's shop in Ratcliff Highway, crowded with the unruly crew of another ship, as well that joining *Pharos*.

Standing by aboard the ship, Tommy had soon become aware that things were not right. Those crew still aboard from the previous passage included the mate, who completely neglected the cargo, spending his time drinking with cronies; the second mate, aged about twenty, who concerned himself with the rigging, taking no interest in the cargo; and the carpenter and the cook, who whiled away the time in the galley, drinking. In time the mate parted company from the ship. There was no attempt at tallying cargo at all. Another mate joined a few days before sailing. In all, *Pharos* probably carried a master, first mate, second mate, carpenter, steward, cook and eighteen ABs.[3] At the signing on, each crew member was automatically given an advance note of two months' wages, cashable (at a discount) at the tailors' shop. Tommy was signed on as ordinary seaman (a promotion for him) at thirty shillings a month, and found himself in possession of an advance note worth £3. He tried several places to cash it, but resorted in the end to an old friend, a tradesman, who charged no discount. He fared much better than the rest of the crew. The larger the advance, the more the likelihood of the seafarer not turning up aboard ship. Seven men failed to join *Pharos* on sailing day, and she went down to Gravesend short-handed, where replacements were found.

Pharos lay at anchor at Red Buoy, some way from Gravesend, to take in a cargo of fifty tons of explosives from a special lighter. Despite the reputation of American ships for bullying crew treatment, this proved to be a quiet ship, neither the master nor the mates being of that character, although there were some hard cases among the crew. A Channel pilot joined to take the ship to Portland, but was soon at odds with the master. Off the Isle of Wight, the pilot altered course to close the land so he could disembark, but was countermanded by the master, who refused to go out of his way to land him. Understandably, the pilot became frantic. The ship had seven passengers, but there was trouble with them. As far as the crew was concerned, this was a good feeding ship. The passengers had believed they would be very well fed. Instead, they would have to pay the cook for their food, which would be the same as that doled out to the crew. The steward was banned from waiting on them, and their presence in the saloon annoyed the master, who told them that it was no business of his to provide for their sustenance. Thereafter they fended for themselves and ignored the master. The pilot was kept on board for five days before being put on a homeward ship in the Bay of Biscay.

The work of the ship went on with automatic regularity, but Tommy found that, although graded an ordinary seaman, and sleeping in the fo'c'sle with the crew, he was not assigned any duties.[4] So he chummed up with the steward, fed with him, and did small services for the passengers. After a fortnight, he felt compelled to give up his quarters, and take refuge in the cabin, sleeping under the saloon table, the captain not seeming to notice. Another curiosity was that at the least sign of bad weather, and despite the fact that *Pharos* was a fairly new vessel and had been well equipped, sail was immediately reduced to lower topsails and a staysail. Captain Collier was prone to breaking out into the worst blasphemies and guttural cursings, scaring Tommy to the bone. Also, he was a master who kept the navigation to himself, not even trusting the mate, Mr Small, who Bullen thought a good officer and seaman. It became the practice for the officers never to go forward anywhere near the crew quarters at night, and Tommy soon realised that the general cargo was systematically being broached of canned meats and condiments, drink and tobacco. No one showed any drunkenness, and pilfering these luxuries went on for the three months of the passage to Melbourne without the officers becoming aware of it. Even the passengers shared in the spoils. There was a leader in the fo'c'sle keeping control of the illicit activity, so that evidence of the depreciations, such as empty wooden cases, were burnt in the galley stove.

Rounding the Cape of Good Hope, instead of heading into the roaring forties to catch the winds, the master kept north in the Indian Ocean among the calm weather, greatly extending the passage. Nearing the end of the passage, the leader of the pilfering relaxed his control, and gave a bottle of spirits to the carpenter, who proceeded to get himself roaring drunk, running to the master's accommodation to call him out for a fight. Clapping him into irons proved to be the only way he could be controlled. The evidence of pilferage was found and presented to Captain Collier, and at last the hold was searched. Tommy was becoming increasingly anxious about the outcome once in port. Some of the crew were making preparations to leave the ship. The ship arrived at Melbourne 155 days out. At the Williamstown anchorage for four days until the explosives were removed, the ship then moved up to the Sandridge pier. The master strangely took no action to have the losses investigated. The main protagonists of the pilferage packed bags and walked ashore in the captain's view, without any word from him. Of course, as deserters they forfeited their accumulated wages, but they had profited with two months' advance of wages. Determining to desert, Tommy befriended the cook of the coastal steamer *Wonga Wonga*, also tied up at the pier, who agreed to help him to stow away for the passage from Melbourne to Sydney. He managed to get his possessions aboard the steamer before spending a final night aboard *Pharos*.

The black steward of *Pharos*, the religious man with whom Tommy had become friendly, guessed that something was up.[5] Tommy revealed his intentions, and the steward, agreeing that *Pharos* was not a suitable vessel for him, presented him with ten dollars to tide him over. Hearing *Wonga Wonga*'s whistle signal for her departure, also from Sandridge Pier, he mingled with the crowd of passengers who were joining for the passage to Sydney, and slipped aboard undetected. In that ship's galley (engaged in serving dinner), his contact, the cook, gave him some bread and meat, and pointed him to the chain locker as a hideaway. Only then did Tommy fully realise that he had become no more than a stowaway. He must have fallen asleep with his legs protruding out of the chain locker, probably into a forepeak store. The mate of the *Wonga Wonga* found him, woke him up and quizzed him about where he had come from. Then he was ordered on deck, where he was fitted into the crew and put to work. The ship carried the master and three deck officers, fourteen deckhands, eleven catering hands, three engineers and twelve engine-room hands. Passengers could number at least fifty-six.[6] *Wonga Wonga*'s cook, whom Bullen names as Mr White, ignored him until nearing the end of the short passage of some forty-eight hours, when he offered to accommodate him ashore and help him find a berth in another of the coastal steamers, by then linking Australia's major and minor ports. As he left *Wonga Wonga*, the mate gave him a sovereign, warned him about crimps infesting Sydney's port district, and said he would try to get him a berth as a lamp trimmer in a steamer. Writing twenty-seven years later, Bullen says that he was convinced 'that Sydney was the most shamelessly immoral place I had ever seen.' The cook's home was a house in Lower York Street, a basic but adequate dwelling, where he was welcomed by Mrs White. A week later Tommy secured a berth as lamp trimmer in the small steamer *Helen McGregor*, at £2 10s 0d a month.

Official Agreements and Account of Crew (the same as those in use in Britain) for these coastal steamers seem not to have survived, though one crew list for immigration on arrival does bear Tommy's name. Following the requirements of the Board of Trade in London, the steamers should have been classed as home-trade passenger ships and to have carried certificated masters, mates and engineers. The Agreement would likely have been a running agreement renewable each January and July. Men joining and leaving such ships between each renewal would be signed on and off under the master's authority and he would pay the balance of wages and issue certificates of discharge. Tommy was probably not put on the agreement of *Wonga Wonga*, but he ought to have been named on *Helen McGregor*'s and *Wentworth*'s (see below) agreements. However, of the crew and passenger lists compiled for the immigration authorities, only one for the *Helen McGregor* seems to exist. This lists a crew of master, mate, four ABs, an engineer and four firemen, cook and steward.[7] The number of deckhands seems very few, even though this was a much smaller vessel than *Wonga Wonga*. As each of the Australian colonies were separate from each other, coastal vessels moving from a port in one colony to a port in another could be treated as arriving from overseas. This may have happened to *Wentworth* on her voyages from Sydney to Auckland, New Zealand.

The *Helen McGregor* maintained a regular service between Sydney and the town of Grafton up the Clarence River, calling en route at Newcastle, also in New South Wales, and if there was demand, at quays or jetties along the river. But she was not really fit for the potentially mountainous seas that could occur on the sections of ocean that had to be crossed. They were a common experience, the ship's motions frightful and making everyone on board seasick. Passengers were battened down in the saloon or second cabin. The poor cook had a minute galley, where somehow in such conditions he managed to create meals for seventy or eighty people, after butchering some of the livestock the ship carried out on the open deck. At night Tommy got no respite for he had to keep the navigation lights and binnacle lights burning, which were often bounced out of their mountings. Tending all of them forced him to cross the open deck while the seas swept aboard. In the engine room, the chief engineer was forced to hand-govern the engine, easing the throttle as the propeller came out of the water, and opening it when it plunged back into the sea. Perhaps worst affected of all were the firemen trying to keep steam up while tending the furnaces, involving clearing out ash and clinker and feeding in coal from the bunkers.

The Clarence River was blocked by a bar, which could only be crossed when the tide was high enough. This tricky operation was only attempted in daylight. Arriving at night meant steaming slowly up and down outside until tide and daylight served. Then all hands took up secure positions on deck, and even in the rigging, as the steamer faced the breakers marking the bar. This was pilotage and ship-handling of the highest order, and the master kept a man in the chains with the hand lead, shouting the depths of water. Often, the ship touched bottom, but once over the bar in calm water, normal routine was resumed. Inside, conning the ship to keep her in the deepest water, often using fixed objects, even trees, as leading marks, required the teamwork of the master and the best helmsman over the remaining distance. Intermediate calls, mostly to rickety jetties, demanded manoeuvring the ship with rudder and engine movements, but this was not a strength of the master, who managed it rather roughly. Packages for delivery were quickly landed and then the ship was away. At Grafton *Helen McGregor* tied up to a more substantial jetty, where Tommy had a quick, uninterested look at the town, and on board spent his spare time fishing.

In the stay of about a week, the mixed cargo of manufactured goods and imports was unloaded, and the return cargo of maize, preserved beef, mutton and tin ore in bags was loaded. Last-minute items of food produce included several hundred bunches of bananas. Departure for Sydney was timed so as to reach the bar when the tide served, but about twenty miles downriver on one passage they had to pass a section of bush fire which threatened to jump to the ship. After this and crossing the bar, the return passage to Sydney was a routine affair. One of the twenty-plus trips Tommy made in that steamer was notable for the amount of heavy rain affecting cargo-handling at Grafton. The river was running very rapidly and the master moved the ship to anchor in the middle of the stream. Now a torrent, the river was bringing down trees and floating islands of debris torn from the banks. Further, it rose about twenty feet to the level of its bank, and the ship could have floated over the jetty. The flooding was extensive over a wide area. Houses were isolated as islands, and in the countryside there was widespread devastation of crops and property. But there was also severe flooding on the Hunter River, at the mouth of which lies Newcastle, which took the attention of the Sydney press.

Helen McGregor managed about two such trips each month, and Tommy says he probably made at least twenty of them, which would have taken the best part of a year.[8] He became dissatisfied with his treatment in the ship, as he was expected to work as a normal crew member as well as tending the lights. At the minor jetties, cargo was handled by the crew, and Tommy was injured on several occasions. Resigning his position in Sydney, he lodged for three weeks with a shoemaker, living on his accumulated earnings. He admits to taking to drink and imbibing heavily. Having run out of money, he secured a position as lamp trimmer again, aboard a new steamer named *Wentworth* belonging to the Australian Steam Navigation Company. Here, the mate of the ship gave him clear instructions that his duties consisted solely of attending to the lamps and polishing the ornamental brass-work about the decks. His wages were to be £3 10s 0d per month. Polishing the brass became an obsession, as he strove to make the ship's brass the shiniest of all the ships in harbour. He was accommodated in a cubicle off the lamp room, separate from the rest of the crew. He also trimmed the cook's lamps, and in return he was fed from the saloon fare prepared for the passengers and officers. This was not to say that the crew fed badly. They also did very well. There was considerable waste of food, due perhaps to the fact that shore contractors supplied the ship's food at a price per head. The ship's cooks and stewards were also provided by the contractors. At all costs complaints must be avoided lest the contract be lost. It was easy for crew members to invent complaints in which meals partly consumed might be discarded. ABs could command £7 0s 0d per month plus 1s 6d per hour overtime. The working day was eight hours. Firemen were paid £10 and trimmers £8 per month. But they appreciated their privileged position and mostly avoided the debauchery of deep-sea ratings.

Wentworth's crew probably was similar to that of *Wonga Wonga*. In 1874 it comprised the master and three mates, twelve deckhands, three engineers, ten engine-room hands and seven catering hands, thirty-six in all.[9] Aboard *Wentworth* Bullen says he led a 'gentleman's life'. The restriction on his duties meant that polishing brass and refuelling the oil navigation lights were usually completed by 10am. Of course, during the night he needed to tend the lights. So during days at sea he took in washing from sailors and firemen at 3s 6d per dozen, worth to him about thirty shillings weekly, about twice his monthly wage. He confesses to having frittered away most of his earnings, and to not thinking of his needs in the future. One benefit of such good times was that his stature developed and he looked more the experienced seafarer.

The round trip between *Wentworth*'s terminal ports of Melbourne and Sydney occupied about eight to ten days. The announcement of an experimental voyage to Auckland in New Zealand generated keen anticipation for Tommy, as the ship's normal passages had become so familiar as to feel boring. *Wentworth* left Sydney on Christmas Eve 1873 and would be at sea the following day. Although carrying mail, festivities began early and developed into a full debauch, with massive meals seemingly being indulged by all on board, along with free-flowing alcohol. The weather was remarkably calm. The firemen slowly became less energetic and steam pressure dropped such that by 4pm the propeller was turning very feebly. Some recovery was achieved on the day following, but the ship reached Auckland a day late. It was the convention then when a ship of some interest called first at a colonial port, for open ship to be granted to the local population and for personages of influence to be treated to a reception aboard. There was a good crowd on the quayside to welcome the ship. With Tommy aboard, *Wentworth* made three visits to Auckland lasting about a week each, but his interest lay chiefly in fishing, and he caught enormous numbers of mackerel and other species from the vast shoals in the harbour. The town did not catch his interest.

His cushy job came to an end abruptly, despite his growing disenchantment with the lack of sailorising in the steamer, and perhaps a little homesickness for London, though, of course, he had no home. The ship left Sydney for Melbourne in a gale, carrying mails and needing to 'show willing'. Just outside the harbour she was unable to make any headway. The engine's governor was carried away, and repair proved ineffectual. The master decided to run back into shelter and successfully anchored. Tommy prepared the anchor light as darkness fell, then forgot to hoist it into position on the forestay. Noticing the light was missing, the master told off the mate and the mate demanded of Tommy, 'Why?' Tommy made a facetious excuse, reported that the light was already lit, and went off to hoist it. The voyage to Melbourne and back was completed, when the mate discharged him for neglect of his duties, though he paid his balance of wages. Tommy Bullen was named on a surviving *Wentworth* immigration list for Sydney, which was probably for his last passage in the ship.

Steamer life lost its interest for Tommy Bullen, and he went searching for a ship in the vicinity of Circular Quay, where many of the overseas sailing vessels berthed. A chance encounter with the second mate of an ancient barque looking for hands, and directions to the pub where the master could be found, meant he was soon being interrogated about his experience. Bullen names him as Captain Bunker. He signed on the barque *Harrowby* in Sydney on 4 March 1874. Tommy was accepted as an ordinary seaman at £3 per month, and he joined *Harrowby* immediately.[10] Her crew size was half that of *Wentworth*. Arriving at Sydney from Mauritius, possibly with a cargo of sugar on 30 December 1873, it comprised the master, first mate, second mate, carpenter, cook and steward, two ordinary seamen and seven able seamen, a boy and three apprentices, eighteen in total. The master's real name was William Renshaw.[11] Ten of these stayed with the ship after the passage from Mauritius, and eight new men, including Tommy, joined in Sydney for the passage to Rangoon in ballast, and then to London. *Harrowby* had been ready for sea for a fortnight before she finally sailed, the master enjoying the comforts of the pub too much to be in a hurry. The replacements signed on and the ship at anchor in the channel about to sail, she was arrested at the behest of the landlady of the St Margaret's Hotel, for the bill for the master's board and lodging to be settled. Captain Renshaw had to pay up.

There are two routes between Sydney and Rangoon from which to choose. One was northwards through the Great Barrier Reef, the Torres Strait and the East Indies, the other was south and west across the Great Australian Bight, and north through the Indian Ocean to the Bay of Bengal. Captain Renshaw chose the latter. Tommy was happy to have been chosen for the second mate Mr Whitehead's watch. Tommy considered that the first mate, Mr Messenger, was worse off, as he had one of the ordinary seamen who could not steer. He found the voyage weary work, not helped by the fact that *Harrowby* was fitted with old-fashioned studding sails (sail extensions), with their complicated rigging making them difficult to set. They were dangerous and also upset the balance of the steering. In any case, the steering was heavy with the old-fashioned chain and barrel steering gear which was fitted. Captain Renshaw had taken against Tommy, whom he had engaged at £3 per month. He resented not having managed to have the sum reduced. On a wet night, with the ship jumping around awkwardly, he came on deck, berated Tommy for not steering a straight course and ordering him 'to meet her' and other such remarks. A stern sea, always a danger to the ship and the man at the helm, swamped the poop and Tommy was ordered away from the wheel. The master threatened to log Tommy (a negative entry in the official log), and there was a heated exchange, broken by another huge sea swamping the ship, throwing the rigging into disarray, and making it urgent for sail to be shortened. The logging took place and his wages reduced to £1 per month. The second mate countersigned the entry, but Tommy refused to sign it, asserting that the action was unfair. All the deckhands were dissatisfied with the turn of events, and this occurred just at the time that fresh food supplies ran out and meals reverted to hard tack.[12]

The cook, new to the ship, was quite hopeless, and when he produced a supposed duff which was little more than flour and water, a solid mass and quite inedible, one of the crew marched with it to the master in the saloon. A furious row took place. But the cook apologised, and produced 'a tin of soup and bully' as soon as the master disappeared. That incident passed over, but the ship began to run short of stores about six weeks out of Sydney; this despite the owner's instructions to the master to provision the ship fully in the colonies. It became a regular practice to raid the pantry for 'goodies' among the master's private stores, with Tommy often taking the lead. About a week from reaching the mouth of the Irrawaddy River leading to Rangoon, about the time for taking the noon sights of the sun, a seaman sent to call the master was turned away with the phrase, 'Go away I'm at my devotions.' Peering through the keyhole, he caught a glimpse of the master sitting with a biscuit tin between his knees and a pot of jam open by his side. In next to no time, the tale was all over the ship, memory of it entertaining the crew for the rest of the voyage. On reaching the pilot station, the master's parsimony extended to not taking a tug for a tow upriver, forcing the pilot who had joined to undertake complicated manoeuvres while working the ship gradually upriver. This told heavily on the crew. A running moor in a crowded anchorage off Rangoon completed the passage from Sydney.

The master promptly took himself ashore, while the crew were allowed an easy time after their arrival exertions. Tommy was impressed by the skill of the local boatmen, who practised the same rowing style as the gondoliers in Venice. He was also fascinated by the much larger river craft carrying some fifty tons of rice to Rangoon from upriver for export. He noted the richly carved bow and stern carvings, and the tiny deck aft for the steersman manipulating the large steering oar. These Burmese bore elaborately decorated bodies with complicated designs, in colours, all over them. The crew could see a sawmill across the river where a dozen elephants drew teak logs from the log rafts which had been floated downriver, piling them in stacks above the high-water mark apparently unsupervised. At the sound of the sawmill's whistle, all the elephants dropped their logs and departed to their quarters.

Aboard *Harrowby*, work went ahead normally, preparing the holds for the homeward cargo. As at all anchorages, an anchor watch was kept all night by one man who served the whole night, having the day off. Then orders came from ashore to revert to the practice when at a temporary anchorage, by which the whole crew worked throughout the day, and at night, in addition, each took the watch for one hour in turn. One night in the middle of a violent storm, Captain Renshaw unexpectedly came aboard in the pouring rain when Tommy, on night watch, met him at the gangway sensibly stripped of his sole garment. The master, in a drunken rage, berated the mate, who took a strip off Tommy. However, anchor watch arrangements were reviewed, and the crew were allowed to start day work an hour later each morning.

The youngest members of the crew did get ashore quite frequently, tending the ship's boat taking the mate or second mate ashore on ship's business, the master again staying permanently ashore. Watching *Harrowby*'s boat, Tommy got in the habit of chatting with the local boatmen, by signs, nods and grunts owing to the lack of a common language.[13] He remembered some stories of Hindu mythology he had read as a child in *Chambers's Miscellany*, and started telling the tale 'Avatar of the Fish', which he could remember. His audience were delighted, particularly so when his naming of the figures Rama, Vishnu, Siva, Ganesh and the like touched a chord. Demonstrating his strength in a show of bravado led to the only time he was attacked abroad, by a man emerging from the water following religious bathing. Fortunately, his group of friends came to his rescue.

Anxiety had grown among the crew about when they would be granted a run ashore, and they concocted the idea of a letter of request being sent to the master ashore at the British Burmah Bar, which accommodated him. Tommy Bullen was persuaded to write the letter, but there was great reluctance to sign it. No one wanted the responsibility, but perhaps also because of lack of writing ability. However, the eldest AB, John Hansen, put his name to the document. Once again, Captain Renshaw appeared aboard in a drunken temper, calling out Hansen and soon after the now-exposed Bullen, to receive his telling-off. However, the leave was granted with a sub of twenty rupees to each man, except Tommy, who was not to have leave. With the master ashore, the mate let him have his turn, minus the ready cash.

Accompanied by Bill the apprentice, Tommy determined to see the Golden Pagoda, involving a long walk out of town and a stiff climb to the temple complex at the summit. Amongst the numerous sights was a massive bell, some twenty feet in circumference, from which they could get no sound. Worshippers made donations in gold leaf, and the process of gilding was going on by workmen on flimsy scaffolding. Tommy was awestruck. Then, while viewing the scene, he heard a voice asking whether he was a believer. His interrogator appeared to be Chinese, beautifully but simply dressed in oriental fashion. In a short conversation about western and eastern religions, it emerged that the gentleman had taken a degree at Cambridge and simply accepted the religion into which he had been born. Tommy was not the only visitor from the ship, as he bumped into the second mate, who gave him two rupees. Back aboard *Harrowby*, Bill and Tommy saw that some crew, as usual, returned the worse for wear.

By now the cargo loading was complete and departure was being anticipated.[14] While the crew had lived well in port, there was no sign of any stores being taken for the homeward passage. Then a new cook joined to replace the one who had ended up in gaol. With him came a boatload of stores. Nevertheless, the reserve of stores aboard was sparse. *Harrowby* duly set off downriver, only to be overtaken by a steam launch and boarded by a European official, who presented a bill to the master. History was repeating itself, as Captain Renshaw had fled his accommodation ashore without paying the bill of 150 rupees. Having no cash, the master paid with ship's stores of bolts of canvas and coils of rope. The creditor probably had the better of the deal. Of course, the crew had little respect left for the master, but gave every deference to the mates, so the work of the ship went ahead smoothly, and the ship was able to clear the Bay of Bengal before the southwest monsoon broke.

Tommy spent the passage across the Indian Ocean, which was uneventful, ruminating about his experiences since he had left London in *Pharos*. He regretted his wasted opportunities in Australia, had slipped into the habits of the common seaman, drinking and swearing, though not the all-too-common debauchery of men ashore. Without a home base, he was working without purpose. His simple religion of early childhood was neglected, though he did have a Bible with him, but no other reading matter. The crew were particularly sceptical of religion. They knew that *Harrowby*'s owners were highly religious and expected that in their masters and aboard their ships. They believed that Captain Renshaw was a holy man. But his behaviour belied that. Closing Africa, the shortage of food became serious again. The Rangoon flour was inedible, the cargo of rice was unsuitable as food, and the meat aboard appalling. Could there be a call at East London for stores? But the weather conditions became increasingly variable and miserable. Unsure of her position and in poor visibility, *Harrowby* nearly ran aground. Somehow she made Algoa Bay, the location of Port Elizabeth, and anchored in the very exposed anchorage with other shipping.

Captain Renshaw soon disappeared ashore in a surf boat which came alongside, expecting to be back within a few hours.[15] But a southeasterly gale blowing into the harbours sprang up, for which ships at anchor needed to be fitted with a coir spring, which *Harrowby* did not have. Several vessels were swept ashore, but somehow the ship survived a deeply anxious period for the crew. The master returned promptly with fresh beef, lamb and vegetables plus only three packages of peas, flour and lime juice, hardly an addition to the ship's preserved stores. A desperate struggle to weigh the anchor followed, and having achieved that and set sail, the loose anchor suddenly ran out and was lost. The passage south along the African coast and into the Atlantic Ocean passed, while the fresh provisions were used up. Normally, in homeward ships now was the time to overhaul the rigging and spruce up the ship generally. But the reserves of cordage, canvas and other bosun's stores were not there. The crew became more and more irritable. Sam, the newest recruit to the vessel, took the galley's offering, a kind of soup, aft, invaded the saloon and poured it over the master's head before making his retreat while the master spluttered his wrath. St Helena was sighted about the time the whole crew was making another deputation to the master, this time to call at the island for fresh supplies. Captain Renshaw countered with navigation arguments against calling at that island, but conceded a call at Ascension Island. As *Harrowby* approached Ascension, a naval officer boarded, listened to the reason for calling, and inspected the storeroom, before piloting the ship to an anchorage. The master was taken ashore, the authorities decided on the level of supplies needed, and within hours he returned with a boatload and orders to leave immediately.

The passage to Falmouth for orders continued on an even keel for all on board, the master keeping out of sight. *Harrowby* chanced upon the *Stanley Sleath* of London, 160 days from San Francisco, festooned in weed and desperate for water, which *Harrowby*'s master supplied in return for a fat sow and bottles labelled lime juice, though actually filled with spirits. Captain Renshaw went on the spree again. Progress homewards was slow, with stops to speak to other vessels and the threat, countered by the mate, of calling in at the Azores. Fair weather continued and finally *Harrowby* came to anchor in Falmouth's harbour.[16] After a couple of days, orders came for London, and she was towed out of the harbour for the passage up Channel. The weather turned for the worse from the northeast and the temperature dropped. It was a fifteen-day struggle to Dungeness. After some hard negotiations about the fee, the tug *Robert Bruce* took the ship in tow to Gravesend. After a period at anchor, another tow in foggy conditions took *Harrowby* upriver to Millwall Dock, and the crew were dismissed from the ship, the unwary falling into the hands of the crimps.

While at anchor at Gravesend, an Anglican seamen's missionary visited the ship, and with her master's permission, came to see the men in the fo'c'sle. The crew, ready to vent their annoyance at the captain's behaviour throughout the voyage, reacted to the missionary with speechless anger. Eventually, Tommy Bullen broke fo'c'sle etiquette, which prevented junior seamen speaking while seniors were silent, and spoke up on their behalf.[17]

'I'm afraid, sir, you wonder at your reception ... This vessel is owned by a firm notorious for their profession of religion, and we are told that one member of the firm preaches every Sunday. The skipper was chosen to command because he professed to be a Christian and a teetotaller ... Yet during the whole voyage the skipper had, whenever possible, been drunk; he was notorious in every port the vessel has called at for his lecherous behaviour, and his attempts to swindle public-house keepers and others of the same class. Through this conduct ... rightly or wrongly, but quite excusably, I think, we've considered skipper and owners as beastly hypocrites altogether ... You are not surprised now, are you, sir, that the men do not look upon you as a minister of religion with favour? A long course of this treatment, which they believe to have been meted out to them under cover of religion, has made them feel revengefully towards all professors of religion whatever'.

Having also been shown a lump of hard tack (elderly preserved beef) and a vermin-infested ship's biscuit, the missionary made his apologies and departed.

6

A Voyage in Whaling

17 December 1874 to 5 May 1877

Tommy Bullen left *Harrowby* in the company of Bill, the apprentice, and a boy or ordinary seaman he names as Oliver.[1] Bill soon separated to return to his family home in Bermondsey, while Tommy and Oliver headed for an eating house Tommy knew in West India Dock Road. But at the first pub they passed Oliver could not resist temptation, squandering some of the little sum he had on a glass of rum. In the eating house Tommy ordered haddocks, rolls, butter and coffee, but Oliver could not eat, the rum having upset his stomach, and gave his share to a nearby carman. With hardly any money between them, the search for somewhere to stay meant a place catering for seafarers. Oliver's lead took them to Ratcliff Highway and a dingy beer house where Tommy left his bag of few belongings in a corner. With £1 from the landlord (a loan until pay-off), Tommy cleared out for the rest of the day by train from Shadwell to Fenchurch Street, returning in the evening after wandering the familiar streets. Unsavoury loafers and down-and-outs crowded the common areas of the house, and Tommy had to create a fuss to get to his bed, which turned out to be less unsavoury than he expected. The next day, leaving his baggage with Bailey, the master of the house, he escaped and found satisfactory lodgings in Newman Street, off Oxford Street.

The time lapse for pay-off over, Tommy and the rest of the crew re-assembled at Green's Home shipping office for the pay-off. As each man signed, he gave Captain Renshaw, standing behind the service grill counter, a piece of his mind. Next to last of the crew, Tommy identified himself to the clerk and the captain told him he had a good mind to stop his wages as he had promised. Tommy looked at the certificate of discharge he was given and saw that he had been graded excellent for conduct and given a bad character for ability. This wholly unfair malignity might well hinder his future employment, as masters paid little attention to the conduct grading, but took the ability grading seriously. Bill, the apprentice, was there, but how he was entitled to some cash is unclear. Perhaps his indentures had expired and he had been graded AB for the remainder of the voyage, or his owners might have given him some return of his parents' premium, for, if still an apprentice, they remained responsible for him in the home port as well as at sea. Outside the office, Bill and Tommy counted their money, and Bill found he had £5 too much. They quickly took themselves away from the building, and Tommy felt he had a bit of revenge for the behaviour of the master. During three weeks ashore, Bullen kept away from sailortown, visiting museums, galleries and theatres. He also made sure he had books to hand. Despite the unpleasantness, he had received £16 in the shipping office.

Bullen says little about his search for another ship, except that he was accepted in the *Rangitiki* as an ordinary seaman. This was a completely different class of vessel compared with his previous experience, being purchased in December 1873 by the newly formed New Zealand Shipping Company as their third vessel, who had had her completely overhauled. She had been built in 1863 as the *Scimitar*.[2] Bullen probably joined her for what would be her second voyage under the new ownership, in South West India Dock, prior to sailing for Port Chalmers in New Zealand. She would make a call off Plymouth to land her pilot. Despite the vessel's superior status as a first-class passenger and cargo ship, on leaving London the majority of the deckhands joined her the worse for wear through drink. The ship, like many others, left the River Thames temporarily desperately short-handed for a day or two until the men sobered up. Bullen was by that passage well up to all the tasks demanded of sailing ship ratings both in skill and physical development, though still rated as an ordinary seaman. The only member of the crew he mentions was an unlikely youth, also aged about seventeen, who had rapidly become the butt of all hands owing to his uncouth appearance, awkwardness and general uselessness, and who suffered the scourge of seasickness for an unusually long period. The two became friends, and Bullen learned that he had been a postulant at Llanthony Abbey, and was something of an artist, a lover of poetry and a reader, having the education of a gentleman. In moments of spare time Bullen listened to him avidly, responding to the poetic and religious discourse he offered.

Bullen credits *Rangitiki* with making a very rapid passage to Port Chalmers, near the southern end of New Zealand South Island, but newspaper reports give a passage of ninety-six days, slightly longer than the average voyage.[3] She arrived at Port Chalmers on 24 March 1875, having experienced a mix of favourable and adverse weather during the passage. At over twenty feet in draught, she was heavily loaded with a deadweight cargo from London, and was immediately towed into port on arrival in the roads. Normally, in an overseas port, crews remained tied to their ships, though individual discharges 'by mutual consent' were not unusual. *Rangitiki*'s crew seem to have been put on day work, a normal practice, and out of working hours allowed freely ashore, which was more unusual. Then rumours suggested that the current master would be leaving, and crew members certainly had the impression that as a result the crew would be discharged. There was nothing in the Agreement and Account of Crew to support this idea, but nevertheless when the rumours proved true, an offer of discharge was made to them. The New Zealand Shipping Company, which had been formed in New Zealand and was at that time managed in New Zealand, was rotating its masters between its ships, and Captain Fox had agreed to move to command the *Waimate*.[4] Captain Boyd would assume command of *Rangitiki*. Bullen, who was undergoing a religious conversion, was among those who asked to be discharged.

The seeds of religious belief had probably been sown in Bullen's subconscious through regular attendance at the Lock Chapel services and Sunday School during the earliest period of his childhood. He was clearly musical, and during his cabin-boy years he readily remembered the words and the tunes of popular hymns and songs, which, on more than one ship, he was asked to sing to the crew. Among other influences aboard the generally 'heathen' ships in which he was serving, he often mentions being befriended by a crew member not given to drunken behaviour and of a religious bent, who reminded him of the behaviours and beliefs from his early years. Port Chalmers offered the usual attractions designed for seafarers, and conspicuous from the ship appeared to be one labelled 'Port Hotel' from which, on his first run ashore, came the sound of music and singing. With a shipmate, Bullen ventured into the back room of the hotel where the sing-songs were taking place. It turned out to be well supervised, with no drunkenness, and all present were encouraged to take a turn. He became a regular. On Sundays, instead of that event, the room was used for a religious meeting with plenty of singing; Tommy and his shipmate ventured in to find a ready welcome. The hymns were interspersed with extempore prayers, and Bible readings. There was a small choir which led the singing. The two seafarers were strongly moved by the experience, and lingered behind at the end. With the help of two of their new friends, Tommy Bullen underwent the conversion.

Aboard ship and at work, he found he was no longer swearing. A reason for leaving *Rangitiki* was to escape the bad language and uncouth behaviours which dominated ratings' lives aboard ship. Free of the ship from about the beginning of April 1875, and with perhaps less than two months' wages in his pocket after deductions, he would soon need paid employment, but was disconcerted to find that he had no skills which employers ashore wanted. Nevertheless, more than a month passed before he was engaged in the whaler *Splendid* on 13 May 1875.[5] This date is found in his listing of his sea service in his applications to be examined for the Board of Trade Certificates of Competency as Second Mate (13 March 1878) and as First Mate (5 August 1880). As the service had to be supported by evidence in the form of certificates of discharge and testimonials from ships' masters, this confirms his service in *Splendid*.

Although Bullen offers insights into his religious activity ashore in Port Chalmers after leaving *Rangitiki*, apart from noting his failure to gain employment ashore, there appears to be nothing in his output about his search for sea employment in a port with a steady turnover of shipping. True, in a few of his early pieces on whaling, he names the whaler *Splendid* as his next ship, but when he came to write about his year in the ship, he adopted the fictitious name 'Cachalot' (French for sperm whale), and set his experiences in a fictitious round-the-world voyage from, and back to, the American whaling port, New Bedford.[6] Written in the first person, *The Cruise of the Cachalot* also conceals the names of the masters and some of the crew, but the majority of the readers without this contextual knowledge, and there were many in New Zealand, would have read the book as autobiography. Researchers, however, comparing the movements of *Splendid* with those of 'Cachalot', immediately realised that *Splendid*, based in Port Chalmers in 1875/6, cruised entirely in the Pacific Ocean.[7]

Splendid was a barque built in Massachusetts, USA, in 1835. She completed about a dozen whaling voyages under the American flag, before a Port Chalmers consortium purchased her to develop a whaling 'fishery' operating from that port. *Splendid* must have been sailed from New Bedford, the heart of the US whaling industry, by a delivery crew of American master, officers and deckhands, departing on 5 September 1873. Storm damage in the Atlantic Ocean forced her to put into St Thomas, West Indies, for major repairs. She then had to round Cape Horn and cross the Pacific Ocean, finally reaching Port Chalmers at the end of August 1874. The change of ownership and flag completed her registration as a British ship dated 23 October 1874 in the registry port of Dunedin, the fourteenth vessel to be registered there in 1874. Her registered tonnage would have been re-measured according to British practice, and this was cited as 358. She was allocated a ship's official number of 61018. Bullen misquotes this on his certificate applications as 6018.[8] The Americans, master Captain Thomas Mellon and First Mate William Earle remained with the ship, but how many others of the delivery crew remained in the ship by May 1875 is unknown. We can be certain that the officials of the Marine Department of New Zealand based at the shipping office/custom house in Dunedin/ Port Chalmers, would have tested the fitness of the master and mates to serve in those positions when the time came to engage the crew formally for *Splendid*'s first voyage as a British ship, and that an Agreement and Account of Crew would have been filled out. Testimonials and certificates of discharge, proving previous service as master and mate respectively, would have been sufficient proof of experience, and it is possible that they might have been issued with certificates of service, without formal examination. American government manning procedures were much less developed than those in Britain, which would have been alien to the two Americans. Unfortunately, Agreements and Account of Crew from *Splendid*'s voyages in the 1870s, which would have contained data on the composition and turnover of her crews, have not been discovered.

The re-equipping of *Splendid* following her arrival in Port Chalmers in 1874 was summarised in the press, concentrating on the processing equipment:[9]

Preparing the whaler *Splendid* for her first cruise for 'ile' out of the port progresses apace, and by the end of this week she will be ready for sea. Her try works, comprising two pots, a cooler, and a receiver, are in position, and a ground of tier of casks has been laid and filled with salt water, to act as ballast for the ship, and her four boats have been put in first-rate order, together with the requisite gear for each. The *Splendid* is provided with a bomb harpoon, a deadly and efficacious implement used in the capture of whales. The harpoon, to the staff of which is attached the bomb-gun, is thrown by hand, and when it enters the fish a certain distance, a piece of mechanism attached to the gun is acted upon, and this pulls a trigger, exploding the gun, and the bomb-arrow, headed with sharp steel, is driven with great force into the whale. The explosion of the gun ignites the slow match or fuse of the bomb, and in about ten minutes the latter explodes, and, as a rule, instantaneously kills the fish. The try works in which the oil is extracted from the blubber are notable features of the *Splendid*'s appointments. Two huge iron pots firmly set in brick work occupy the centre of the main deck. Each has its furnace, and the latter are so arranged that when the fires are going a layer of water can be kept between them and the deck, thus obviating the danger of the deck taking fire. A huge oblong copper vessel, into which the boiling oil is ladled for cooling purposes, is fixed on one side of the try works, and is connected with a receiver, into which the oil is baled in turn when it is cool enough to be poured into casks below. The owners of the *Splendid* are evidently resolved to spare no expense in fitting their vessel for sea, and if the venture should happen to be unsuccessful the blame cannot be laid at the door of niggardly outfit. We hope, however, that the *Splendid* will find no scarcity of fish in her cruising grounds, and in that case we are very sure that those on board he will be able to give a good account of them.

Bullen's *The Cruise of the Cachalot* was an immediate and international success which matched the fame of Herman Melville's *Moby Dick* of half a century earlier. Whaling history researchers, especially those in New Zealand, have studied the text closely, trying to match the movements of the fictitious 'Cachalot', and such crew data as Bullen gives, with data from other sources, notably newspaper reports. *Splendid*'s name soon emerged as a reasonable match for the data on the ship in Pacific waters, but that seemed only to cover at most about a third of the text. However, a crew member of *Splendid* from late 1874, then a 13-year-old boy newly apprenticed under the ship's carpenter, R P Mackay, reading Bullen's text in the late 1890s, recognised many of the incidents described by Bullen, and was convinced that they were based on real events he had experienced in *Splendid*.[10] Mackay kept a personal diary, making his own notes, which included listing the names of members of the crew. He annotated his copy of *The Cruise of the Cachalot*. After his death in 1948, this, the diaries and other papers were deposited in the Alexander Turnbull Library in Wellington, New Zealand.

While the Mackay diary seems to confirm some crew names mentioned by Bullen, the names of other whalers sighted and some of the whale catches, his crew listing does not include Bullen's name. This omission led to speculation that Bullen might have used a false name aboard *Splendid* and that he had some misdemeanour to conceal. However, given his religious conversion, presenting an honest face would surely have marked his behaviour. We must also question the reliability of an informal listing by a teenager new to seafaring. In personal relations between individual crew members aboard ship, nicknames were common and, unless referring to an officer, surnames might never be used. In his certificate application naming *Splendid*, Bullen's capacity is given as AB (able-bodied seaman), an appropriate grading for someone having over four years at sea. His dates of joining and leaving *Splendid* fit within the dates she was in Port Chalmers. During Bullen's first cruise (May 1875 to February 1876), a number of crew refused to work, and back in Port Chalmers were arraigned before a magistrate for mutiny.[11] Only three of the seven men named can positively be identified in the Mackay crew listing. The matter was settled out of court and the men returned to the ship. As none are listed in Mackay's crew list for the subsequent cruise, it can be inferred that these men were discharged by mutual agreement.

One further aspect of Bullen's invention in *The Cruise of the Cachalot* concerns the language apparently attributed to Mr Earle (first mate and master in *Splendid*), whom Bullen names as 'Mister (later Captain) Count'. Earle's relatives in New York, on understanding that Count was Earle, took offence, arguing that such language would never have been used by an educated man, and threatened to sue for defamation of character.[12] The New York newspaper, *Brooklyn Daily Eagle*, publicised the issue in a number of articles in 1901, quoting extracts from correspondence between the complainant and Bullen, and extracts from letters to the editor by whaling shipmasters.[13] The complainant seems to have taken offence at only two episodes. On page 36, taking his place in the launch of the first mate's whaleboat, Mr Count addressed Bullen, 'Y'r a smart youngster, an' I've kinder took t'yer; but don't yer look ahead an' get gallied, 'r I'll knock ye stiff wi' th'tiller; y'hear me? N' don't ye dare to make to make thet sheet fast, 'r ye'll die so sudden y' won't know whar y'r hurted.' This seems sound advice to this reader. On page 157, Captain Slocum being injured in an accident chasing a whale, during which a crew member had been killed, Mr Count had to stand in to read the burial service. Finding himself not up to the task, Bullen has him say, 'This thing's to many for me; kin any of ye do it? Ef not, I guess we'll hev ter take it as read.' After a silent pause Bullen offered to read the words in the prayer book, adding for the reader that he had been a chorister in the old Lock Chapel, Harrow Road (in London). The complainant might also have alighted on the description of Mr Count during a whale chase in which his boat was holed: 'Our chief, foaming at the mouth with rage and excitement, was screeching inarticulate blasphemy at the other mate, who, not knowing what was the matter, was yelling back all his copious vocabulary of abuse. 'Was'nt Mr Count mad? I really thought he would split with rage ...' Bullen probably puts more doubtful language in the mouth of Captain Slocum than these examples, whom he kills off in a brawl with the fourth mate, who also dies when both topple overboard. In fact, the real original master, Captain Mellen, resigned at the end of Bullen's first cruise in *Splendid*, following which Mr Earle was appointed master for Bullen's second cruise.

In *The Cruise of the Cachalot*, Bullen, presumably on the crew agreement as an AB, says he was appointed boat steerer and fourth mate (page 197). If he was really given that appointment, it must have been after Captain Mellen had departed, and for Bullen's second cruise. The complainant also requested proof that Bullen had held that position. It was certainly not unusual for a capable apprentice with four years' sea time to be appointed the most junior mate after his indentures had expired, or for an AB to be upgraded to fill a vacancy owing to the holder's illness or death. Further, appointments as third or fourth mate did not legally require certificates of competency. Correspondents to the *Brooklyn Eagle* in 1901, claiming to know something of *Splendid* in about 1875, could not remember a Bullen among her crew. Bullen in a letter to the complainant expresses willingness to show his discharge and testimonial to the paper's London correspondent, but whether that actually happened is not known. As noted above, the matter was resurrected in the New Zealand press in 1943, as another dimension adding to Mackay's diary and crew listing, and casting a shadow on Bullen's service. Apparently, that matter went no further, but the article in *Dominion* (1943), and the note in the *Brooklyn Eagle* (1901) that Captain Earle had kept a personal diary, which had disappeared in Port Chalmers, led to the uncalled-for implication that somehow Bullen was involved.

Independent information about the two cruises when Bullen was aboard *Splendid* is found in the diary kept by Mackay, extracts from which are given in the table on page 84, and less detailed outlines are found in the New Zealand press, based on ships' masters' reports to their owners, after many ocean-going vessels' arrivals. That for the end of *Splendid*'s cruise between May 1875 and February 1776 reads:[14]

The whaling barque *Splendid*, locally owned, has returned from her second whaling cruise with, we regret to say, but a poor return upon the venture of her owners. She had been absent from May last, hence went to the Pacific islands, and cruised during the winter months, and in December put into the Bay of Islands (NZ North Isle). Thence she received instructions to proceed to the cruising ground of the Solander and Stewart's Island, and obeyed them, but met with very poor luck there, taking only one sperm whale, part of which was lost through a gale of wind coming on. During another gale off Stewart's Island she was rather roughly handled – two of her boats, with the davits being washed away. Mr Nicoll, one of her owners, went up to Port William, Stewart's Island, to meet her, and came in with her to Port Chalmers, where she is to refit. She left Port William on Saturday morning, had light, variable and southerly winds along, arrived off the Heads yesterday morning, and sailed in on the flood tide, bringing up half-way down the Cross Channel. We hear that the utmost dissatisfaction exists among her hands, and that they are in a state of all but mutiny. Various reports are in circulation, but as a statement of facts will be, in all probability, elicited before the Resident Magistrate of the Port, we shall be silent until the case or cases come on for hearing, nothing doubting but that the investigation will be thoroughly searching. The *Splendid* brings 14 tons of sperm oil, the fruits of her cruise.

Locations visited by the whaler *Splendid* during her May 1875 to February 1876 cruise from Port Chalmers, New Zealand

19 May 1875	Sailed from Port Chalmers
27 May 1875	Off Sunday Island, Kermadoc Isles approx 29°S 178°W
2 July 1875	Anchored off Vav'au, Tonga Islands approx 19°S 174°W
3 September 1875	Weighed anchor
6 September 1875	Cruising the Vasquez Ground around Kermadoc Is
13 September 1875	Horn Island [Futuna], Fiji, approx 17°S 175°E
18 September 1875	Off Tonga-tapu [then back to Vasques Ground]
16 October 1875	Off Sunday Island
28 October 1875	Off French Rock
10 November 1875	Off French Rock
30 November 1875	Anchored at Bay of Islands off Russell
10 December 1875	Sailed from bay of Islands for Solander Ground
31 December 1875	Off Solander Isle
3 January 1876	Off Solander Island near SW Cape and Preservation Inlet
5 January 1876	Off SW Cape of New Zealand
10 January 1876	Anchored at Port William, Stewart I
14 January 1876	Sailed from Port William for Solander ground
13 February 1876	Off Traps to Snares Islands approx 48°S 169°E
14 February 1876	Off Ruapuke I, Foveaux Strait
15 February 1876	At Anchor Patterson Inlet, Stewart Island
19 February 1876	Anchored in Port William
26 February 1876	Sailed from Port William for Port Chalmers
28 February 1876	Arrived Port Chalmers

Source: Diary of Robert Percy Mackay, deck apprentice, whaler *Splendid* c1874–77, courtesy of Rhys Richards (ed), 'Robert Percival Mackay: Carpenter's Boy on the *Splendid*, 1875–1877' (nd), containing his transcription of the manuscript diary held at the Alexander Turnbull Library, Wellington, New Zealand, Papers relating to the whaler *Splendid*, MSX-4007 to MSX-2009, MS micro copy.

From these two sources this first cruise, with Bullen aboard, took *Splendid* to cruising grounds north-northeast of New Zealand to the vicinity of the Tonga and Fiji island groups, cruising back and forth roughly on a north-south axis. She did not venture further east to Honolulu in the Hawaiian Isles, where, according to Bullen, the 'Cachalot' went to refit and picked up a number of 'Kanakas' to return them to their own islands. *Splendid* picked them up at Horn Island. Running back to New Zealand North Isle, to the Bay of Islands, *Splendid* received instructions to go south to the Solander whaling ground and the completion of the cruise. Other whalers, some of which Bullen names, were encountered in most of the locations visited. Mackay names several: to north and east of New Zealand, *Splendid* met the whalers *Coral, Lagoda, Petrel, Matilda Sears* and *James Arnold*, and south of New Zealand, *Matilda Sears, Tamerlane, Eliza Adams, Chance* and *Swordfish*. The whalers never missed an opportunity to socialise, exchanging experiences and levels of success.

It is clear that *Splendid*'s nine-month absence from Port Chalmers produced very small returns in the form of whale oil. The lack of success not only affected the owning consortium. The crew were engaged on a share basis and their dissatisfaction must have been a factor in the unrest that erupted in a refusal of some to 'turn to', and to a court hearing in Russell when one member was sent to gaol. There was a further outburst by half a dozen men when anchored in Port William, who refused to help weigh anchor. This may have triggered the master's decision to return to Port Chalmers, where the seven culprits were arraigned before a magistrate. Only three of the names occur in the Mackay list. The case was postponed, and was quickly settled out of court. This may have been achieved partly because the American master either resigned his command, or was dismissed. It seems he was something of a 'bucko' master in the American tradition, who ruled partly through brutality, including physical maltreatment. But another factor may have been his discomfort with the British merchant seafaring regulations. The following cruise of some three months, restricted to the Solander whaling ground, with Mr Earle promoted to Captain Earle, in command, was in marked contrast to the previous cruise, and is reflected in the published voyage report.[15]

ARRIVAL OF THE WHALING BARQUE *SPLENDID*

The whaling barque *Splendid*, which left this port on the 10th of March [1876], was towed up to the anchorage by the steam tug *Geelong* on the 5th inst. We congratulate her owners on the success which has attended her, as also on the altered appearance of the ship's company, who, instead of coming into port thoroughly dissatisfied, are now quite jubilant at the termination of their cruise, and anxiously desirous to start again. Captain Earle on his part expresses his satisfaction at the behaviour of his crew, and altogether the owners of the *Splendid* are to be congratulated on their change of management of the vessel. Her prior trip to this occupied fully eight months, with a result of not quite thirteen tuns of oil, while the present trip of less than half that time brings her into port with fully 22 tuns. This, we hope, will pay both the owners and crew for their exertions. We have been favoured by Mr. Elder with the following abstract from Captain Earle's journal, from which we gather:- The *Splendid* left this port on 10th March, passed the Bluff on the 12th, and after knocking about the [Foveaux] Strait for three days encountered a stiff W.N.W. gale, which forced her to run for Port William [Stewart Island] for shelter. After a detention of 12 days, caused by stress of weather, she left for the Solander [Islands] on the 27th; cruised about till April 2nd, when she raised a school of sperm whales. The boats were instantly lowered and gave chase striking and killing one whale besides getting one of her boats badly stove in the encounter. She took the whale in tow, and ran with a strong N.W. gale for Port William, anchoring there on the 7th; tryed out and stowed down her oil; left again on the 16th for the whaling grounds; cruised about for three days, and on the 19th when about eight miles off the Solander, she raised a second school of fish; lowered her boats, and after a very exciting chase, succeeded in securing two whales, with which she ran back to Port William, and tryed out. Nearly the entire month of May she was detained at Port William through heavy westerly gales, and only succeeded in putting to sea on the 27th ult. She cruised about until 2nd inst, when she again raised a school of whales, but did not succeed in striking a fish owing to the unsettled weather. On the following day a strong N.W. gale was experienced. Captain Earle determined to keep the ship away for Port Chalmers. She passed through Foveaux Strait at 5.20 p.m. same day, and passed the ship *Beautiful Star* hove-to off Centre Island. Dog Island was sighted at 8.20 pm, and the Nuggets passed at 2 a.m. on the 4th. Thence she encountered a terrific gale from the S.W., and hove-to off Cape Saunders at 5p.m., with thick rainy weather and the gale blowing great guns. The weather moderating the next day, she made the heads in the forenoon, and was towed up as above.

Locations visited by the whaler *Splendid* during her March 1876 to June 1876 cruise from Port Chalmers, New Zealand

10 March 1876	Sailed from Port Chalmers for the Solander ground
15 March 1876	Anchored in Port William for shelter
17 March 1876	Sailed from Port William to the Solander ground
30 March 1876	Off Preservation Inlet
7 April 1876	Anchored in Port William
16 April 1876	Sailed from Port William to the Solander ground
26 April 1876	Arrived at Port William to boil and stow, also shelter
9 May 1876	Still sheltering at Port William [Diary blank thereafter]
5 June 1876	Returned to Port Chalmers

Source: See table on page 84.

Whaling on the Solander ground at about latitude 47° S was inevitably subject to the full force of the Southern Ocean weather. Shelter was principally found at Port William and vessels remained there weather-bound for lengthy periods. If the harbour was entered with a whale alongside, it was a safe and easy place to complete the processing of the carcass, trying out and boiling. The Mackay diary again names *Chance, Tamerlane, Eliza Adams* sheltering or processing with *Splendid* in Port William, and out on the Solander ground, names which also occur in *Cruise of the Cachalot*.

Bullen's earliest short essays, 'A Day on the Solander Whaling Ground' and 'Humpbacking in the Friendly Isles', addressed episodes in the whaling scene which Bullen experienced.[16] Altogether some twenty such essays addressed whaling, as well as a couple of novels. So he made the subject something of his own. His decision to leave *Splendid* is as much a mystery as his engagement a year earlier. In *With Christ at Sea* he jumps from his conversion to picking up again his association with the Christian folk in Port Chalmers 'after a long absence'. Yet it was only three months since *Splendid* had made a short stay there between the two cruises when he was supposed to be aboard. Surely if he held the position of fourth mate so soon after being graded AB, with a master he clearly respected, there was every reason to hold on to that appointment, and to build up his sea time if he now had hopes of obtaining a certificate of competency. However, a factor might have been the practice for whaling crews to be paid by the 'lay' or share in the profits of the voyage which often led to crew members being short-changed when the voyage finally ended.[17] Bullen's resumed religious association brought him into the Episcopalian fold, with a new Anglican priest who intended to work among seamen, the Revd Lorenzo Moore. This led to him undergoing the rite of confirmation, at a service led by the Bishop of Dunedin, and following that to taking communion. A likely date for this might be the Confirmation Service held on 23 July 1876 at Holy Trinity Church, Port Chalmers, by the Anglican Bishop of Dunedin, Bishop Neville, when there were nineteen candidates, thirteen male and six female.[18]

Bullen spent three months ashore between signing off *Splendid* and signing on *West York*. His narrative accounts for perhaps about a month of that period. Much of the balance may have been the abortive period when he took employment as a farm labourer, only to be dismissed as a dismal failure. So he returned to what he knew best, and agreed a wage to ship in the *Orpheus* of Greenock, if he could live aboard before signing on. He found the crew comprised one other British seaman, all the other hands being of foreign nationalities. She eventually sailed from Port Chalmers on 16 August 1876 in ballast for Java.[19] Meanwhile, Bullen had fallen in with a Norwegian seaman, Rasmus Rasmussen, referred to as Jem, who was also moved by religion. A vacancy in his ship's crew tempted Bullen and, not legally committed to *Orpheus*, he signed on *West York* at a lower wage than in *Orpheus*, in order to sail with Jem. This ship sailed in ballast for Portland, Oregon, on 15 September 1876. His religious friends were pleased he had found work, but questioned his lack of loyalty to the *Orpheus*, having given his word.

Bullen was concerned about the reception he might receive, as a 'holy Joe' of the most extreme kind.[20] The day before sailing he had joined *West York*'s crew for the evening meal, openly saying to himself a private prayer as a grace. He had then joined in the conversation as an agreeable and amusing shipmate, relating stories of his experiences, thereby gaining their acceptance. He writes: 'And so auspiciously commenced the most delightful voyage I ever made'. His shipmates also noticed the change in Jem, who had begged him to sign on the ship. Early in the passage Jem had badly stubbed his foot against some ironwork, but had controlled a possible torrent of blasphemy by dropping to his knees and praying aloud. Bullen soon proved himself a thorough seaman, removing any fears they might have had that he might not pull his weight. In stormy conditions he had a near-death experience sitting astride the jibboom, hauling down the flying jib for furling. The down haul gave way unexpectedly, the sail ran through his fingers and he found himself hanging below the boom by one foot over the water. With a struggle back to his position above the boom he completed the furl, giving thanks for his salvation. The ship's master was a sincere Christian, who on Sundays dressed in shore-going clothing and conducted a service for the crew, Tommy's first experience of such an occurrence. He knew some of the hymns from the Moody and Sankey collection, and raised the tune when a hymn was announced. However, he was bitterly disappointed by the manner of the master's reading of the Morning Service from the Book of

Common Prayer, and also puzzled that a Methodist should use a Church of England form of worship. Bullen still had a lot to learn about the different variants of Christian worship. At the end of the first service the master picked out a man from the port watch, whom Bullen calls 'Cockney', for neglecting his cleanliness and not dressing properly for Sunday.

Life aboard was, of course, not always a 'bed of roses'. The second mate (the master's son) took every opportunity to haze Jem, although the core of the starboard watch, Jem, Ballentyne, Bob and Tommy, prided themselves in being a smart team, of which the master was certainly aware. With the ship sailing easily in fine weather, Tommy was surprised to be confronted with Willie Ballentyne undergoing his own conversion experience. Men in the port watch did not understand, but learned to tolerate the group in the starboard watch, though clearing out of the fo'c'sle if conversation took a religious turn.

The *West York* took a drawn-out period of sixty-four days to Portland, Oregon, but the group in the starboard watch were never bored with the routine of the ship. Tommy was also attempting to teach himself navigation, so it is clear that he had decided to better himself and attempt the certificate of competency examination for second mate. *West York* was towed into the Columbia River and they were pleased they were to go upriver to Portland rather than berth near the mouth of the river at Astoria, where they saw a ship named *Desdemona*. Another tug took them in tow, named *Williamette Chief*. Still under way, the ship was boarded by a crimp of the worst kind called James Turk, who thought he could get the crew to desert for the delights of Portland's sailortown. When the religious bent of *West York*'s crew became clear to him, he cleared out and did not trouble them again. The crew's behaviour spread on land, and they were soon invited to join the meetings of religious denominations ashore, where they were assured of a warm welcome throughout their time in that port. The voyage back to the United Kingdom around Cape Horn was blessed with fair weather, though the passage was rather drawn out. *West York* called at Falmouth, UK, for orders, and was visited by religious relatives and friends of the master, whose home was in St Ives was not very far away. The ship was ordered to Belfast, where the voyage ended, the crew dispersed, and Tommy lost contact with the friends he had made. He took a deck passage in the steam ferry *Voltaic* to Liverpool.

7

Another Voyage in a Single Ship
25 May 1877 to 2 March 1878

A day in Liverpool was enough to allow Bullen to revisit familiar locations, and the following day he caught a train to London, leaving it at Willesden and going on to Liverpool Street where he left his 'dunnage', presumably in the left luggage office.[1] With nowhere in particular to go, he wandered familiar streets for the rest of the day, before making his way to the King's Cross area where he found decent lodgings, as one of twenty single men in the same building, which served him for a stay of about three weeks. Avoiding theatres and music halls, he occupied himself with visits to all the museums and parks, and a considerable amount of reading. He visited the docks one day, leaving his discharge with the mate of a barque named *Dartmouth* bound for Hong Kong, via Cardiff. He avoided sailors' institutions, of which he had a low opinion, but attended several churches, including Westminster Abbey and St Paul's Cathedral, enjoying none of them except the singing. He was shy about entering Nonconformist chapels, which he thought of as private places where a stranger had no business. When sailing time came again, he was rather glad get away again with some purpose to life.

Bullen's assessment of the crew of which he now became a member was that there was not a single man on board with the slightest of Christian sympathies, but that apart and except for one individual, they were a very good lot of fellows; and *Dartmouth* was well-manned for a sailing ship of that period with six ABs and one OS in each watch. Bullen was number eighteen on the Agreement and Account of Crew out of the total crew, including the master, of twenty-five aboard leaving Cardiff after loading the outward cargo. He signed himself F T Bullen, which might be considered a step towards the form he later used with all his publications, Frank T Bullen. He gave his age correctly as twenty, and the 'Capacity', or rating, stated was AB. The wage given, at £3 5s 0d per month, was higher than that given for ABs in his previous ships. Like the rest of the ABs this voyage, he took an advance of wages of £2. He lists the foreign-born crew members as one each from Sweden, Denmark, Finland (then a part of Russia), Alsace (the bosun), Mauritius, France (two), America (three). His memory is quite good as, according the AAC, there were men from Prussia, Jamaica (two), Finland, Denmark, Belgium, Mauritius and Nova Scotia. All others aboard were from Britain or Ireland. The one bad egg, though a good seaman, alluded to above, he describes as a 'gaunt Irishman, Michael O'Dwyer'. Of the two Irishmen aboard it was John Tierney who was discharged at Hong Kong, and is presumably the man. The master, John Robertson from Aberdeen, aged sixty-five, held a Master's Certificate, Second Class, awarded in 1848 under the voluntary examination scheme introduced in 1845, and superseded by the compulsory scheme from 1 January 1851. It is thought that about three thousand certificates were issued under that scheme, overseen by Trinity House, London, and local port administrations. A second-class master was qualified to navigate ships north of the equator, and the standard demanded was higher than under the compulsory scheme. Bullen is full of praise for the master:[2] 'And we had a superlatively excellent skipper, who possessed that genius for command without which no master, however seamanlike, can hope to maintain discipline in a merchant ship, we were really fairly comfortable.'

Bullen found his fellow crew members tolerant of such religious utterances he might make, and their unfailing good-fellowship enervating. It seemed in conflict with his religious perspective, perhaps an expectation that he ought to assert his beliefs more strongly, and he 'grew cold spiritually'. Had there been more forceful opposition, he could have fought that.

Bullen says little about the passage to Hong Kong. The weather was generally favourable and *Dartmouth* made a fairly rapid passage. The route taken was the typical southward heading from the English Channel, and then around the Cape of Good Hope into the Indian Ocean. The Java and China seas, areas new to Bullen, were entered through the Sunda Straits between Sumatra and Java.[3] Passing through the strait he must have seen the smoking volcano, Krakatoa. This was before its catastrophic explosion in 1883 and the resultant affects felt worldwide. A newspaper report places *Dartmouth* off Anjer, Java, on 4 September 1877.[4]

Much more might have been made of the tricky navigation, especially for a sailing ship, through the reef- and island-bespattered equatorial region between the two seas, where the Gaspar Strait wrecked many a vessel. In the more open China Sea, but still with unmarked reefs to negotiate, there was an ever-present threat from local pirates from Borneo, and Chinese pirates as the ship came closer to China. However, *Dartmouth* reached Hong Kong safely in early October.

Most shipping found a berth in the anchorage between Hong Kong Island and the mainland. Cargo handling was by crowds of Chinese workers, so *Dartmouth's* cargo of coal would have been speedily unloaded into junks for landing ashore, and had there been any homeward cargo offering, that would have been loaded from junks. Steam shipping serving Hong Kong was already dominating homeward cargo bookings to Britain and Europe, and *Dartmouth* had to make do with a shipment of hemp in Manila in the Philippine Islands, which would involve a ballast passage across the China Sea.

Only a day or two after arriving, a seamen's missionary from a launch flying the Bethel flag boarded and asked permission for crew members to be allowed to attend a service to be held aboard another ship.[5] Only Bullen volunteered. Generally, the response from other ships was similarly poor, with some twenty seamen attending altogether. The host ship's second mate was instructed to get the crew to rig the church. A bunch of dirty, bruised men emerged, and took half an hour to complete the task, after which they disappeared. A missionary read the Church of England service very badly; no hymns were sung, and someone else read a sermon from a book, also badly. Not a good example of religious work among seafarers. Nevertheless, this was a manifestation of the globalisation of the seamen's mission movement originating in London in 1818, in which 'seamen's friend and Bethel union societies' made religious provision and some social welfare provision, with examples by the 1870s in ports worldwide. Bethel means 'house of God', premises ashore became known as seamen's Bethels, and the movement's flag had the word Bethel emblazoned in white on a blue ground. The societies in Hong Kong in the 1870s can be traced back to provision in Whampoa near Canton, decades before Hong Kong became a British colony.

Liberty day came round, and Bullen went ashore with his watch. He tried to look after the seaman from Finland, but soon missed him, and later found himself looking for him in a street with the worst of reputations. He got into some trouble with some Chinese, and escaping them, made for the wharf where sampans lay for hire. Here he was stopped by a white policeman and he learned of the risk of being murdered on his own in such a boat. A system of registration was in force, and the policeman took his name and the name of his ship, the time and the registration number of the sampan. Safely back on board, the mate asked him about the rest of his watch, about whom he had no information. They turned up the following morning in a most dissipated state. Two days later *Dartmouth*, in ballast, left for Manila in the Philippine Islands, to load her cargo of hemp for home. Because he had published a tale on Manila in 1898, Bullen has little to say about the call at Manila in *With Christ at Sea*.[6] But in the alternative source, he is not impressed with the oversight and treatment of the indigenous peoples by the administration of what was still a Spanish colony.

The passage to Manila was being made during the southwest monsoon and the weather was predictably stormy. Being light ship and with, no doubt, the minimum of ballast, *Dartmouth* had 'much ado to hold her own against the fierce beam wind'. Ever live to the fauna he saw around him, Bullen relates an incident he observed while at the helm:[7]

It was just after sunset on a very gloomy evening, with a half gale of wind blowing, and the old *Dartmouth* laying over till her lee rail dipped occasionally. I was at the wheel and saw to my surprise, a stork come labouring on a heavy wing up from to leeward, apparently bent upon taking shelter on board. Several times he fetched up under the lee of the spanker, catching the down-draught of the great sail and being whirled away again, only just able to avoid the curling crests of the cross sea. Once or twice he reached astern and came cautiously to windward, but he was evidently afraid of being driven on board against his will, and resumed his fruitless struggle up under our lee. My sympathies were so strongly excited that I could hardly breathe when he managed to get within a few feet of the lee rail, and it was with a real pang of sorrow that I saw the gallant bird grow weaker and weaker until, making one more attempt to get under the lee of the spanker, he lost his steerage way, the eddy caught him and whirled him, a ragged bundle of feathers, into the yeasty smother beneath, where he instantly disappeared.

After a passage of ten days, *Dartmouth* was beating into the 'magnificent Bay of Manila', a fine, easy of access harbour, with a gradually shallowing seabed making for great ease of navigation. Her master picked upon the widest, that south of Caballo Island, of the two access channels, as there was an offshore wind and evening twilight was approaching. Suddenly, out of nowhere as it were, a guard boat appeared alongside, ordering the ship to heave-to and demanding the ship's business and intentions. Having given satisfactory answers, *Dartmouth* was ordered not to enter by the south channel lest she be fired upon from another nearby island named Corregidor. Although the islands were marked with lights, entry was made that more difficult by a black night and the sudden appearance of a 'milk sea'. In this natural phenomenon the water became like a lake of flame and every wave crest shot up showers of diamonds as it broke. The ship's spars and rigging were lit up more brightly than an electric searchlight.

The next official encounter, at anchor the following day, was the visit of the health officer, demanding answers to a long list of questions which satisfied him and the ship was granted full pratique. He was followed by the customs officials who ordered a full 'rummage', even though the manifest had only the ballast as cargo to declare. The real purpose was revealed when the searchers explored the personal possessions of the crew. All soap was confiscated, as were all the trinkets that had been purchased as take-home gifts. This made quite a pile out on deck. Bullen protested in Spanish, but to no avail, and the master would be informed of the fine that had to be paid. The group left behind a ragged soldier with a rusty rifle as some kind of guard. In time, Bullen got round to chatting to him in the Spanish he had picked up in the West Indies, and he discovered that *Dartmouth*'s master had failed to provide the usual 'cumshaw' (present) to the officer in charge of the searching party. Bullen learned that the soldier really hated the Spanish colonists for their cruelty and maltreatment of the indigenous peoples, and the extent to which the soldier's life had been scarred by the disappearance of his family and his forced recruitment into the army.

Bullen seems to have managed a run ashore. He was struck with the absence of any energy among the population, except where the English, American and German merchants were to be found. The ordinary peoples avoided the old city of Manila where their Spanish rulers held sway. In fact, it was the Chinese, as a group, who seemed most industrious. The supply of water seemed to be in the hands of large men from northern Manchuria, who distributed water in two barrels slung from the ends of flexible bamboo poles. In the port district the 'godowns' (warehouses) were in a poor state of repair. Exports mainly went in Spanish steamships to Spain, but two former staples, sugar and tobacco, were being suppressed through excess taxation and production. Bullen thought that hemp was becoming a leading export. Cordage made from the local hemp, Manila hemp, was light and silky, yet enviably strong. The Americans especially favoured it and were the experts in the production of cordage for use in ships. Unlike the Americans, British shipping was going over to flexible steel wire rope wherever that could be tolerated in the rigging. He also thought that much business was in the hands of 'half-breeds' always ready to cheat in their dealings, and shipmasters in particular were robbed right and left until they had developed a sharp awareness of the tricks of trading. The Philippine Islands were ripe for a change of rule, which could only be one of three nations who might do justice to the inhabitants: Japan, Great Britain or the United States. The last already had a strong foothold in the country and was the best customer for Philippine products.

Two replacement crew had been shipped in Hong Kong, an AB and an OS. Bullen had become friendly with the AB, D C Eddy, an American who had exhausted a good inheritance with heavy drinking and debauchery, and had taken to the sea, in a sense as Bullen himself had, to put food in his mouth. He discovered that Eddy had a low opinion of Christians, as sanctimonious hypocrites, but he did not understand Eddy's reasoning. Eventually, the long labour of filling Dartmouth with bales of hemp was completed. Bullen says nothing about the return passage to London. She sailed from Manila on 17 November 1877 and was entered inwards at London on 2 March 1878.[8] She might have crossed the Pacific Ocean to take the Cape Horn route around South America, or more likely, simply retraced her outward route through the China and Java seas, Indian Ocean and round the Cape of Good Hope.

He does say that he pursued his study of navigation by looking in on a navigation teacher, and by passing for second mate soon after *Dartmouth* berthed in London. His opinion of the process was:[9]

Once school work is over the candidate's real trial begins. Now he finds the value of having attended to his business while at sea and the futility of cramming up seamanship from manuals written for that purpose. For the examiners are all old captains, and the examination is *viva voce*. In my own case I followed the usual routine. As soon as I came home I went to a navigation school, or crammer's, and paid my fee, not imagining that I should learn anything, but expecting to have what I did know marshalled in the most useful order. I afterwards found that I need not have spent my money. I can honestly declare that in my case, at any rate, I got no good whatever.

It is worth taking note of the what these steps entailed. Having decided to attempt the Board of Trade Examination for the Certificate of Competency as Second Mate, Bullen would have to have purchased a copy of the examination regulations, and navigation and seamanship textbooks, and a set of nautical tables.[10] By 1878, a great many private teachers of navigation had published their own textbooks, and often included excerpts from the Board of Trade Regulations. Stripped of the detail, the master of every British foreign-going ship clearing a British port had to possess the certificate as master, and his first mate at least the certificate as first mate, and his second mate the certificate as second mate. There was no prescribed course of study, but regulations included an outline syllabus. The principal criteria for admission to the examination were proof of sea experience totalling four years 'before the mast' (as an apprentice or deckhand) for second mate, a year in charge of a watch and a certificate as second mate for first mate, and a year in charge of a watch and a certificate as first mate for the master's examination. Sea time had to be proved with an array of certificates of discharge and testimonials of sobriety, experience and ability, from the master of each ship. The examinations were offered at all the British ports having Local Marine Boards, as frequently as weekly. Success led to the issue of a paper cloth certificate in London about a week after the examination, which was sent to the Mercantile Marine Office nominated by the candidate.

However, if he did not know already, possession of a certificate did not guarantee being employed at the grade named. Bullen shipped several times as an AB. A high standard of behaviour was expected of holders of the government certificate, and misdemeanours, social or professional, were recorded in a 'black book', and certificates could be cancelled. Failure in the examination did not prevent repeated attempts (there was a fee to pay), but penalties of additional sea time might be imposed.

There were two parts to the examination, the written navigation paper solving navigation calculations with quite a long period of time allowed, and the oral (seamanship), answering questions put verbally by the examiner. This could last an hour or more. By the mid 1870s, the written scripts were being sent to a marking team in London from the various ports, but the oral was conducted by examiners based in each port. Candidates could fail at the application stage, if their application form had not been filled out correctly or evidence was missing in support for the sea time claimed. The latter was calculated to the exact number of days. The syllabus given in the 1863 Regulations would not have been much different in 1878:

8 A SECOND MATE must be seventeen years of age, and must have been four years at sea.

In NAVIGATION.– He must write a legible hand, and understand the first five rules of arithmetic, and the use of logarithms. He must be able to work a day's work complete, including the bearings and distance of the port he is bound to, by Mercator's method; to correct the sun's declination for longitude, and find his latitude by meridian altitude of the sun; and work such other easy problems of a like nature as may be put to him. He must understand the use of the sextant, and be able to observe with it, and read off the arc.

In SEAMANSHIP.– He must give satisfactory answers as to the rigging and unrigging of ships, stowing of holds, etc; must understand the measurement of the log-line, glass and lead-line; be conversant with the rule of the road, as regards both steamers and sailing vessels, and the lights and fog signals carried by them.

This abbreviated and somewhat confusing syllabus conceals the scope of both the written and oral examinations. Logarithms, for example, includes the trigonometrical ratios. The use of heavenly bodies demands familiarity with the nautical almanac. The observation calculations involve an understanding of the earth sphere and the celestial sphere, and familiarity with their co-ordinate systems. Course and distance calculations allow for the differences between the sphere and plane charts known as projection. Navigation by nautical charts involves geometric methods of solution, and familiarity with the symbolic presentation of charts. The oral covers all the tasks and responsibilities which might devolve on a second mate in charge of a watch: appreciation of weather conditions, trimming of sails, reduction of sails, supervision of steering, direction of the ratings on watch, look out, collision avoidance, the relatively new rule of the road (ie Highway Code at sea) which had to be quoted by heart, routine navigation, logging actions. There was considerable scope for the examiners to produce new questions or interpretations.

Navigation teachers from 1851, when the examinations were introduced, collected great pools of past questions, and could predict when a question might be reused. They also soon knew of examiners' favourite themes and even differences in answers between one examiner and the other. This experience was one good reason for paying to attend a navigation school, where teaching was mainly by personal tutorial, with students at different stages in their familiarity with the syllabus. We can be sure that Bullen knew of teachers based around Tower Hill and in the East End of London.

Despite this, candidates did attempt the examinations without taking the guidance of a local navigation teacher, and from the little he says about his experience, Bullen was one of these. He put in his application to the office at Tower Hill, London, on 9 March 1878, *Dartmouth* having arrived on 1 March, paying the fee of £1 0s 0d. He listed his service in *Western Belle, Harrowby, Splendid, West York* and *Dartmouth*, with the sea time totalled as four years, two months and eight days. Each entry was ticked by an examiner, and the discharge slips and testimonials must have been found satisfactory. He passed the examination on 12 March and the examiner's certificate (a section on the application form) with the supporting discharges and testimonials were forwarded to the Registrar General of Seamen to make out the certificate. His Certificate of Competency as Second Mate was approved on 13 March and issued to him at the Mercantile Marine Office, St Katherine's Dock on 15 March 1878, his discharges and testimonials being returned to him at the same time. The master of *Dartmouth* had given him a 'really splendid testimonial', telling him that he had kept his eye on him all the voyage. His final comment was that he found the examination ridiculously easy, though he had dreaded it much. Perhaps walking on air on passing the examination, for the first time in his life he fell in love, with feelings reciprocated, and began to dream of a home of his own.

8

Mixed Experiences in Five Ships

19 March 1878 to 9 August 1879

Even though he now had an attachment and he now held the statutory certificate enabling him to hold a position as an officer in a British, foreign-going merchant ship, Bullen did not extend his time ashore to be with his girl, or to extend the fruitless search to be engaged as a second mate. He knew the latter depended upon being already known to prospective ships' masters or shipowners. It was insufficient to possess a favourable testimonial from the master of *Dartmouth*. So, a mere three weeks after his return to London, he contented himself with accepting a berth as an AB in a ship named *Columbus*, which had loaded a general cargo, including 400 tons of iron, for Lyttleton in New Zealand. This was the port for Canterbury, the principal town in New Zealand's South Island. It could be up to two years before this ship returned to London according to the AAC that the crew were signing. He was pleased to find that two of his shipmates from the *Dartmouth* had also signed on, John Stadey from Finland and Londoner William Palmer. He explains that he did not name *Columbus* in his writing out of consideration for its owner, named on the agreement as George Lidgett, whom he believed was 'a very good Christian man', who would grieve to know how utterly godless was the life on board one of his ships.[1] Instead, he adopted the name 'Magellan', thus leaving a hint about the real name as both are names of famous late medieval world explorers.[2]

In his short essay 'The Chums', Bullen explains his affection for 'Jack Stadey', extolling the merits of Finnish seafarers as 'the finest all-round mariners in the world', and having something of a reputation as wizards owing to their practical skills. Stadey was, however, ungainly of movement and lacking the skills Finns were supposed to possess. Bullen and Stadey had become friends in the *Dartmouth*, even though Stadey could never be given sailorising jobs. In London, after that voyage, he had accompanied Bullen, who had introduced him to the delights of museums and the like, away from sailortown. The two had stocked up on food delicacies, joining 'Magellan', but those only lasted a few days, as, of course, the food had to be shared among the hands as a whole. Unfortunately, the pair were not picked for the same watch. Bullen eventually discovered that Stadey was being picked upon by a Shetlander he names as Sandy Rorison, who might be Arthur Morrisson, aged twenty-three from Lerwick, on the AAC. A stand-up argument between Bullen and Rorison, which might have led to fisticuffs, ended in the aggressor breaking down with his face in his hands. The bullying ceased and Rorison and Stadey became friends, always sailing together.

Columbus sailed from Gravesend on 21 March 1878 with a crew that was, for once, sober, and which quickly formed a working team, so that soon after, encountering a severe squall in which other ships foundered, the crew made light of the work involved.[3] *Columbus* carried two adult and a girl passengers in the saloon and four in second class, who were accommodated in part of the apprentices' house on the fore deck. When the ship encountered a heavy sea, they really felt the clumsy movement of the ship, probably caused by the amount of heavy iron in the cargo.[4] She was not particularly well manned, having left the River Thames with only fifteen in the crew, including the master. He was William Esson, aged thirty-four from Aberdeen. The first mate was from Hull and the second mate came from Lerwick in the Shetland Isles. The carpenter came from Banff in Scotland. The cook and steward were from Jamaica and Dominica. Of the nine ABs, five were from overseas, Sweden, St Vincent, Belgium, Denmark and Finland, and four were British. This was a not unusual mix of nationalities in the crew of a British sailing vessel by the 1870s.

The master and the first mate, according to Bullen, both drank to excess in bad weather. But worse than that, they were inconsiderate of their small deckhand resources, often keeping both watches on deck unnecessarily, following a sail handling which demanded both watches. Further, at times carrying over long excessive sail, the crew were often kept waiting around in expectation of being called out. At times the pair were in the cabin 'rolling drunk', when they should have been on deck with an eye on the weather. Yet despite the areligious atmosphere, strangely there was far less profanity among the deckhands than usual.

Running the easting down, a term seafarers used to encompass the part of the passage between the Cape of Good Hope and Australia, often roughly in latitude 40° S, and running with westerly gales from astern, so much water from following seas came aboard the poop that it was found necessary to build a barricade of planks to prevent flooding in the poop accommodation. The ship was running in this manner for some six weeks, and the crew were living in oilskins and sea boots, and a grimy sea grass began to grow over the upper deck. It was on Easter Sunday that conditions became so severe that it became impossible to keep *Columbus* ahead of the sea, and that the most dangerous of manoeuvres, 'heaving to' had to be attempted. Here is Bullen's description:[5]

Now this term, though highly technical, is, I think, susceptible of explanation to landsmen. It means that, as the ship is built to breast the sea, her safest position in a gale is with her bows pointing as nearly in the direction from which the wind and sea are coming as possible, for she then rises to meet the waves, whereas when the waves are overtaking her the stern has a tendency to cower down before them and let them rage over the deck, doing dreadful damage. But after a ship has been running before wind and sea until both have risen to a fearful height, it becomes a task of great danger and difficulty to 'heave-to', that is to turn her round to face the elements she has been fleeing from. First of all, as it means the reduction of sail to almost nothing, which, as it reduces the vessel's speed, is in itself a serious danger, as the halting vessel may be over whelmed. Next, in the actual process of turning the ship round she must of necessity be for a brief space be broadside on to those tremendous waves, presenting her most vulnerable part to their awful attack.

A snow-laden squall swept over the ship, followed by three enormous seas, and when the decks emerged from the torrent, the bulwarks had burst outwards most of the length of the ship, and the temporary breakwater had disappeared from the poop, causing serious flooding below decks. The manoeuvre was ordered, and the ship succeeded in coming round safely. But for the next forty-eight hours *Columbus*' behaviour was even more frightening than before. Eventually, the weather eased and the passage was completed in reasonable time.

Columbus arrived in Lyttleton on 15 July 1878, after a passage of 115 days.[6] Bullen found a friend from his time in Port Chalmers, and had a pleasant experience when he was able to get ashore. Then *Columbus*' master sent for him, telling him that there was a ship in port in need of a second mate, and that he had recommended Bullen for the post. However, as Bullen would be bettering himself and a replacement would cost the master over thirty shillings a month extra than retaining Bullen, he could not give Bullen his balance of wages. Bullen says it cost him £10. Perhaps *Columbus*' master made a minor concession, as the AAC shows a balance of wages payment of £1, additionally he had benefited from his one month's advance and whatever, if anything, he may have purchased from the master's slop chest. Bullen's wage was £3 5s 0d per month, but in Lyttleton *Columbus*' master signed on one AB at £6 per month and two other ABs at £5 per month.

Bullen's new ship, named *Bulwark*, which he joined on 7 August 1878, turned out to be full of surprises and a most welcome appointment for his first experience as an officer.[7] Her master, Captain George Trail Seator, from the Orkney Islands, was 'overflowing with benevolence, a sincere Christian and an excellent seaman'. No longer a young man, he gave Bullen a warm reception and was full of encouragement. Bullen's service under his command strengthened his deep respect for him; Bullen comments: 'He was a man whom I am proud to have lived to know'. Captain Seator was almost certainly well-known in New Zealand and Australian ports. While in Lyttleton he was called as nautical assessor for an inquiry chaired by the Collector of Customs, A Rose, into the return to port of the *Duke of Argyll* owing to tender stability.[8]

Bulwark had already been away from Britain for over two years, yet still retained her original crew, who were nearly all British, and was that rarity 'an emphatically happy ship'. Bullen was not yet to know it, but *Bulwark* was at the end of her career with famous owners in the New Zealand emigrant trade, Shaw, Saville, & Co. Having unloaded her inward cargo at No 3 wharf in Lyttleton, *Bulwark* was moved to the Gladstone Pier to fulfil a charter with the New Zealand government to load 1500 tons measurement of broad-gauge railway stock for delivery in Adelaide, following which she was put up for sale. Bullen's first task aboard her was to supervise the loading and stowage of railway wagons and locomotives.

With loading complete and *Bulwark* out in the stream came one of those chance events offering something of a step up. The ship's old first mate suffered a serious fall, confining him to his room, and Bullen was forced to act as chief officer. As second mate at sea, Bullen was already in charge of the starboard watch, so someone else would have to be found to take the port watch. The master might have elected to take that watch himself, especially as the passage should not be very long. Or he might have appointed the bosun or carpenter, as probably the most experienced of the petty officers. As well as keeping his watch, the responsibility of directing the running programme of maintenance now became Bullen's, which normally included the duties of the dayworkers such as carpenter, bosun, sailmaker or cook, who reported to the first mate. Of course, as first mate he would take verbal guidance from the injured first mate (if he was not insensible) and, of course, the master. It seems likely that Bullen readily rose to the occasion. Still anchored in the stream, the master ashore, and the ship showing signs of dragging her anchor in a rising gale, he ordered the other anchor to be dropped to steady the situation. The master returning aboard seemed pleased with his initiative. Once at sea, Captain Seator, about to go below to bed, advised him, 'If you want me don't hesitate to call me at once. But don't call me if you can help it, as I am very tired; and besides, I want you to feel free to do your own work'. *Bulwark* finally sailed from Lyttleton on 5 August 1878, but did not reach Adelaide until 5 October 1878, when she berthed at the Metcalf Wharf.[9]

The big surprise was Bullen's discovery that all the ship's company were teetotallers and that several of them were members of lodges, or branches, of the Independent Order of Good Templars (IOGT). This had been founded in 1851 in New York with roots in the temperance movement. IOGT spread rapidly internationally, and by 1878 the movement was well established in Britain and Australia, and lodges were key pillars of the worldwide temperance movement. Aboard *Bulwark* numbers justified forming their own lodge. It is possible that advice was taken from the IOTG Grand Lodge of Australia. A second-hand set of regalia was purchased, and officers for the 'Bulwark of England' lodge were elected: Chaplain – the master; Treasurer – first mate; Secretary – Bullen; with other roles taken by ABs. Lodge meetings and services were held in the saloon. News of the existence of the shipboard lodge excited considerable interest in Adelaide, particularly the IOGT lodges, who welcomed *Bulwark*'s members and gave them use of their accommodation for meetings.[10] Then came the news that *Bulwark* was to be sold and that the crew would be paid off, thus breaking up the cohesion of the Bulwark of England Lodge. In a final meeting, the Lodge was formally dissolved and the regalia given away. Captain Seator, the ship's steward and Bullen himself were retained on board to care for the ship until she was purchased. *Bulwark* remained laid up in Adelaide and for sale at least into 1880, when she was again reported in the press, still commanded by Captain Seator, and loaded with timber. But by that time Bullen was long gone.

Bullen soon left *Bulwark* with Captain Seator's blessing, when the master, Captain Ward, of the barque *Day Dawn* of Adelaide, appealed for Bullen to be released to join his ship, as none of his officers had certificates.[11] This was a vessel of much the same size as *Caroline*, Bullen's first ship. British shipping law, which applied in its colonies such as South Australia, demanded that foreign-going merchant ships sailed with a second certificated officer in addition to the master. Curiously, vessels in the British home trade were not required to be served by masters or mates holding certificates of competency unless they carried passengers. How that rule extended to the maritime scene in South Australia is unknown, but because the intended destination was the port Noumea in the French colonial island of New Caledonia, the shipping officer in Adelaide may have made compliance a condition of clearing *Day Dawn* outwards. Bullen almost suffered a 'pier head jump' as the ship sailed almost immediately. He also found that despite only holding a certificate as second mate, he was signed on as first mate at £7 per month.

It was only after the rush of towing down the River Torrens and getting all sail set once the open sea was reached that Bullen had time to take in the peculiar circumstances that prevailed aboard *Day Dawn*. The nominal master was a young man who did not hold a certificate. He was the son of the owner, a long retired shipmaster, who had chosen to make the voyage, perhaps because he held a certificate of service as master, through having been in command before 1851 when certificates of competency were introduced. The son had brought his new wife with him, and the three occupied the master's and the first mate's accommodation.

Bullen would have to occupy the two-berth second mate's cabin, with the Swedish second mate who had been in the ship many years, effectively combining the roles of bosun, sailmaker and watchkeeper. The crew were experienced coastal hands who, with the second mate, were not to be interfered with. The nominal master was treated as a novice by his father, and was not able to respond to that treatment, but could be expected to take his feelings out on the compulsory recruit. The young master interfered with Bullen's handling of routine tasks, and it became apparent that for the running of the ship he was not really needed; but in the one area of navigation he was left in peace.

Day Dawn had a fine passage to Noumea and took a French pilot to tack through the reef into the harbour. At his station as first mate, on the fo'c'sle, and the ship on the fourth tack, Bullen realised she was heading for a spur from the reef, and that no action was being taken by the pilot or master. Bullen shouted, 'Hard up,' and the master helped the helmsman to turn the wheel hard over, the ship turning just in time, though a scraping sound showed that *Day Dawn* had briefly touched bottom. It's a rarity that a pilot's con of the ship is interfered with, but in this case, due to his inaction, it was amply justified. *Day Dawn* safely negotiated her way past a fleet of French warships to a convenient anchorage. In port Bullen commenced the task of setting up, or tightening, the rigging, which had become far too slack. Finding this work going on, the master countermanded Bullen's instructions for that essential task, and ordered the ship's hull to be painted.[12] As unloading by the bosun and deckhands was under the supervision of the master, Bullen really had nothing to do. He recalls a run ashore when he missed the liberty boat's departure from the shore. The rapid tropical night had set in, and he had a fear of not being aboard his ship at night. Seeing some boats moored offshore, on the spur of the moment he swam out to the nearest, where he set about releasing, with difficulty, the boat from her chain moorings.[13] Finding no oars, he improvised a paddle with a bottom board, and slowly and quietly manoeuvred the boat past several vessels at anchor until he reached *Day Dawn* among the vessels further out. Sending the boat adrift, he climbed aboard and turned in. He immediately regretted this minor act of piracy, but never heard anything about the missing boat.

In the prevailing unsatisfactory state of affairs aboard *Day Dawn*, it was obvious that he was not wanted, and that the master and owner probably resented having to pay his wage. Should he ask for his discharge, and take a chance of finding another ship? On Christmas Day he had permission for a run ashore. In the boat to the landing, he noticed a pair of pretty white schooners, which might have been gentlemen's yachts. Towards the end of the day, and back in the town which was coming to life, he was invited into the George Washington Hotel by the proprietor, speaking with an American accent. Learning that Christmas dinner was to be served, Bullen decided to stay and ordered an iced soft drink. He was joined by a number of Britons and Americans. One of the company turned out to be the master of one of the white schooners, and another its mate. They were looking for a sailing master to do all the navigation on a run to the New Hebrides, and offered Bullen £15 a month. Assuming it was a trading voyage for cargoes such as sandalwood, copra or pearl shell and the like, Bullen saw a way out of his current situation, and accepted. *Day Dawn*'s owner was happy to comply with his request for his release, and he was soon on his way ashore with his belongings, to the hotel. It seems unlikely that his discharge was completed in proper form, or that similar procedures were followed aboard the unnamed schooner.

En route to the hotel, Bullen witnessed a string of near-naked men and women linked together by a cord. After booking his room he traced the group to a marketplace where he learned that they were being apprenticed for three years at £5 annually and food. He immediately thought of the scene as slavery. This certainly coloured his view of the schooner's real cargo when he knew what it was. Two days later he was aboard the schooner when it sailed. Its deckhands were a group of islanders from Rarotonga, very smart at their work, which Bullen, a passenger apart from navigation, watched with admiration. A very pleasant passage to Mallicolo in the New Hebrides was spoilt for Bullen by the incessant drinking of the white mate and master, and their blasphemous conversation. He was horrified to realise that he was, as he thought, in a 'blackbirder', the nickname for a slaving vessel. As well as coasting locations on Mallicolo, the schooner also called at an adjacent island, Tanna, altogether taking on board 204 islanders of both sexes. Six died on the passage back to Noumea, and were buried at sea without any formalities.

To equate the schooner's shipment of these two hundred South Sea islanders with slavery is probably too strong an assumption. The employment of islanders from a wide range of Pacific island groups was widespread in the nineteenth century, but it involved the transportation of workers to other islands where there was a shortage of labour, and to Australia's east coast.[14] In the more tropical latitudes, Australian farmers turned to imported labour because of labour shortages. The islanders were contracted for fixed periods and for an agreed income including food and accommodation, plus guaranteed return passages to their home islands. Engagement could be for as short a period as one year. The arrangements were akin to those for bonded servants, but were likewise susceptible to bullying and ill-treatment. The Australian press carried a number of reports of imported labour in New Caledonia creating unrest through drinking, and there are also several reports about the merits or otherwise of using such labour in Australia.[15] Islanders were also employed in sailing vessels, as Bullen's experience in *Splendid* had shown. To keep passages when carrying labour as short as possible, fast vessels, such as schooners were preferred, and a number of vessels made a living from the two-way business. However, one trader was reported taking five months to gather together a shipment from various islands.

Needless to say, Bullen got away from the French schooner as quickly as possible, Although he does not clearly name her again, *Day Dawn* was still in *Noumea* and about to sail to Pam on the northwest end of New Caledonia for a cargo of copper ore. Captain Ward seems to have been willing to re-employ him, which might have been convenient if he had not really been signed off. Before reaching Pam, taking the wheel temporarily, Bullen lost his hat and suddenly passed out. He hints at sunstroke, but the master was also ill with fever. He was delirious for a good many days and without any proper medical care. Meanwhile, *Day Dawn* had anchored off Pam, and the crew loaded the ore without any attempt at proper stowage, but in the hope of an early departure. Now short of a navigator, an officer was borrowed from a French mail boat for the passage to Newcastle, New South Wales. After two days on passage, they encountered a serious storm, the ship labouring through the concentration of weight low down in her hold.

Regaining some sensibility, Bullen learned that about 150 tons of ore had been jettisoned, that the main topmast had gone, that the 'tween deck beams were awash, and that the French officer had forgotten his navigation. Somehow Bullen was helped on deck with his sextant, managing eventually to take a sight of the sun and have someone read the time by the chronometer. This had to be followed by a sight of the sun on the meridian at noon, and the two combined by spherical calculation to get a position. The position obtained showed that Cape Moreton (near Brisbane) was WSW and 80 nautical miles away. After that labour Bullen passed out again. The weather had eased and the light in time was sighted. *Day Dawn* was picked up by a coastal steamer on 8 February 1879, and towed to the Brisbane pilot station where a tug took over and towed her up the river.[16] Bullen was ordered into hospital, and so parted company with *Day Dawn*, its master, owner and crew. The Australian newspapers continued to list movements of *Day Dawn* continuing to trade to New Caledonia, so she must have been repaired in Brisbane after Bullen had left her.

The hospital surgeon gradually nursed Bullen back to health, but as soon as he was allowed out for a walk, he made for the shipping office to be paid off, and then booked a passage to Adelaide in a coastal steamer. So serious had been the illness that he now weighed seven stone instead of eleven stone. Of course, the hospital surgeon was not pleased, arguing that he had a lien on *Day Dawn*'s owner for continued treatment. However, the steamer passage served for convalescence, and Bullen was much fitter arriving in Adelaide.

There he was put up by a friend made while he was still attached to *Bulwark*. Captain Seator, who heard he was in town, took it upon himself to find Bullen a berth, securing it as second mate in the fine Anderson, Anderson ship, *Harbinger*, of 1500 tons bound for London, whose second mate on the outward passage had taken his discharge in Adelaide.[17]

Harbinger, according to Basil Lubbock, was the last sailing ship specially built for the carriage of passengers.[18] Its owners, Anderson and Anderson of London, had had the ship built in Greenock to the most advanced specification technically, and for the first-class passenger trade between Britain and Australia. This was a trade in which the company had entered in 1853, with its first ship named *Orient*.[19] By the 1870s, it operated several sailing ships under their Orient Line banner, and was already introducing steamers on the route. The investment and the faith in the continued passenger desire to travel in sail is impressive against the inroads which steam propulsion would make in the coming years. Bullen was 'bowled over' by almost all aspects of the ship:[20]

She was to my mind one of the noblest specimens of modern shipbuilding that ever floated. For all her huge bulk she was as easy to handle as any ten-ton yacht – far easier than some – and in any kind of weather her docility was amazing ... She was so clean in the entrance that you never saw a foaming spread of broken water ahead, driven in front by the onset of the hull. She parted the waves before her pleasantly, as an arrow in the air; but it needed a tempest to show her 'way' in its perfection. In a grand and gracious fashion, she seemed to claim affinity with the waves, and they in their wildest tumult met her as if they knew and loved her. She was the only ship I ever knew or heard of that would 'stay' under storm stay sails, reefed topsails and a reefed foresail in a gale of wind. In fact, I never saw anything that she would not do that a ship should do. She was so truly a child of the ocean that even a bungler could hardly mishandle her; she would work in spite of him. And lastly, she would steer when you could hardly detect an air out of the heavens, with a sea like a mirror, and the sails hanging apparently motionless. The men used to say that she would go a knot with only a quartermaster whistling at the wheel for a wind.

Harbinger was built of iron, and for details of her masting and rigging harked back to an earlier period. She was a lofty vessel crossing skysail yards, with a long bowsprit, jibboom and flying jibboom. Her standing rigging was not set up with stretching or bottle screws, but by the lanyard and deadeye method of the past. Underhill offers a detailed description of the idiosyncrasies which were introduced by her builder, Robert Steele. She was first a passenger ship, and passenger comfort was a primary consideration in her build and operation. Yet, as Bullen argues, above it all worked. *Harbinger* had the finest of wooden deck fittings and saloon accommodation. Her deckhouse accommodated the galley, carpenter's shop, petty officers' quarters, donkey engine (for which she carried a driver) and condenser, together with accommodation for thirty passengers. There was a cow house, teak-wood pens for thirty sheep, and fowl coops for poultry, ducks and geese. For those a butcher was carried. In the crew fo'c'sle there were three tiers of bunks, and on her outward passage she had carried fifty crew including four quartermasters (helmsmen), twenty ABs and six apprentices. Passenger numbers were about two hundred, including third class or steerage. Eight crew were carried to handle catering and cabin services. The surgeon was Dr Andrew Norrie, who had recently qualified on 6 May 1878 at the University of Edinburgh.

Because passenger comfort was the Orient Line's prime concern, its ships were not pushed hard to make the fastest passages. Further port calls were made en route to allow a little shore going and restock with fresh food. Nevertheless, Bullen clearly thought more effort and attention by the master could have achieved faster passages. Bullen tells us that *Harbinger*'s master, Lieutenant Henry Y Slader, RNR, was 'a learned man but his experience of sailing ships was of the slightest'.[21] As far as possible he tried to impose man-o'-war conditions, and never interfered with the work of the ship. Commendably, he supervised the training and education of the six apprentices, who were made responsible for tending the mizzenmast (sails and rigging). One apprentice was to be always on duty on the poop, understudying the officer of the watch. He held a weekly navigation class, and invited them in turn to dine with him. He was well supplied with weather and current charts and followed their guidance. But *Harbinger* made a four and half month passage to Britain, while a smaller ship leaving Adelaide three weeks after *Harbinger*, arrived in London four weeks before her. That ship's master, Bullen asserts:[22]

> ... had been sailing ships between England and Australia for many years, all the while accumulating first-hand knowledge of the conditions obtaining over all those seas he traversed, learning by experience the weather-signs and all the grammar of the language that the ocean speaks to its intimate friends. This knowledge it is that constitutes the fine flower of seamanship as it was (and is still in ships that depend upon sail only), but which will soon be looked upon as a lost art ...

Bullen, in his writing, frequently commends the importance of practical experience among merchant ship crews. Bullen had secured his appointment as *Harbinger*'s second mate, on Captain Seator's recommendation for his experience and ability. But the move put the ship's third mate 'out of joint', as he might otherwise have expected appointment as second mate. *Harbinger*'s master seems not to have taken the third mate, Frank Lawton, in hand for his inexperience and behaviour. On the homeward passage the third mate effectively abandoned his duties, though this slack behaviour seemed not to be corrected by the first mate or the master. However, calling at Cape Town (28 May 1879), the third mate was discharged, and not replaced. Bullen was much more impressed with *Harbinger*'s bosun, Thomas Keys, aged twenty-nine, a giant in stature and strength, and a complete master of his profession. He was most perfect as far as rigging work was concerned, and in handling the ship's deck ratings. 'Watching him splice a two-inch wire grummet round the goose-neck of the spanker boom,' Bullen asked him if he had received some special instruction in handling wire. Keys told him that he was a trained Blackwall rigger, and that he only went to sea when he found a ship that suited him. Clearly, he matched the standards Anderson, Anderson expected in the key men appointed to their ships.[23]

At a personal level, though, Bullen found service in *Harbinger* less satisfying. Despite the numbers aboard, he was really deprived of society altogether. He might not entertain passengers in his berth; he was barred from going forward into the second cabin; the chief officer was associating with nobody; and the third mate resented him. There was no one else with whom he might forgather. A peculiar watchkeeping arrangement was imposed on him 'eight hours out', presumably meaning he always kept the evening 8 to 12 watch and the early morning 4 to 8 watch. He must also have kept the afternoon 12 to 4 watch. The normal four hours on and four hours off, the so called double-watch system, made provision for rotating the pattern, so the 12 to 4 watch was only kept on alternate days. Under the 'eight hours out' system he found himself on the same watches continuously. He also comments that no acts of worship were organised, and that among the passengers were some suffering with consumption, making the voyage for medical reasons. Their deaths ought to have been recorded in the official log, but that was only done by the shipping master at the end of the voyage. A quartermaster (helmsman) also died at St Helena from the same cause and was buried ashore (12 June 1879). This was also found to be missing from the official log, and seems to suggest that the master was unfamiliar with the legal requirement for the recording of untoward events.

After a pleasant, though slow passage, *Harbinger* reached Gravesend on 9 August 1879, berthing in West India South Dock. It seems likely that the crew were signed off at Gravesend, under the new Transmission of Wages scheme, whereby shipping office officials boarded homeward-bound ships to carry out the discharge formalities. Crew members could opt to have their balance of wages paid at a shipping office of their choice once they were on leave, receiving only a travel warrant and a small sum in hand. After long voyages in particular, they might leave the shipping office with considerable sums, and were thus targets for the machinations of the crimps. Of those ABs who completed the round voyage in *Harbinger* almost all paid off with about £20. Bullen, as second mate on £6 per month for half the voyage, paid off with £21 6s 2d. The scheme meant that seafarers left the ship with little cash in hand, and so frustrated the crimps, who were also banned from boarding ships downriver.

Bullen signed off with his now regular signature, Frank T Bullen. His second name was clearly in use during his early voyages, but it is not clear whether he continued to use Thomas or Tommy with friends and associates, or whether he now became known as Frank. Before leaving *Harbinger*, an opportunity occurred for him to have a word with the ship's husband (managing owner), about the possibility of continued employment with Anderson, Anderson. The reply was in the negative as 'we have so many of our own young officers to provide for, that we are unable to employ outsiders'. Perhaps there might be a chance when Bullen held a certificate as first mate. It was hopeless, as he already knew.

On leaving *Harbinger*, uppermost in his mind must have been the renewing of his association with his girl, which must have immediately led to the decision that they should marry, as the marriage took place on 1 September 1879, a bare three weeks after his return, at St Marylebone Church in London, not that far from the Paddington area where his life had started. His wife was Amelia Grimwood, daughter of Voltaire Lucifer Grimwood, deceased. Amelia was born about 1860. Their address in the register was given as 8 Castle Street, probably just the room, charged at five shillings per week including some furnishings.[24] He says in *With Christ at Sea* that he then passed his examination for the first mate

118

certificate. However, that is in error as the certificate is dated 5 August 1880. He had actually signed on *Herat*, a Liverpool ship on 30 August 1879, to be on board on 3 September 1879, before the wedding took place. Bullen's description of his wife's distress on hearing he was going back to sea so soon, certainly rings true, as does his explanations that he was running out of money.

9

A Voyage in Two Ships

30 August 1879 to 6 July 1880

One of the reasons that the British government took full charge of the arrangements for engaging and discharging merchant seafarers in the Mercantile Marine Act of 1850 was to ensure that their remuneration and conditions of service were properly recorded, and that they received their full entitlement at the end of the voyage. There was optional provision for the payment of debts, and support of seafarers' dependants, normally wives and parents, through the advance note and the allotment note systems. Both were made out whilst signing on. Both were ultimately payable by the ship's owners. The former, typically one month's wages, was only payable after the ship had sailed and if the seafarer was aboard. Traders, such as boarding-house keepers and seafarers' outfitters, would accept the advance note as payment of debt and perhaps return a small proportion in cash, but at a sizeable discount of the value of the note. Probably only the managing owner of the ship, or possibly a seafarers' charity, would pay the full value. The allotment note catered for ongoing monthly payments to the named relative, but only after two months had elapsed after the ship had sailed, as both the month's advance had to be worked off, and a further month's earnings accumulated. So did Bullen make provision for his new wife?[1] Bullen tells us that signing on as an AB he was paid £3 per month, but the *Herat*'s AAC shows all the ABs being paid only £2 10s 0d monthly and being given an advance note for that sum. He might have given her his last sovereign or two, and the advance note for her to take to the shipowner's office when it became due. Without naming any provision for an allotment note,

Bullen hints at its existence by indicating that his £3 per month produced a weekly income for his wife of eight shillings, which is roughly thirty shillings per month. He could not have allotted more, as the authorities imposed a limit of half the monthly wage. However, not only was Bullen earning less than £3 per month, he made no provision for an allotment payment. There can be no doubt that he knew of the ability to make allotments. *Herat's* first mate, second mate, carpenter, sailmaker and bosun all made provision for dependants, though none of the remaining crew did so. This pattern is representative of the use of the allotment note in other sailing vessels of the period. Bullen took his responsibilities for his wife's support seriously. However, he hoped to be lucky and obtain a second mate's berth overseas; it might be better to avoid the complication of cancelling an allotment note relating to *Herat*. Further, she may already have held the resident servant's position as a general domestic at Zion House, Lewisham, Kent, given in the 1881 Census.[2]

Sailing from the River Thames, *Herat* was off Deal on 4 September 1879, still under tow.[3] He writes about the crew of nineteen or twenty, but the AAC has twenty-five names, including the master, but omitting apprentices if carried. Most of the ABs were more or less drunk on sailing, only four being fit for work. But all who signed on had joined, and there was no anchoring at Gravesend, which would have allowed a break for getting things shipshape. The tug let go off Beachy Head. Bullen labels his fellow occupants of the fo'c'sle as a godless and evil crowd. In contrast, however, the master, Captain Charles Robertson, was a sincere Christian but Bullen regrets to say that:[4]

> ... he did not possess that instinct for command which would have enabled him to make his ship as happy as the *West York* ... he was lacking in that most essential quality of a seaman, courage ... [which] could not be hidden from the crew when the first gale was encountered, and thence-forward his authority over them was a thing of naught.

Robertson, aged forty-nine, was born in Port Glasgow. Signed on as third mate was Charles Robertson junior, aged twenty and born in Sydney (NSW), who was probably the master's son, and who had probably served under his father as an apprentice, as he names *Herat* as his last ship. The four-year term as apprentice (or possibly before the mast) would have been completed. His birthplace suggests that possibly the master had married in Sydney or that his wife had been sailing with him. The first mate, E E Jeffery, aged thirty from Plymouth, had also served in the ship the previous voyage. The second mate, William Crowhurst, aged thirty-two from Longworth, Oxfordshire, was new to the ship. The carpenter, sailmaker, bosun and cook were also new faces, and of the petty officers, only the steward had been in the crew the previous voyage. The engagement of sixteen ABs, including Bullen, indicates that *Herat* was a full-rigged ship similar to Bullen's recent vessels, *Bulwark* and *Harbinger*, and at about 1400 tons measurement, among the largest of his ships. Unusually, there were no hands aboard from the continent of Europe, though there were two from Nova Scotia and an American.

Herat's managing owner was Edward P Bates of Liverpool, where the ship was registered.[5] Trading regularly to India, the owners chose to name many of their ships after cities and areas in or beyond northern India. Herat is a city in Afghanistan. Bates family members had practised as merchants in Calcutta and Bombay in the early part of the nineteenth century, but by the 1850s the business was based in Liverpool, having moved into shipowning. Although Edward P Bates was named as *Herat*'s managing owner, shares in the ship were probably spread among several other members of the family. Though India was a trading focus, their ships were operated more as general traders, tramping wherever the next cargo took them.

That the crew was wholly English-speaking did not prevent a considerable turnover once *Herat* reached Calcutta. After arriving at Calcutta on 31 December 1879, ten of the crew left the ship, four as deserters, six, including Bullen and the bosun, being discharged by mutual consent. Nine ABs and a new bosun were engaged for the return passage to Liverpool, arriving on 10 June 1880.[6] That, of course, was after Bullen had been discharged in Calcutta.

Bullen has little to say about the outward passage, except to relate events which resulted in him being 'sent to Coventry' by all the other deckhands. In the shipping office Bullen had done a 'small favour' to a man who was well past deckhand's work. This might have been a few favourable words which prevented the man being turned away when he was about to be signed on. The man, Edward Wilson, aged fifty-four on the AAC but according to Bullen fifty-eight, was very willing, but unfit and banned by the mate from going aloft. Bullen comments on the rarity of finding a hale old deckhand among the ABs, caused by the bad food, the atmosphere in the fo'c'sle, changes in climate, variations in levels of exertion, and debauchery while ashore. Before joining the man had been turned away from the Sailors' Home (London, Dock & Well Street) being unable to pay, and had been sleeping rough. He was in Bullen's watch and, of course, they chatted in slack moments. Called to shorten sail, Wilson went aloft on a minor task, ignoring Bullen, who said he would do it, only to fall to the deck and be killed (7 September 1879). The master read the burial service with great feeling, the sailmaker having prepared the body for the committal.

Immediately after, the master held a church service in the saloon at which no one was missing except those on watch. Bullen raised the tune for a hymn, which set the other deckhands against him. Another factor was that the master had asked him if he would select the hymns in future. Afterwards the chat in the fo'c'sle was all at Bullen's expense. Things reached such a state that Bullen avoided going into that space as much as possible. Further, the master chatted with him when he was at the wheel, a mark of favouritism which the crew resented. Bullen asserts that the three mates were also behaving in an unfriendly manner towards him, though there was no cause in relation to his work. Matters culminated when the master ordered 'field work' (extra work during the watch below), to change the whole suit of sails. Bullen turned to, but the rest of his watch refused to leave the fo'c'sle. However, despite threats of violence, he came to no harm. It turned out that one of the crew thought better of him than the rest, asking Bullen for an explanation of his religion and beliefs. That conversation took place on deck, but entering the fo'c'sle his new friend told the others off with all the expletives he usually mustered. There was an immediate uproar, but the pair lay in their bunks ignoring the remarks, and things quietened down. Once in Calcutta, the 'refusers' (Bullen uses 'mutineers') were taken before the shipping master and fined two days' pay, though Bullen doubted that would have any effect.

The master, who obviously recognised that Bullen was a cut above the rest of the deckhands, and knew that he held a certificate as second mate, allowed Bullen ashore as often as he liked, typically evenings and Sundays. For once, he mentions taking advantage of the facilities offered to seafarers by the then worldwide networks of seamen's missions of various denominations and local individual provision. He divided his time 'between Colonel Haig's Mission in Radha Bazaar, visiting the beautiful [Anglican] cathedral ... and the English Church Mission ship'.[7] Largely through the American missionaries working out of the Radha Bazaar Seamen's Rest, there was something of a revival taking place among seafarers visiting Calcutta, with groups singing sacred songs in the streets making their way back to their ships. Bullen argues that as a result the men worked better, gave no trouble by returning aboard drunk, were in better health, and were obviously happy.[8]

Something over a fortnight after arriving in Calcutta, *Herat's* master sent for Bullen to tell him he had signed off the bosun for incompetency, and was thinking of offering him the vacancy, but knowing what had happened in the fo'c'sle thought it better to find him a berth as second mate. Successful in this, Bullen was offered his discharge if he forwent the residual pay he was due, or remain as an AB in *Herat*. Of course, he accepted the offer, and was signed on *Britannia*, another 1400-ton ship. Bullen says the pay agreed was £5 10s 0d per month, but the entry in *Britannia's* AAC is £5, with an advance of £5. His discharge from *Herat*, on 26 January 1880, shows a payment of 51 rupees 12 annas, or about £5. His earnings for five months' service in *Herat* were about £12 10s 0d, leaving him about £10, allowing for the month's advance. So about £5 was spent on slop chest purchases aboard *Herat*, or the master took £5 as his fee for releasing him. Given the discrepancies between Bullen's memory of the two experiences so far when he left a ship to take a better position, it seems quite possible that he conflated the two events, and that Captain Robertson did not treat him so badly after all. So Bullen joined *Britannia* with £10 (about 100 rupees) in his pocket (pay-off and advance), and he was certainly wondering how his wife was managing. It had become possible to make cash remittances by telegraph, and he took the opportunity to send his advance of £5 (50 rupees) home.[9]

At first sight on joining *Britannia* (26 January 1880), Bullen thought he had landed on his feet as he was given a warm welcome by the first mate, William Robertson, aged thirty from Fife, and by the master. Bullen mentions a third mate, but one was not listed on the AAC. The master was J Hamilton, thirty, born in Liverpool. Possibly he was the son of the managing owner, William Hamilton of Lancaster. *Britannia* was loading jute for Dundee. He found himself superintending the stowage, but was otherwise free to go ashore at will. The ship's outward voyage had been to Colombo, but for her next cargo she had probably sailed in ballast round to Calcutta. Bullen's predecessor as second mate, Charles Ford from Jersey, had died on the outward passage from internal injuries (presumably following a fall from aloft), on 20 October 1879 in latitude 26° S 77° E (to the east of Mauritius). *Britannia* sailed from Calcutta on 14 February 1880.[10] At sea, the master chatted familiarly with Bullen, making him feel at home. But there was an undercurrent of which Bullen now became aware. It was not that Bullen soon understood his commanding officer was not a believer. The core of the undercurrent was that

Between the skipper and the steward there existed a strange fraternity, which had its result in the latter behaving towards the officers with a gross and insolent familiarity, such as I never before or since seen on board ship ... one afternoon he came to my cabin door and, with out any preliminary, flung it wide open, saying 'Here, you, get me a cask o' beef when ye go on deck, 's quick 's the devil 'll let ye.' Aghast at this salutation, I could hardly speak for a moment ... At last I said, 'How dare you address me like that?' ... he coolly said, 'oh, you go t'hell. Just do as I told you, that's all.'

Bullen immediately reported the steward to the master for gross insolence and foul abuse. His reply was astounding:

'Look here, don't you get interfering with my steward, or it will be the worse for you. He's a dam sight better man than you are any day'. 'That may be true, sir,' Bullen answered; 'but at the same time I must remind you that you engaged me as third in command of this ship, and that during the six weeks I have been on board you have had no fault to find with me. Why, then, do you now propose to subject me to the coarse domination of a domestic servant, knowing, as you must do that I shall at the same time lose all power of command over my watch, down to the smallest boy?' The master responded, 'You seem to have an infernal lot of back slack. Go away.'

The master thereafter took every opportunity to belittle Bullen, including taking his cabin door off its hinges, imposing extra duties during his watch below, and dressing him down in public. This continued for the remainder of the voyage, a further four months or so.[11] As a final thrust, the master endorsed his discharge slip with a 'G', for 'Good', which had come to mean in the case of an officer 'No Good'. In that period there was a footnote on pages four and five of the official logbook, headed 'List of Crew and Report of Character', instructing masters to use one of the following abbreviations: 'VG for 'Very Good', G, 'Good', M, 'Middling', and I, 'Indifferent'. One of these had to be used in the columns headed 'for General Conduct' and 'for Ability in Seamanship'. Masters could also decline to report, for which the abbreviation 'DR' came into use. These abbreviations were also entered on the certificate of discharge issued to each seafarer when signing off. Before 1900, when Continuous Certificate of Discharge Books were introduced, discharge certificates not bearing 'VG' were often conveniently lost. As a result, only 'VG' or 'DR' were ever used in the twentieth century.

Britannia finally reached Dundee on 6 July 1880 when the crew were signed off.[12] Bullen's discharge is labelled Dis 3b, the Transmission of Seamen's Wages form. This allows entries for names, port of destination and sums to be deducted from the pay-off. Bullen's deductions were 12s 6d rail fare (Dundee to London), cash in hand £1, and ship's deductions £4 3s. He collected his pay-off of £21 1s 2d on 9 July 1880 at the Tower Hill shipping office. Then the Dis 3 form was returned to Dundee for attachment to the AAC.

Bullen rounds off his discussion of this voyage, remarking that fortunately he already had his mate's certificate, as the best discharge from his most recent ship and a favourable testimonial was essential for admission to the examination. He submitted Application to be Examined, Form Exn 2, on 23 July 1880, to the Mercantile Marine Office at St Katherine's Dock in London and paid the examination fee for the first mate's examination of ten shillings. On the reverse in Section G, he was required to list his sea service from first going to sea. The first five entries were the same as on his application for the second mate's examination, *Western Belle*, *Harrowby*, *Splendid*, *West York* and *Dartmouth*. So he effectively concealed his time in *Caroline*, *Investigator*, *Sea Gem*, *Brinkburn* and the steamer, possibly owing to lack of documentation. To this list he added his time in *Columbus*, *Bulwark*, *Harbinger*, *Herat* and *Britannia*. What mattered was his time as second mate in charge of the watch, which needed to add up to twelve months in foreign-going ships. This meant that his time as an AB in *Columbus* and *Herat* did not count, though it had to be declared. We do not know whether he received a testimonial from *Britannia*'s master, or the extent to which it was unfavourable, but the sea time in *Britannia* was needed to make up the twelve months. With it Bullen had served as second mate for one year, one month and twenty days. He did have the discharge paper, but that lacked 'VG'. The examiner, James Rankin, must have reviewed Bullen's application almost immediately, as he endorsed it 'Unsatisfactory testimonials'. He also noticed that Bullen could not produce a testimonial from the master of *Columbus* or *Herat*. However, there was a fallback. He could launch and appeal to the Local Marine Board of London, which operated the examination provision for the Port of London. The application was further annotated 'Granted by Special Application to the Local Marine Board 29 July 1880'. It was by no means uncommon for applications to be rejected on similar grounds. Another future maritime writer, Joseph Conrad, six months younger than Bullen but also born in 1857, suffered a similar indignity with respect to his sea time in French ships. He studied under John Newton at the Sailors' Home (London) for all three of his certificates in the 1880s.[13]

Bullen took the examination on 4 August 1880: the written paper in navigation followed the viva voce examination in seamanship. The examiner was James Rankin, who had reviewed Bullen's application, and would endorse Section H of the application 'passed' in both sections of the test. The oral examination could be as wide ranging as the examiner cared to make it. Given the referral of the application, it seems likely that Bullen was closely questioned about his experiences in *Britannia*. The syllabus for the whole examination in 1863, probably little different in 1880, was:[14]

10. A FIRST MATE must be nineteen years of age, and have served five years at sea, of which one year must have been as either Second or Only Mate, or as both.

In Navigation – In addition to the qualification required for a Second Mate, he must be able to observe and calculate the amplitude of the sun, and deduce the variation of the compass therefrom, to be able to observe azimuths: and be able to find the longitude by chronometer from an observation of the sun by the usual methods; to work the latitude by single altitude of the sun off the meridian; to compare chronometers and keep their rates. He must know how to lay off the place of the ship on the chart, both by bearings of known objects, and by latitude and longitude. He must be able to determine the error of a sextant and to adjust it, also to find the time of high water from the known time at full and change.

In Seamanship – In addition to what is required for a Second Mate, he must know how to moor and unmoor, and to keep a clear anchor; to carry out an anchor; to stow a hold; and to make the requisite entries in the ship's log. He will also be questioned as to his knowledge of the use and management of the mortar and rocket lines in the case of the stranding of a vessel, as explained in the official logbook. A more extensive knowledge of seamanship will be required, as to shifting large spars and sails, shifting yards and masts, etc, and getting heavy weights, anchors, etc, in and out. Casting a ship on a lee shore; securing masts in case of accident to the bowsprit.

Bullen tells us that he found the examination for first mate much easier than that for second mate.[15] It is not clear whether he attended a navigation school at all, but if he did, it was for a very short period. Perhaps because a network of navigation teachers skilled in the mathematics of spherical trigonometry had been planted around the country, without ever having been to sea, he did not consider that they had anything to offer for the seamanship oral, viewed then as more important than the written navigation paper.[16] Despite his success in the examination for his Certificate of Competency as First Mate, and his delight in having a home, Bullen's time at home was soon cut short through the consumption of his pay-off. Before that he had to collect his certificate. It was dated 5 August 1880. He collected it on 6 August at the Tower Hill Mercantile Marine Office. At this period the same certificate number was retained for each certificate grade, in Bullen's case 04758 (the zero is part of the number), entered on the reverse of the certificate with his given address, 12 Bonny Street, Camden Town, London.

10

Two Voyages in Six Ships

17 August 1880 to 30 September 1882

With so much shipping using the port of London, and the resultant considerable turnover of seafaring manpower, it might be thought comparatively easy to secure a berth as a first or second mate of an outward-bound ship. Bullen's time ashore continued to be limited by the cash in hand from his previous voyage, with home expenses and the cost of his latest qualification making inroads. He was once again reduced to accepting a berth as an AB, and trusting to luck that somewhere overseas he might secure a berth as an officer. His search probably began immediately after he had collected his Certificate of Competency as First Mate on 6 August 1880, at the shipping office. It was a heartless and degrading business inquiring aboard ship after ship, calling at public houses where shipmasters congregated and leaving his name at shipping offices on the off-chance there might be a vacancy. After perhaps a fortnight of that drudgery, rumour of the possibility of a vacancy in a ship in the Surrey Commercial Dock complex on the south side of the River Thames took him away from the familiar territory of the St Katherine, London and West and East India docks, into an area having connections with the Baltic Sea area. There he found the vacancy had already been filled. Then modest good fortune came his way aboard a vessel which had only arrived from Montreal on 6 August, but after unloading would be sailing west to Nova Scotia in ballast. Bullen secured the berth as AB, available because part of the crew had been signed off. So Bullen found himself outward bound again on 17 August 1880.[1]

Bullen does not name the vessel in *With Christ at Sea*, where he describes it as a small Nova Scotian brigantine bound for Sydney, Cape Breton (CB).[2] However, he did name her in a short essay reprinted in *A Sack of Shakings* a year later, as the *Wanderer*.[3] A vessel of 249 tons, and rigged as a brigantine, her crew, including the master, numbered eleven. An Agreement and Account of Crew (AAC) embracing the passage from London has not been found, but a List C 'Account of Crew …' names the crew arriving in London, and shows the pay-off of two of her ABs. With the dates involved, this pinpoints this *Wanderer* among several other vessels named *Wanderer* at this time. Bullen had grave doubts about the sailing quality of the vessel, but was pleasantly surprised. Instead of towing downriver, his new ship was 'worked' in a surprisingly handy fashion, which delighted the pilot and Bullen himself. Zigzagging in easy tacks took them downriver and through the Downs, and into the Channel. In the gales to be expected of an Atlantic crossing in the autumn, *Wanderer* rose easily over the waves, continuing to answer readily to the smallest touch of the helm. Despite her small freeboard, 'never a wave broke on deck', and she behaved like 'one of the sea people' (the gulls and petrels) riding the wind. A well-balanced set of sails allow, in steadier weather, such a vessel to be steered with wheel movements of 'a spoke' or 'half a spoke', and a helmsman might say to his relief 'she's taking half a spoke starboard (or port)'. The helmsman finds the balance point and it was not unknown for ten or fifteen minutes to pass without wheel movement, with the ship maintaining the desired heading. Such a vessel was *Wanderer*.

The master, John Gallihar, aged thirty-three from Guysboro, Nova Scotia, was also managing owner. His certificate number (923) suggests he passed the examination perhaps in Halifax Nova Scotia, while, that of his first mate, Joseph Lewis (08006), was probably passed in Britain. David Gallihar, twenty-eight, also from Guysboro, might have been the master's brother. Six ABs and a cook/steward completed the manning. The delightful passage to Sydney, CB, took twenty-nine days.[4] The one adverse element was the cook, who 'was so grotesquely incapable of doing anything in the cooking way, and so foully unclean besides' that the crew had to prepare their own food. The master was a kind-hearted man and would not allow the imposter cook to be maltreated. Often the master took over the cooking.[5] *Wanderer* had arrived on 15 September, and would sail on 18 September for Lingan, NS, to load a cargo of coal for St John, New Brunswick, by which time Bullen had moved on to make a passage which must have been heavily engraved in his memory.

Before embarking on Bullen's next ship, it is necessary to clear up the confusion which can exist between certain port locations in this part of the world. St John's is the main city in Newfoundland, which was never visited by Bullen. St John, NB, a port in the Bay of Fundy on its west coast, and St John's, Antigua, in the West Indies, are both destination ports for Bullen in this chapter. Winters were harsh in the Canadian east-coast regions where Bullen's ships took him, with the remains of tropical hurricanes bringing severe gales, and complicated by the extreme tidal conditions which prevail in the Bay of Fundy. There the tidal rise and fall can reach the largest in the world, over fifty feet, and produce the related tidal streams, whirlpools, rapids and bore. In St John, NB, tides can reach twenty-six feet, while there are many parts of the region where at low water vessels may be left high and dry. These are the conditions that Bullen's change of ship in Sydney, CB, would lead him to experience.

As *Wanderer* entered the more-or-less empty Sydney harbour, no one could miss the strangely rigged, antiquated and clumsy-looking vessel among the very few ships there. It was only on the evening of *Wanderer*'s departure from the anchorage to take up the next charter, that the first mate, Joseph Lewis, called out Bullen to check that he held a first mate's certificate, and tell him that the strange craft wanted a first mate.[6] *Wanderer*'s master would let him go, but could not be bothered with the formalities of discharge, so he would have to 'jump ship' (desert). Owing to his advance in London, Bullen knew he would not be losing very much of his earnings in *Wanderer*, so he gathered his possessions, jumped into a waiting boat, and soon found himself ashore, in the pitch dark in freezing weather, with no idea of where to go. Following the first glimpse of light, he asked for shelter, and was welcomed into a room with someone else, where he could have the sofa, which he soon discovered was flea-ridden. The following day he soon found an hotel, where he left his bag, while he went searching for the master needing a first mate.

Bullen does not name the strangely rigged vessel in *With Christ at Sea*, while in his short story, 'The Skipper of the Amulet', he calls her 'Amulet', a synonymous term for *Keepsake*, the real name of the vessel. She is variously described as a brig or a snow, and was registered in Workington, Cumberland. Her managing owner was Thomas Middleton, a member of the Middleton shipbuilding and shipowning extended family of the Cumberland coast, though correspondence in 1881 shows him writing from Cardiff.[7] Calling at the Sydney, CB, shipping office gave Bullen his new ship's name and probably the information that her master was living ashore. After something of a search, Bullen found *Keepsake*'s master, whom he names as Captain Jones, though newspaper reports of *Keepsake*'s movements give the name Davies, ensconced in a drinking dive with a glass of brandy in his hand. Following an exchange of credentials and agreeing a salary of £6 per month, Bullen was signed on in the shipping office, which was part of a general store. *Keepsake*'s last passage had been from Santos in Brazil to Sydney, CB, and now she was to load a cargo of coal destined for St John, NB. Bullen obtained an advance, presumably the usual month's wages, which he was able to despatch, presumably by telegraph, to his wife. The master, in a permanent state of intoxication, did not accompany Bullen aboard, simply telling him to go and take charge, and to report to him where he was.

Bullen was in for a shock when he reached the *Keepsake*, which seems at that stage at least to have been at anchor, as at the landing place he ran into a group of men dragging the body of a young seaman out of the water, who had fallen out of *Keepsake*'s boat the previous night. A couple of days later he had to go ashore with crew members to attend the funeral in the local churchyard, without a priest, and none of the crew knowing what to do. The deceased was from Cork, and respected by his shipmates for his devotion. The body was lowered into the grave, and one man knelt and made a brief commendation. Discovering the death of one of the crew could hardly be a more inauspicious beginning to Bullen's service in *Keepsake*. Arriving on board his worst fears were confirmed:[8]

> The second mate was on board, certainly; but in a state of fury against the skipper, and firmly resolved never to do a stroke of work on board again. He told me a yarn about the condition of things on board; how they lived just from hand to mouth, buying a few pounds of stores here and there; how they had been out from England nearly two years, during which time they had shipped five different [first] mates. And how the skipper had drunk every penny of freight earned by the ship ... The condition of the vessel was deplorable ... My heart sank within me when I saw the filth everywhere and noticed the sullen looks of the five men forrad, doubly miserable now from the loss of their shipmate ... with a short prayer for courage and ability to see the thing through, I began.

Bullen began on the large amount of outstanding work. The crew turned to, though with a good deal of muttering, and two days' cleaning made things more shipshape and the vessel looked a little more seaworthy. The near absence of ship materials for restoring the rigging made it difficult to make rigging repairs. A visit ashore to report progress to the master forced Bullen to go to his room where he found his commanding officer in bed with a half-emptied bottle of brandy and certainly in a state of drunkenness. Bullen was ordered not to trouble him, but to get the cargo in and the ship ready for sea. Bullen managed to get to a doctor to have a whitlow removed from his left thumb, but he was left in pain, literally single-handed and with a permanently damaged thumb. With the ship under the coal tips, loading was completed, the ship moved back out to anchor, and she was ready for sea. Although this was duly reported to the master, there was no immediate effort to get aboard and sail. Captain Davies continued his carouse for another three weeks, according to Bullen. Meanwhile, the consignee of the cargo in St John, NB, was agitating for its delivery. The local agent who had booked the shipment came aboard to find out about the delay, and ordered Bullen to take the ship to sea without the master if he did not board immediately. The agent would have had to consult the owner in Britain about his threat. At last the master came aboard, ordered the ship to get under way, and disappeared to his cabin with his supply of spirits, and orders not to be disturbed.

With the second mate refusing to do anything at all, Bullen was effectively in total charge and continuously on watch, though snatching some sleep while the most experienced AB kept lookout. Keeping clear of the land where he could, and trying to fix position with stellar navigation, he immediately discovered that the ship's chronometer was hopelessly out of order. He resorted to taking soundings with the deep-sea lead, and asking the fishing schooners he met with for their positions. He narrowly avoided running ashore off Cape Roseway (south coast Nova Scotia), where the beam of its light shone across the ship. Somehow the ship was manoeuvred around Cape Sable (southern tip of Nova Scotia), with its tide races and currents, into the Bay of Fundy and the search for a pilot. The weather kept fine and clear until that was achieved and Bullen was able to get some decent rest.

On arrival at St John, NB, Captain Davies immediately went ashore, only to return after dark and, ignoring the lighted gangway, walked over the quay edge and fell some fifty feet, feet first into the mud on which *Keepsake* was lying, the tide with its some thirty feet fall having completely ebbed. His cries alerted the crew, who rescued him uninjured except for a few bruises, and still drunk. He returned ashore and once again set up in a local hotel. So Bullen was again left in full charge. He was soon being pestered by 'longshoremen' who somehow had discovered that there was a large amount of 'junk' aboard. The ship had been re-rigged in Santos with wire rigging where possible, and the old rope fibre had not been sold off. These men were pestering to buy it at a low price, with a personal backhander to the mate. His principles ensured that he turned them down, but the men went to the master, who took the bribe and signed a disposal order forcing Bullen's compliance.

The second mate and one of the seamen managed to get their discharge out of the master, and departed in great glee. But Bullen was tied to the ship while unloading was completed. His one short relaxation was to attend morning service at a nearby Church of England church, which was a peaceful place, though the service was gabbled and the preaching very poor. No one spoke to him. Despite his inebriation, the master did attend to ship's business, finally appearing on board with the information that *Keepsake* was to load a cargo of timber for a winter passage to Europe, at Parrsboro, NS, across the Bay of Fundy from St John in the Minas Basin, entered from the eastern branch of the Bay of Fundy. A tug, for the overnight tow across, and a pilot had been booked. After setting off, the master and an associate, for whom Bullen uses the word 'tagarene', perhaps meaning wastrel, boarded, and soon disappeared below to continue drinking. Bullen relaxed as the pilot kept watch all night, with a local pilot taken for the awkward wriggle into the Basin. No one on board knew where the ship should berth, so she was laid alongside the first wharf they came to. With the pilot, Bullen trudged through the snow and eventually found the wharfinger, who gave instructions to the wharf where the timber cargo was to be loaded. It is not clear how the ship was moved, unless the tug remained to complete the tow while *Keepsake* was still afloat.

Captain Davies with his friend disappeared ashore the day after arrival to settle in to another hotel and continue drinking. Bullen did not find out where he was for ten days. Timber started coming aboard, but of proper stowage there was none. Bullen's authority over the loading was completely undermined, and despite his threat not to sail in *Keepsake*, supervision of loading was entirely given over to the drunken stevedore drinking pal of the master.

The lack of proper stowage undermined the seaworthiness of the ship in the eyes of British maritime law, as timber deck cargoes were subject to special regulations. Deck cargoes were normal with complete cargoes of timber. As early as 1837 a Select Committee on Shipwrecks of Timber Ships had made recommendations on the stowage of timber cargoes.[9] Soon after Bullen made his complaint, Captain Davies came down to visit the ship. The crew were alerted by the crash of breaking ice. Once again the master had fallen between the wharf and the ship, without much physical damage, which curtailed his visit to return to his hotel without a change of clothing. When loading was complete:[10]

> ... she had a deck load of deals four feet above the rails – that is about eight feet in height – and was so 'crank' and top heavy that she would scarcely stand upright at the wharf. Her sails were like muslin for thinness, besides being clouted, or patched ... The men were afraid to put their weight on a rope for fear of bringing something tumbling about their ears. And she was almost bare of provisions. So I sat down and wrote a letter to the owner, briefly setting forth the state of affairs, telling him that I was firmly convinced that it was the skipper's intention to cast the ship away, and that, under all the circumstances, I did not feel justified in going to sea in such a vessel.

Bullen then visited the master, finding him in bed with his friend and thoroughly besotted, and demanded his discharge. His request was refused. Nevertheless, Bullen removed his belongings to another hotel and effectively had to jump ship. Having consulted a lawyer, he managed to have the master served with a writ of Capias, as he was about to board *Keepsake* for a tow to St John. In the ensuing hearing, the master and his friends asserted that he was a sober person, and the argument that his drinking endangered the ship's company failed completely. The master was allowed to sail still in command of *Keepsake*.

Bullen quotes a figure of £12 as the amount of wages he lost by becoming a deserter. Meanwhile, *Keepsake*, clearly short-handed, was towed back to St John, ostensibly to recruit the missing crew members, but also an excuse for the master to continue his debauchery ashore. The ship arrived at St John on 9 December 1880, and sailed thence for Mumbles (for orders) on 17 December 1880.[11] She was run aground and wrecked at Little River (Maine US) on 27 December 1880 with the loss of three lives.[12] Bullen, now without a ship, found himself high and dry in a remote minor port in midwinter, surviving on credit until he could find employment.[13] He found a welcome among the Episcopalians of the town and sang with their choir. He times his stay ashore in Parrsboro at about three weeks, when a stranger introduced himself. The man had built a schooner of 24 tons measurement, loaded it with potatoes grown on his own farm and planned to take her to the West Indies, to sell both the ship and the cargo. He needed a navigator: would Bullen accept at $25 [Canadian] a month? Accepting, Bullen requested a month's advance, and agreed $15 in cash, to settle his bills and send something home. The 'crew' turned out to be the owner's son, aged twelve, and a boy of fifteen. The vessel was named *Daisy*, and had been properly registered at Parrsboro, NS, as No 1/24 in 1877. Its official number was 71389 and the owner, James George of Parrsboro.[14]

Clearing the Minas Basin was managed easily, but once out in the Bay of Fundy the weather became very severe, with intense cold and 'frost smoke' rising from the sea.[15] Spray condensed all over the rigging and the movements of the vessel caused ice droplets to sprinkle down. Reaching the far side of the bay, *Daisy* slipped into Musquash harbour, NB, close southeast of St John, to ship supplies of wood and water. Moving cautiously south, *Daisy* crossed back over towards Nova Scotia, the rigging becoming so frozen up that the vessel could not be worked. Christmas Day 1880 found them anchored outside Yarmouth Harbour (southwest NS). Then she reached an anchorage behind Cape Sable Island, where she lay for week until a serious storm blew itself out, with the tide drying out at low water. Then they managed to get ashore to replenish their supply of wood. They also cut a young tree without trimming its branches and lashed it across the deck. Eventually, with a fair wind, *Daisy* managed to get away from Nova Scotia, heading south and soon sailed into the much warmer Gulf Stream. A gale set in, blowing across the set of the Gulf Stream and generating very serious waves. A cable was shackled to the spruce tree, which was then passed overboard to act as a sea anchor, with the ship hove-to for three days. The tree had served its purpose, becoming nearly worn through. Creeping gradually southwards, *Daisy* found fine warm weather. Eventually, *Daisy* sailed in to St John's, Antigua, among the Leeward Islands.

Bullen had very early discovered that the owner and master was a physically filthy, cruel and blasphemous man, and quite uncouth. He found being crammed up with the man most unpleasant, and he could hardly wait to clear out again. In St John's he went to the shipping office and promptly signed off the *Daisy*. There was little shipping movement of the international trading kind there, and the shipping master advised him to leave as soon as he could. There happened to be a schooner about to sail, and Bullen was given a note of introduction for a passage to Bridgetown, Barbados.[16]

The schooner bore the name *Migumooweesoo*, and was listed in the *Mercantile Navy List 1880* as owned by Archibald S Bonyun of Bridgetown, Barbados, though built in Freeport Nova Scotia in 1872. Her official number was 64019. Her master was suffering from a bout of dysentery, and he was delighted to have Bullen aboard to stand in for him and direct the crew of islanders. The cargo was twenty horses for Barbados, which, at the time of his arrival on board, were calmly floating with their heads just out of the water alongside. The crew had started loading the horses. Someone in the water dived with slings to pass them under the horses' bodies. Others on deck manned the tackle, hauling the animals up to be swung aboard and landed on the deck. With all aboard there was little room on deck for working the vessel. The schooner sailed with a fair breeze, but then calms and baffling airs hampered the passage for three days, such that the fodder and water for the animals threatened to run out. With the return of the wind, it was necessary to head for the nearest port, Prince Rupert in Dominica, where fodder (sugar cane tops) and water was purchased for the animals and fish for the crew. Two days later the ship reached Bridgetown, Barbados. It is not clear whether Bullen was formally signed on *Migumooweesoo*, but he certainly played a key part in that short passage.

Bullen had only been in Bridgetown for ten days when the shipping office passed him news of a barquentine in harbour which needed a first mate.[17] *Campanero* was a 'splendid yacht-like craft and one that it would be a delight to command'. But there was a sad tale to tell. On the passage up and across the Atlantic Ocean from Port Natal (southeast Africa) and probably in ballast, her master, Captain John Pawtell, born in 1840 in Clapton, London, who was accompanied by his expectant wife and son, had been struck down with disease.[18] His wife had given birth to a second son during the passage, but neither she nor the original first mate knew enough to treat the master, and four days before arriving in Bridgetown the master had died. Pawtell was highly respected by the crew for his ability as a seaman and navigator, and as a 'simple-minded, great-hearted Christian.' The first mate, George Thomas, from Fowey, born in 1850, who held a master's certificate, had naturally assumed command, and was probably confirmed in that position by telegraph by the owners, Foulds & Bone of Greenock.

The call at Bridgetown had been made solely for orders, but it provided an opportunity for the widow and children to transfer to a homeward mail steamer. The orders were to sail to the Mexican coast for a cargo of mahogany, the region of Bullen's first voyage experiences (Chapter 2). Bullen's master in this ship, newly promoted, was cheerful, companiable and sober. The bosun/second mate (Bullen's phrase), who seemed clearly responsible for the fine condition of the vessel, was a rough diamond, and perhaps a little too 'chummy' with the master. However, no bosun is named on the AAC, and the original certificated second mate was discharged at

Natal. It is not possible to identify which senior AB had assumed the role of watchkeeper. However, for Bullen, this was a comfortable berth, certainly compared with the horrors of *Keepsake* and *Daisy*. Bullen, however, regretted that he had not immediately made clear that he was a practising Christian, and found himself unable to show it thereafter.

Campanero's voyage had commenced in Liverpool on 7 June 1879, and crew changes on the AAC placed her successively at Cardiff, Penarth, Natal, Port Adelaide, Port Louis, Mauritius, Melbourne, Natal, Barbados, and Rotterdam. Bullen names the Tonola River, Mexico, as the loading location. This was in the centre of the Bay of Campeche. There the master and the bosun took to day-long rambles ashore, leaving Bullen in charge, but expecting him to be sociable when they returned. He has little to say about the passage from Barbados or the progress of the loading, except to note that when deliveries of logs lagged, the crew were sent scouring the creeks for damaged timber, which could be used as broken stowage to fill the inevitable spaces between and at ends of logs. He was kept fully occupied with little chance of getting ashore, not that he really wanted to, as the place was 'devilish', with nothing of the religion usually found in the Spanish Americas. At last there was no space left, and the 'full ship' flag could be hoisted as a signal to the log rafts that no more could be received.

Work now turned to routine watchkeeping and navigation. Bullen clearly maintained systematic positioning, with bearings when in sight of land, and otherwise using astro-navigation. He had free access to two good chronometers, but the master would never compare working or positions. Tonola was no more than three hundred nautical miles from Cayo Arena where *Investigator* had been lost, so Bullen had personal experience to make him wary of those offshore reefs northwest of the Yukatan peninsula. One night, just after coming on watch, with the ship sailing well at perhaps 11 knots, he detected a strong 'reef smell' and immediately ran aloft. On the fore topsail yard he saw breakers ahead, and shouted an abrupt alteration of course, which, just in time, took *Campanero* away from the danger. The rest of the passage to Falmouth for orders was uneventful. *Campanero* arrived there on 12 July, the second of seven vessels arriving that day, and after a two-day stay, she sailed for Rotterdam.[19] There, nine men were signed off, indicating the sum total of the crew. Bullen was the last man to be signed off, on 3 August 1881, probably because he had to remain to see the cargo discharged. His pay off was £7 14s 5d. The only two ABs who completed the whole voyage since June 1879 paid off with £67 and £60 each. While in Rotterdam, Bullen had a repeat experience with 'longshoremen' attempting to bribe him to sell ship's 'junk' cheaply. This he again declined, with the same result of the master accepting the bribe to his detriment. He was not offered continued employment, and took the ferry back to London.

With little cash in hand, Bullen's time at home was probably as curtailed as on previous occasions. He was almost certainly weighing up his options. If he was to attempt the examination for the master certificate of competency, he did not yet have sufficient sea time, with testimonials, as first mate and must make another voyage in that capacity, if he could get it. There is little doubt that his experience and ability, and attention to studying navigation, offered hope of success in that examination, but, even with the certificate, his lack of patronage might continue to block his appointment in senior positions as first mate and master. Of his time in London between *Campanero* and *Somerville*, he leaves no comment. Equally, there is little or nothing in his output about his eleven months in *Somerville*, which took him to a part of the world which he had not previously experienced, Madagascar and Zanzibar.

Somerville was a small schooner of 264 tons, whose managing owner was James Porter of Fenchurch Street in London. Her master was Thomas Wootton, aged thirty-six, born in Margate. Bullen secured his only outward-bound appointment as her first mate, partly by accepting a condition which was 'to sign an agreement to be responsible for all cargo short delivered.'[20] Such a condition harks back to medieval times when, under the maritime Laws of Oléron, whole crews of merchant ships could be held responsible for loss of, or damage to cargoes, and the practice of deducting the missing cargo value from their final account of wages.[21] The limitation of liability of shipowners was covered in the Merchant Shipping Acts, the principal Act in 1881 being the Merchant Shipping Act of 1854. State oversight of the payment of seafarers' wages was introduced in part to prevent the fraudulent treatment of wages payment through such devices as charging financial loss to the crew. The condition which Bullen signed up to was not part of the conditions agreed in the AAC, but a private matter which bound Bullen to the owner. As it would have taken very little shortage of cargo to completely wipe out his pay-off at the end of the voyage, the device may simply have been to encourage the first mate to take extra care for the cargo in terms of stowage and tallying (recording quantities loaded and discharged).

Bullen signed on with most other crew members on 15 October 1881, two months and eighteen days after leaving *Campanero*. We might speculate that such a long period between ships might have been due to his difficulty in securing a mate's berth, as well as exploring opportunities for employment ashore. *Somerville* was loading in St Katherine's Dock for Tamatave, a port city on the east coast of Madagascar. With a total crew, including the master, of eleven, her manning was similar to that of *Campanero*.[22] There was a bosun, who probably acted also as second mate, a cook/steward, four ABs, two boys and an ordinary seaman. Four of these were discharged in Tamatave or Zanzibar where replacements were engaged. From these crew movements it seems likely that from Tamatave, *Somerville* sailed to Zanzibar, and sailed back to Tamatave before returning to London.

Outward, she had sailed from Gravesend on 19 October 1881, and homeward, she passed Deal in tow of the tug *Robert Bruce* on 29 September 1882.[23] Whilst at Zanzibar, Captain Wootton had been laid up with fever most of the time, so more of the ship's business than normal may have fallen on Bullen.[24] On this, Bullen's comment is that every member of the crew succumbed to fever except himself and the bosun. He describes this man, a Finn aged thirty-nine, who signed himself as Charles J Newman, as the splendid and priceless bosun/carpenter/second mate.[25] In his short story, 'The Slaver', Bullen tells of encountering, one dark night, an Arab dhow carrying slaves.[26] Knowing that there was a Royal Naval gunboat on anti-slavery patrol in the area, Bullen dived below to fetch a rocket which he set off in the hope it would be seen. It lit up the dhow, which was soon captured by the gunboat which, passing close to *Somerville*, shouted thanks for the warning. He also tells of an exploit in Tamatave, Madagascar. He went ashore one evening to fetch the master, who had an invitation ashore. Waiting for the master to turn up, he went for a swim with the boatmen, leaving their light clothing on the shore. Emerging to dress, a troop of ferocious dogs rushed at the group. Running for the nearest refuge, a pyramid of bones, they avoided dog bites, and pelted the dogs away with a salvos of bones. Safely descended, they found their legs badly scratched by the bones. The bones turned out to be part of *Somerville's* homeward cargo, which came swarming with tropical insects, such as centipedes, scorpions and even a tarantula.[27]

It seems that Bullen made no more remarks about this voyage, when in port or whilst on passage. He did not sign off with the rest of the crew but attended the shipping office a week later to sign Form M, Release at the Termination of Voyage. His pay off amounted to £5 17s 10d. His pay was £5 10s 0d monthly, but half of that was his allotment payment to his wife. Had he spent nothing during the voyage his pay-off would have been in excess of £30. He refers in several of his essays to the fact that he smoked, and he may have made other slop chest purchases. There is always the possibility that he forfeited some of his pay-off, and he may also have drawn cash from the master to make personal purchases in port.

This was Bullen's last voyage as a merchant seafarer, but as a passenger he would travel as an author and lecturer to the United States, the West Indies, Australia, New Zealand, Canada and Madeira, where he died in 1915. His sea career can be summarised in terms of the aggregate sea time of his formal engagements in merchant ships, and the total time that elapsed between those engagements. Between 1870 and 1882 his sea time totalled 124 months or a little over ten years.[28] Between engagements he was on shore a total of 27 months or two and a quarter years. However, a significant proportion of shore time was abroad. He was only ashore in Britain some thirteen months. Ten years' sea time may seem a short first career, but it is probably not that far removed from the average sea career of deck officers, while that for ships' engineers, at about eight years, was even shorter.

11

Struggles Making a Life Ashore in London

30 September 1882 to 1899

Following his discharge from the *Somerville* on 30 September
1882, Bullen took the momentous decision to make a family
life ashore. While he was at sea, his wife had had to take such
employment as she could get. The 1881 census records Amelia as a
live-in domestic servant under her maiden name of Grimwood, at
Zion House, Lewisham, Kent.[1] This is relatively close to Deptford,
where she was born, and the general location of other members of
the Grimwood family. In 1861 the Grimwood family were at New
King Street, Deptford, with Amelia, aged one, the youngest of four
children.[2] Her father, Voltaire Lucifer, was a potato salesman. So
when she married Bullen in 1879, she was not without relatives
of her own generation, as Bullen asserts, even though her father
had died. With the return of her husband in 1882, she must have
relinquished the job in Lewisham to begin married life, but until
children arrived, they surely both needed paid employment. By the
time of their first child, Irene born in 1883, they were renting a
basement room in Hazlewood Crescent, Kensal New Town, in the
area of the area of Bullen's early childhood.[3]

High on Bullen's list of priorities must have been his means of
earning a living. Despite the difficulty of securing employment in
London as a merchant ship's officer, he might have been expected
to attempt the Board of Trade examination for a Certificate of
Competency as Master (foreign-going). He had the required sea
time (a year) as officer in charge of the watch, and that qualification
carried some status in maritime circles ashore. A drawback was
certainly the examination fee of £2, which he felt he could not

afford, and tuition fees if he chose to attend one of the navigation schools in London, such Prosser's City of London Navigation School at 99 Minories, or Janet Taylor's Nautical Academy at 104 Minories. He had little respect for the offerings of such cram school teachers, and regarded the examination as well within his capabilities. Understandably, he was bound up with the novelty of establishing a family home, and the expenses that implied. Former merchant seafarers certainly picked up jobs in the extensive range of maritime businesses in port districts, but most might be classed as low-status employment; being accepted for higher status roles of a level matching the responsibilities he had held as a first (or chief) mate meant demonstrating matching prior experience. Certainly, from his point of view, the salary paid needed to be equivalent of what he earned as first mate of *Somerville*, which was £5 10s 0d per month and, of course, included his accommodation and subsistence. This might be valued at, say, £2 10s a month.

We do not know when exactly he was appointed a junior clerk in the Meteorological Office, as Bullen says little about his time there or the duties involved. However, surviving Meteorological Council reports show he was appointed in 1882/3 and resigned in 1899/1900.[4] All he says is that he was a 'computer' (Civil Service junior clerk grade), and that he came to dislike the job intensely, possibly owing to office politics and perhaps even favouritism, and the lack of scope for initiative.[5] The staff list published in the annual *British Imperial Calendar* for 1891 shows a number of clerks sharing the same surnames, so nepotism is one possible example.[6] Bullen's article in *Good Words* entitled 'The Working of the Weather Office' is an excellent description of the functions and structure of the Meteorological Office for a general readership, but says nothing about the staff or his employment there.[7] In the nineteenth century, a 'computer' was a person making calculations, particularly in an observatory: the Meteorological Office was certainly an organisation receiving data from a large number of observing locations, so the more modern term for 'computer' might be 'data analyst'.

Today, his job title suggests low-status office employment, but in the nineteenth century the term covered a wide range of activities. In 1891 the Meteorological Office was governed by a council of six, nominated by the Royal Society, who oversaw the activities of a staff of forty-three. In charge was the Marine Superintendent over a chief clerk, five senior clerks (heads of sections), twenty-one junior clerks and fifteen unclassified clerks. According to Bullen, his appointment paid £2 per week or £104 per year, a sum not much different from the value of his employment in *Somerville*. These Civil Service appointments and rates of pay, promised a steady, if small, income, and possibly a small annual increment. In the early 1890s his annual salary was £110 per annum. His lunch break was forty-five minutes. The working week was Monday to Saturday, with the afternoon off on alternate Saturdays. A further benefit was twenty-eight days' annual leave, with flexibility to take odd days off as part of annual leave. Promotion prospects were limited, and no doubt offered scope for patronage when a vacancy occurred. Compare Bullen's annual wage to the salaries paid to the headmasters and assistant masters in the five training ships moored at that time on the River Thames. Heads' salaries ranged from £100 to £150 per annum and assistants' between £70 and £110.[8]

All marine navigators are 'computers' within the nineteenth-century usage, so with their practical seafaring and weather experience, it is not surprising that former seafarers were attractive as Meteorological Office staff. How many filled that description in that period is not known, but there was at least one, William Allingham (1850–1919), who was a near contemporary to Bullen. Comments in the press suggest that he also had a similarly short merchant seafaring career before taking up his junior clerkship aged twenty-five in 1875, approximately the same age as was Bullen when he started in 1882/3. In the same financial year Allingham, according to the index to the report, was appointed to visit ships in the port of London, which might have been an upgrade. By the time of his sudden death in 1919 he had climbed the ladder and was a chief assistant.[9] Like Bullen, he later in life applied his talents to publishing, though in a more restricted and less popular manner, as the author of several texts, on navigation, seafaring and meteorology, aimed at merchant seafarers.[10] He also gave lectures on these topics to maritime professionals, addressing, in the same period as Bullen, issues of merchant seafaring of the day. There is a suggestion in Bullen's comments that many of the clerks had income-generating sidelines. Securing his position in the Meteorological Office is an indicator of Bullen's advancement intellectually and socially, and breadth of knowledge.

The little that Bullen tells us about his fifteen years at the Meteorological Office is mostly found in *Confessions of a Tradesman*.[11] The bulk of this book is concerned with his various efforts to augment his regular salary out of office hours, and thereby to improve his family living conditions. There the themes are his lack of experience in household management, the mistakes he made and the lessons he learned. His seafarer's naivety and trust in those he had dealings with received some sharp knocks. It is a tale of financial ineptitude heading towards formal bankruptcy, and then financial salvation through the acceptance of his literary output, which allowed him to free himself from office drudgery. He seems to have made financial commitments beyond the cost of accommodation and subsistence, almost from the outset. Initially, these were hire-purchase agreements for furniture, but did, at some stage, extend to a luxury, a piano costing £40 being hire-purchased as a gift to his wife. But such bulky personal effects impinged on the cost of moving from one rented roof over their heads to another. The Bullen home progressed from renting single rooms to renting whole houses, in which at least two floors could be sublet in the hope of recovering the house rental. He found himself with impecunious tenants who, as often as not, fled without paying rent, or made pitiable excuses for delaying payment, so that his house rent fell in arrears. Facing similar problems, the Bullen family was also forced to take landlord-avoiding action, sometimes fleeing to a new address overnight. The table on page 156 lists the addresses which were given when registering family events such as births and marriages, and less precisely for electoral registration and street directories.

A fellow clerk at the Meteorological Office, who had had some success as a door-to-door salesman and picture framer, gave Bullen some instruction in purchasing small quantities of objects and materials from wholesalers, and hawking them partly among fellow employees. Indeed, he was overstretched and passed over some of his lines to Bullen. But Bullen was not a born salesman, and these activities presupposed being able to make the wholesale purchases in advance, as well as the time needed to hawk the objects. At times, making the purchases with a promise to pay meant another level of indebtedness. Bills outstanding, whether for rent, medical treatment, or materials purchased, within the periods normally allowed for payment, led to court orders to pay, and visitations by bailiffs to seize the value owed in household goods.

Another moneymaking activity was a picture framing service. Yet this still meant the advance purchase of mouldings, backing materials, mounts and glass, and occupying space at home for storage and manufacture. Orders did come in spasmodically, and he did become reasonably skilled. This became the most successful of his entrepreneurial activities, and the last to be dropped when he became a full-time author/lecturer in about 1899. He even turned to envelope-addressing and bookkeeping, and a late-evening activity was to sit as an artist's model at 1s 6d per hour, for a book and magazine illustrator with whom he became very friendly, and who in due course provided many of the illustrations in Bullen's books. Although Bullen does not name him, this must surely be Arthur Twidle (1865–1936), a well-known illustrator, who in 1891 had an address in Lordship Lane, where Bullen also had premises.[12] Although he found maintaining a position for long periods quite a trial, he enjoyed his visits to Twidle's home, and after the sitting he was treated to a late evening meal. Once Twidle was engaged by a publisher to illustrate a book by Bullen, it is difficult not to see Bullen explaining maritime aspects of proposed images, and it is not impossible that a facial image of Bullen appears in one or more of his illustrations. Altogether Twidle illustrated fourteen of Bullen's books with seventy-six images.

After their initial residence in the Paddington area, the Bullens occupied a number of properties in the Clerkenwell area of Dulwich, south of the River Thames, and closer to Amelia's home districts of Deptford/Lewisham. However, they made one move out of that familiar territory for a period, into East Ham where rents seemed cheaper. But this change was at the cost of a longer journey to the Meteorological Office in Victoria Street, close to Parliament Square. From the start of his employment there, Bullen had avoided travel expenses by walking to work and was used to walking some five miles each way from Dulwich. There was a cost, in the erosion of his free time as well as his energy, which increased considerably from East Ham. However, that problem was eased when, in the early 1890s, Bullen's wife, Amelia, received a legacy of less than £200, using which they decided to rent an empty shop and to fit it out. The premises was found back in Clerkenwell, on Lordship Lane. One side of the shop would accommodate Bullen's picture-framing business, and the other fitted out to sell fancy goods and embroidery, to be run by his wife. The shop sign read 'Art Needlework Bullen and Picture Framing'. Their first day of opening was not propitious – not one customer came through the door. Things did pick up a little, but the initiative would turn out to be but a larger step towards financial collapse.

The regime of out-of-office hours work on customer orders, late into the night and up early before leaving for work, the worry over finances, and the daily walk to work in all weathers, was taking its toll. One morning (it is not clear whether this was before or after opening the shop), in a quiet shortcut, Bullen collapsed, coming to on the ground after a period unconscious. He struggled to the home of a medical practitioner he knew, who diagnosed heart failure, and kept him in his consulting room resting for a long period, before inquiring about his life, and advocating complete rest. Bullen began to realise his need to change his lifestyle.

Despite his self-imposed regime of out-of-hours labour for additional income, Bullen does admit to only one regular extracurricular activity arising from his religious beliefs for which he set aside Thursday evenings and Sundays. Despite his early Church of England experiences and his confirmation in an Anglican service in New Zealand, he seems not to have become associated with a local Anglican church in his new life ashore. His associations later in life seems to have been with free church groups, and he was particularly drawn to outdoor testimony to the public in general. So it was that, while resident in Paddington in 1883 when his first child, born that year, was a babe in arms, he joined a band of open-air preachers, on the street corner near his home and was called upon to make his first public testimony of Christian belief and salvation.[13] After initial awkwardness, he soon became a fluent advocate, making his contributions more colourful by speaking from memory, reciting passages of scripture without reading from the Bible, and singing verses from well-known hymns. Though, incidentally, this was a good training for his future career as a public lecturer, as he learned to make himself heard and the value of visual aids.

Moving south of the River Thames to Clerkenwell/Dulwich, he became associated with another free church group which had the use of a mission hall in Peckham. Amongst the group's good works was the provision of free teas to needy children of the neighbourhood when enough money could be collected to purchase the materials. As a fundraising device, Bullen offered to give a talk on 'South Sea Whale Fishery'. One of the group advanced £5 from his savings for expenses, allowing Bullen to have some coloured slides made, and the group to book Peckham Public Hall. The hall was let at half price and a lantern enthusiast projected the images without a fee. The hall was packed and profits after expenses came to £13 for the tea fund. Bullen's story of religious life and initiative, *The Apostles of the South East*, is thought to reflect aspects of Bullen's association with such a group in the 1880s and 1890s.[14] The book concerns the population of Lupin Street, Rotherhithe, ignored by the Salvation Army, the Anglicans and Roman Catholics alike, as unredeemable. Desirous of having somewhere to meet for religious interaction, residents of Lupin Street teamed up to rent a derelict cowshed and convert it as a meeting house. Bullen conceals the real location and the names of all the characters, but that apart, his story reflects real events and activities of which he was a part.[15]

Apart from abrupt removals and moments of cash shortage impinging on regular household purchases, household life must have continued. Mentions of his wife and children are rare entries in his literary output, and we do not know whether they accompanied him on Sundays to the religious meetings he attended. Certainly, the birth of five children and their subsequent registration, and annual events such as birthdays, would have been celebratory points in the calendar. Irene Theodore T M was born in 1882 in Shoreditch, London, and Amy in Paddington in 1887. Frank Thomas (junior) was born in 1891 in Upton Park, East Ham. Emanuel John was born in Camberwell, Surrey in 1894, as was Margaret Paula in 1895. But there was also tragedy as John died in 1897, and Frank Thomas in Ancona, Italy, in 1908. He was a 17-year-old apprentice in SS *Hazelmoor*, who, on leave ashore, was killed falling over a cliff.[16]

Religious activity must surely have offered Bullen temporary relief from his financial worries, but there was no denying he was sinking further into insolvency. With no current hope of settling his debts, it only took an unexpected catastrophe to his premises to force a complete stop to his sidelines. The ceiling of his shop collapsed, the plaster and the supporting laths coming down, with a piece striking his head. Quick thinking led him to turn off the gas at the meter. His reply to his wife's inquiry about any harm he might have sustained was:[17]

'No doubt about it. I'm all right, and for good or evil I've done with this business. This means a full stop. I can't go on, however much I might want to ... I shall do the only thing that is now possible, I shall go up to Bankruptcy Buildings in the morning and file my petition.'

The saga of that experience is summarised in four short entries in the *London Gazette*.[18] Bullen's description of his encounters spreads across fifty or more pages. Filing the petition and the court appearances took place in the High Court of Justice in Bankruptcy in Carey Street, the term 'Carey Street' becoming a slang term for bankruptcy. Complicated forms, which needed a legal mind to help in completing, comprised the petition, with the fee in advance from the insolvent petitioner, who also had to pay his adviser. Bullen's public examination was on 10 April 1895, where he was found wanting in answering almost every question. Nevertheless, he became legally bankrupt from that time. But he was protected from his creditors who could only approach the court in the hope of retrieving even a part of the debt. Meanwhile, Bullen's articles were beginning to bring in small sums of money, and once he was contracted to submit several articles each week, at £2 per week, to the London newspaper *The Morning Leader* in 1899 and had his first book *The Cruise of the Cachalot* accepted by the publisher of *Cornhill* magazine, which began taking his articles on a regular basis, he almost suddenly found himself with a surplus of income. His first thought was to repay his creditors, obtaining receipts as evidence to the court that he had paid them off. His visits to Carey Street in 1899 were to petition for his discharge from bankruptcy. There he found that he should have paid the sums he owed into the court (subject to a charge), so his discharge was suspended by two years until 22 November 1901. The summary of Bullen's 'crime' was that his assets were not of value equivalent to ten shillings in the pound of unsecured liabilities; he had neglected to keep such books of account as was normal practice; and he had continued to trade knowing himself to be insolvent. These terms seemed to be recorded against many of the debtors passing through the court.

Although Bullen continued his employment at the Meteorological Office into 1899, his article writing was being recognised as welcome material in a widening range of magazine titles, and the publication of *The Cruise of the Cachalot* in time for Christmas 1898 jumped him to the top of that year's literary ratings. Before the year was out, the literary commentator of one serial was comparing him with Joseph Conrad, whose publications were also becoming recognised:[19]

Mr. Conrad, ... [a] foreigner who has made England his home and working ground, has also during 1898 a new book and a good magazine story. The book is *Tales of Unrest*, a remarkable collection of closely-knit, imaginative studies of humanity, near and far. The story is 'Youth', which was printed in *Blackwood* [magazine] in the summer, and of which we have already spoken in this column. It is to our mind infinitely the best story of the year, and is worthy to rank in the first bunch of short stories that exist. While speaking of Mr Conrad, we would mention Mr Frank T Bullen whose *Cruise of the Cachalot* has a certain resemblance (entirely fortuitous) to Mr Conrad's *Nigger of the Narcissus*. The latter book is more consciously a work of art than Mr Bullen's rich narrative of sperm-whaling, but Mr Bullen scores by his patience as an historian, his tenacity of purpose, and his minute and vivid descriptive powers. Both books are salt with the sea. Mr Bullen is wholly a discovery of 1898 ...

Frank T Bullen, the author, had certainly 'arrived' by December 1898!

Frank T Bullen's Home Addresses

1857	40 Alfred Road, Paddington London [birth certificate]
1861	15 Desborough Terrace, Paddington, London [1861 Census]
1863	23 Alfred Road, Paddington, London [baptismal register; might be cousin's address]
1871	9 Stalham Street, Paddington, London [1871 Census]
1879	8 Castle St, London [marriage register]
1883 approx	Hazlewood Crescent, Kensal New Town (basement room) [*Recollections*, 51]
18??	9 Porthall Road, Paddington, London [*London Gazette* 1895, past address]
1888	An F Thomas Bullen listed at 246 Ashmore Rd, Paddington, but ? same person.
18??	5 Cromwell Road, Upton Park, Essex [*London Gazette*, 1895, past address]
1890	Beattock House, Bristol Rd, East Ham, London [register of electors]
1891	20 Lordship Lane, East Dulwich Camberwell [1891 Census]

1892–4	135 Lordship Lane, East Dulwich, London. Mrs Amelia Bullen, fancy repository, gilder, carver, picture frame maker [local directories]
1895	135 Lordship Lane, Dulwich, Surrey [*London Gazette*, 1895, past address]
1895	134 Lordship Lane, Dulwich, Surrey [*London Gazette*, 1895, present address]
1896–1902	81 Landor Road, Stockwell, London; Mrs Amelia Bullen, dressmaker [local dir]
1897	Dulwich [preface to *Cruise of the Cachalot*]
1897	23 Melbourne Grove, Dulwich, Camberwell [register of electors]
1898	79 Landells Road, Dulwich, Camberwell [register of electors]
1899	7 Graces Road, Dulwich, Camberwell [register of electors]
1899	Camberwell [preface to *Log of a Sea Waif*]
1900	7 Graces Road, Dulwich, Camberwell [register of electors]
1901	89 Barry Road, Dulwich, Camberwell [register of electors]
1901	Dulwich [preface to *Apostles of the South East*]
1901	89 Barry Road, Camberwell [1891 Census]
1904	Millfield, Heathwood Road, Christchurch ? Bournemouth
1904	Millfield Lodge, Melbourn [Kelly Directory of Cambs] FTB FRGS
1905	Millfield, Melbourn, Cambridgeshire [preface to *Back to Sunny Seas*]
1906	Millfield, Melbourn, Cambridgeshire [preface to *Our Heritage the Sea*]
1906	New Road, Melbourn, Cambs [register of electors]
1907	New Road, Melbourn, Cambs [register of electors]
1908	New Road, Melbourn, Cambridgeshire [register of electors]
1908	Millfield, Melbourn, Cambridgeshire [preface to *Confessions of a Tradesman*]
1909	New Road, Melbourn, Cambs [register of electors]
1911	Millfield, Melbourn, Cambs [1911 Census]
1911	New Road, Melbourn, Cambs [register of electors]
1912	New Road, Melbourn, Cambs [register of electors]
1914	Millfield, Heathwood Road, Bournemouth [register of electors]
1915	Millfield, Heathwood Road, Bournemouth; Miss Martha Tappenden, executrix, also resident there. [*Times*, 1915] Subsequently Miss M Tappenden at Ferndene, 9 de Lisle Rd, Bournemouth.

Note: entries in directories and registers of electors were compiled annually and could be up to a year out of date.

12

Success in Self Employment as Lecturer and Author

1899 to 26 February 1915

While 1899 marked his severance from the Meteorological Office and his embarkation in the status of self-employed public lecturer/writer on maritime themes, Bullen had been gradually undergoing an informal training in both roles through his religious activity, and to some extent through his employment in the Meteorological Office, where data analysis would regularly have to be written up. He had read widely throughout his life, and in the 1880s began in a small way writing about his maritime experiences. During this final phase of his life, he continued to stretch his energies to maintain the parallel activities of travelling lecturer and writer, rapidly achieving national and world renown. These activities were soon being managed, at least to some extent, by a lecture agent and a literary agent (A P Watt), and he began receiving invitations to literary as well as religious organisation events, at which he mixed among the learned in those fields. That he became upwardly mobile is reflected in the dedications in his books and in numerous reports of his participation in social events, with his name appearing alongside the likes of Rudyard Kipling, Conan Doyle and Joseph Conrad.

Achieving such fame brought with it numerous invitations to speak or attend charity events, particularly annual meetings. Examples included the Seamen's Christian Friend Society (1901), Queen Victoria Seamen's Rest (foundation stone, 1901), Manchester and Salford Mission (1902) and British and Foreign Bible Society (1903).[1] Other invitations as a guest included the Royal Literary Fund (dinner, 1901), the meeting of the Authors'

Club, with Conan Doyle in the chair (1902), the welcome home dinner for Captain Scott at the Savage Club (1904), the marriage of Sir Arthur Conan Doyle (1907), and the Royal Society of St George meeting (1910).[2] Bullen had been elected a Fellow of the Royal Geographical Society as early as 1898, but recognition at the highest level came in 1908 when he was invited to visit York Cottage, the residence of the then Prince and Princess of Wales (the future King George V and Queen Mary) to entertain the young princes.[3]

These developments affected his mode of dress, class of travel (first) and topics of conversation, while the endless travel saw him frequently absent from home or returning late at night. With much increased income he could afford a home in the country, and overseas travel. These points taken together might well have contributed to his living apart from his wife, perhaps from about 1908 onwards, by which time his surviving children, his daughters, were either married or had reached their late teens.

Apart from some snippets about his earlier life, Bullen's final volume, *Recollections*, is almost wholly concerned with his experiences as a travelling lecturer in the age of acetylene gas lantern illustration. Although the projection of moving images without sound, silent film, had made its appearance by the mid 1890s, facilities for the projection of prepared images, glass slides, were by then widely available, and reasonably portable. The facility could be hired with the services of a projectionist, and remained so in the early decades of the twentieth century. Bullen bought into this, and all his public lectures, which were extremely popular, were illustrated. It was the responsibility of the lecture host organisation to book the projectionist with his equipment, and thus the lecturer had to trust the arrangements which had been made. From time to time projectionists did not turn up or the equipment malfunctioned. Fortunately, Bullen had the ability to deliver his subjects without visual support, as was always the case with his Sunday sermons. Similar problems are faced by today's visiting speakers arriving with their Powerpoint presentations in memory sticks, only to find incompatibilities between computer systems preventing files being opened.

Except for close-to-home speaking engagements, it was probably essential, if Bullen was going to make that part of his employment, that his name should be on the books of an agent. It seems likely that the Lecture Agency Limited, of the Outer Temple, Strand, London, acted for him, as in the late summer, when secretaries were arranging their lecturers for the autumn and spring series, that business advertised widely for bookings, naming lecturers (including Bullen) who already had a profile, and indicating the lecture titles on offer. A free prospectus was available.[4] Probably there was an element of negotiation around bookings which had already been made. As well as the subject and illustration requirements, there were the logistics of the journey to be considered, which might include hotel accommodation, and meals. Bullen appears mostly to have walked from home to a local railway station, followed by a train journey and perhaps a cab to the venue. The further the journey, the more likely that several speaking engagements were arranged within easy reach of a chosen hub. This also allowed the travel costs to be shared by several organisations. Bullen also offered his availability to act as visiting preacher to Nonconformist chapels in the area he was visiting, if he happened to be there over a weekend. In the 1901/2 season he was booked for seventy-eight lecturing engagements. Visiting Dundee, he had travelled throughout Saturday from London, given three sermons on Sunday, and would deliver lectures on Monday and Tuesday.[5] One of his sermons was on the subject of Joy and another on the Gospel of Jonah, with its maritime associations.

Physically, the regime was exhausting, the more as Bullen was undoubtedly weakened by his heart condition, and was experiencing respiratory conditions such as bronchitis. In his discussions of his sea career, he often mentioned his smoking, and it seems likely that habit was continued in later life. Another factor was London's poisonous atmosphere and the days when 'smog' came down. Travelling to and from engagements, Bullen was always encumbered with the weight of his glass slides, and for all his more distant bookings would have with him an overnight bag and his dress suit, into which he changed on arrival. From time to time he was forced to cancel engagements, news which made its way into the newspapers. In January 1901 a report read: '[He] is lying somewhat seriously ill with bronchitis'.[6]

The number and diversity of his lecture hosts reveal the national spread and strength of organisations promoting forms of adult education, almost all of them financed by subscription, and invariably evening events. Examples include branches of the Young Men's Christian Association (YMCA), such as those in Croydon, Sheffield and Aberdeen. Literary or literary and philosophical societies were another category very strongly represented, for example in Camberwell, Enfield and Bristol. Some groups were connected to chapels, such as those in Kensington, Cardiff and Liverpool, where the meeting might start with a hymn and a prayer, and perhaps a voluble chairman, held in the chapel itself, but eating into the visiting lecturer's allotted time. Independent boarding schools were also considerable subscribers. Bullen names Glenalmond College in Perthshire, Fettes College in Edinburgh, Cheltenham Ladies' College, where he was the only male, Charterhouse School (Surrey), and Uppingham School (Rutland). Indeed, his travels also took him into Ireland and Wales, as well as all over England and Scotland.

Bullen frequently had to cope with unexpected events. Arriving at Plymouth railway station, he was given a note from his host who had offered accommodation, that she had, at very short notice, been called away and saying he was to make free of her home on Plymouth Hoe.[7] Leaving the station, he found waiting for him the grandest of carriages. His host was probably associated with Plymouth Fishermen's and Seamen's Bethel, which had a chapel and rooms in Castle Street, by Sutton Harbour. The lecture took place at Plymouth's Mechanics' Institute, which was used by many organisations for public meetings.[8] A comment and summary of the lecture, entitled 'Romance and Reality at Sea', appeared the following day in the *Western Evening Herald*.[9]

161

Mr F T Bullen, the literary champion of the sailorman, delighted a crowded audience at Plymouth last night with a lecture on romance and reality at sea. Mr Bullen, who burst on an astonished world some few years since, with a piece of new realism in the story of the *Cachalot*, is a man who nourishes no illusions about sailors and the sea. He knows both too well. It is his mission in life to correct the prevailing hallucinations about the seaman for which Dibden and co, who know nothing at all of him, are responsible.

The sailorman is not of fell intent a romantic person, he is intently practical, and full of grievances. It is true he also gets full of other things sometimes when on shore. But Mr Bullen entreats those who are seeking to benefit him, not to deal with him as a prodigal son, not to endeavour to reform him with a cup of tea and a bun. He must be treated as a man, as a man who is doing valuable, indispensable national work; he must be made to respect himself by finding that other men can respect him; if he could come, as Mr Bullen suggests, under a reasonable discipline, he would be the better therefor. When he is disciplined, the British sailor is the best in the world. But in the Mercantile Marine, he is not; and 'the general attitude of the crew towards officers is such that I' (says Mr Bullen) 'would rather sweep a London crossing than be mate of a big sailing ship with a crew of British seamen.' There is a great contrast between them and the willing, civil Scandinavians whom British skippers prefer. Mr Bullen is really doing a missionary work in his books and lectures; for it is only by arousing public interest in the case of the fo'c'sle hands out of tramps and sailors, by supressing the crimp and the runner, by levelling up all round, that the sailor can be improved and the inflow of foreigners to our Mercantile Marine be checked.

Some of Bullen's Public Lecture Titles

South Sea Whale Fishing
Romance and Reality at Sea
Whales and Whale Fishing
The Mighty Ocean
The Sea
The Way They Have in the Navy
Deep Sea People at Home
The Lives of Deep-Sea People

Sources: British Newspaper Archive, www.britishnewspaperarchive.co.uk

That in 1901 he was giving so many public lectures might suggest that Bullen had a large store of prepared lecture topics. The list in the table above, derived from an extensive search of newspaper advertisements, and the overlap between some titles, might indicate that he concentrated on perhaps no more than half a dozen topics. Maybe that was all he needed, as every engagement implied a different audience to whom the topic was new, and even if one was a return invitation (such was his popularity), he had another topic for which he could adjust his material to suit the audience. There is no doubt, that, speaking without notes, he was fully conscious of the type of audience he was facing. Asked to address the crew of a naval ship, he drew on his store of seafaring experiences meaningful in particular to the ratings. Speaking in Liverpool in the free lecture series sponsored by the Corporation, the hall filled with 1200 people off the streets who were there mainly to shelter from the weather. In this instance he drew fully on his experiences in Liverpool when he was as down and out as they were.[10] His lectures were lively affairs, interspersed with humorous anecdotes and even a song, as he had a good voice. Comments in the press attest to the information and entertainment value of his talks: 'I heard Mr Bullen lecture ... it was thrilling. The limelight view of a sperm whale swallowing a giant octopus was a sight ... Mr Bullen has marvellous material and uses it right well'.[11] Addressing the Kingston Literary Society, Bullen was 'one of the most popular and entertaining speakers the Society has ever engaged.'[12]

While for some years his intensive life delivering lectures all over Britain and Ireland were important contributors to his income, in the first decade of the twentieth century he fitted in a number of overseas visits which contributed one way or another to his fame as a maritime speaker and author, travelling as a passenger. The first seems to have been to the Mediterranean region, as his 'Preface' to *With Christ at Sea* was dated Malta, September 1900. So far, nothing more about that visit has been discovered. It may have been associated with an appointment as special correspondent for the *Daily Mail*, aboard naval vessels in the Mediterranean. Presumably that newspaper carried a number of Bullen articles. Unfortunately, its private digitised archive has proved inaccessible to the author. However, Bullen has written a little more about his visit to the United States in 1901 when he arrived in Boston from London in SS *New England* on 1 August for a visit of about six weeks. He had most of his family with him, his wife Amelia, daughters Amy and Paula, and son Frank junior, his eldest daughter Irene having married. He gave the immigration return New Bedford as his ultimate destination, and it seems clear that one objective of the visit was at last to have personal knowledge of the whaling port where he had set the start of the voyage described in *Cruise of the Cachalot*. It is clear that as well as an element of tourism he was using some of his free time to progress his current literary output, as he dated *Deep Sea Plunderings* September 1901, at New Bedford, Massachusetts. In 1902 he dedicated his novel *A Whaleman's Wife* to Theodore Roosevelt, then president of the United States, an acknowledgement of a meeting which must have been arranged for him during this visit. That was probably before the assassination of President McKinley in 1901, resulting in Roosevelt, as vice president, being elevated to the presidency. While at Boston and New Bedford, he had preached on Sundays and given lectures. His itinerary included New York, Philadelphia, Niagara, the Buffalo exposition, Longfellow's home at Cambridge, and Harvard University.[13] He was booked to sail from Boston for England on 11 September.

Bullen's next overseas foray was in 1904, when he accepted an offer from Owen Phillips, the shipping magnate, of free passages in the Royal Mail Steam Packet's ships serving the West Indies. He could be accompanied by a secretary, a Miss Taylor, so he could write up his impressions as he went along. They joined the SS *Tagus* in Southampton, sailing on 13 April 1904.[14] *Tagus* called at Barbados and Trinidad outwards, and then Kingston (Jamaica), Colon (Panama), Port Limon (Costa Rica), Savanilla (Columbia), Kingston, Trinidad and Barbados. At Barbados, Bullen left *Tagus* to transfer to a smaller inter-island steamer, SS *Eden*, which serviced some of the islands to the northwest of Barbados, collectively called the Windward Islands, the Leeward Islands, or the Lesser Antilles. The sequence of island calls from Barbados in the *Eden* was St Lucia, Martinique, Dominica, Guadeloupe, Antigua, Nevis, St Kitts, St Thomas, with repeat calls coming south again to Barbados. Then *Eden* called at St Vincent and Tobago before crossing west to Venezuela to call at Carapano, Margarita and La Guayra, then turning eastwards at two of these ports before reaching Trinidad again. There Bullen left *Eden* to await the arrival of SS *Orinoco* in Trinidad, and the return passage via Barbados back to Plymouth, arriving 30 June 1904, where he took the train to London. *Orinoco's* arrival in Trinidad was delayed by a hurricane, while Bullen sat out the delay and atrocious weather in an hotel.

Bullen's travelogue of his time in the three ships was aimed at a general public which had an appetite for descriptions of exotic places abroad, and so is something of a guide for passengers making similar voyages.[15] There is relatively little about the ships, or their personnel, but he is complimentary about the service and facilities they offered. He follows the sequence of ports, describing locations and the population, filling in with some historical data and drawing on his previous time in the area with a little of his experiences of, for example, Kingston (Jamaica), St John's (Antigua), and Bridgetown (Barbados).

In 1906 Bullen embarked on a more ambitious, organised lecture tour of Australia and New Zealand. All the arrangements 'down under', the itinerary, venue and hotel reservations, local transport, publicity, introductions, were placed in the hands of a travelling lecture agent, R S Smythe, who had previously handled the lecture tours of the likes of Mark Twain and H M Stanley.[16] How much of his own capital Bullen invested is unclear, but he certainly expected a proportionate share of the lecture attendance charges. He departed London with an element of insurance in the form of an invitation from *The Standard* newspaper to publish an article series on his impressions of Australia and New Zealand. The twenty-three essays were published after his return, in December 1906 and January 1907, under the collective title 'Australia Revisited'.[17] Bullen sailed from London (Tilbury) in SS *Omrah*, apparently on his own, on 8 March 1906. He was booked as a cabin passenger to Sydney. Port calls en route included Gibraltar, Marseilles, Naples, Port Said, the Suez Canal, Colombo, Fremantle, Adelaide and Melbourne.[18]

Bullen's name was already quite well known in the Antipodes through the newspaper publicity for his books since 1898 and the publication of *Cruise of the Cachalot*. His lecture tour was being trumpeted before he had left London, and at each port reporters were waiting for the gangway to be rigged to catch him before disembarkation. Failing that, they tracked him to his hotel. Ship arrivals were still major news items in that reading age before the development of wireless and, much later, television. The success of the lecture tour depended on newspaper commentaries as well as advertisements, and Bullen seems to have been generous with his time. The resultant articles were often of full column length and range over his sea career, especially his reminiscences of the Australian and New Zealand ports, his present impressions of ports he had hardly set foot in, and sometimes his views on political decisions and initiatives where replies could easily find him wrong-footed. One such was in Fremantle, where he was asked to comment on the sudden rise of the Labour Party in the recent elections in Britain. These extended reports could produce small items of biographical interest, such as how he came to be paid for his first book in 1898. Four chapters were accepted for serialisation in *Cornhill* magazine with a payment of £50, and the promise of a further £50 for the remainder of the book if the sample was well received. But the editor imposed a cut of 30,000 words from the original 100,000. The fully published book was so successful that the publishers subsequently made an *ex gratia* payment of £200. The *Omrah*'s call at Fremantle was very brief, though Bullen managed a couple of hours in Perth, where he had an appointment to meet the premier of Western Australia, Mr Razon, and the proprietor of the newspaper *West Australian*, Dr Hackett.[19] Similar arrangements were made for him at each port of call.

Bullen's lecturing commitments began with the arrival of *Omrah* in Adelaide, and a call of several days which allowed the delivery of four lectures: 'Romance and Reality at Sea', 'Whales and Whale Fishing', 'The Mighty Ocean' and 'The Way They Have in the Navy'. These four would be repeated in Melbourne and then in Sydney, though such was his popularity as a speaker that two repeat lectures were arranged in Melbourne and Sydney, and there were also matinee lectures for children. The lectures at Adelaide and Melbourne were packed out, and duly summarised in the press the following day. In Sydney the weather was wet and there were more competing events taking place. Bullen seems to have left *Omrah* in Adelaide and, following his course of lectures, to have reached Melbourne by train.[20] From Melbourne to Sydney he was able to take passage in the SS *Orotona* (same ownership as *Omrah*), whose time of departure was convenient to him.[21] Apart from the planned introductions, his time in Australian ports appears to have been quite limited, and his ability to make visits to interesting locations was restricted. However, one he was able to make in Sydney was to the stationary training ship *Sobraon*, a one-time famous clipper ship on the run between Britain and Australia. As well as touring the ship, he witnessed a demonstration of physical training exercises, and gave an encouraging address to the 430 boys then aboard. As with the dozen similar training ships in Britain, *Sobraon* gave an elementary education and an industrial training for service at sea as ratings, in seamanship.[22] Having arrived at Fremantle on 12 May

1906, he took passage from Sydney for Auckland (New Zealand) on 30 May in SS *Zealandia*, dates which illustrate the tightness of his schedule.[23]

The stay in Auckland was conditioned by the delivery of the same four lectures before moving on. However, the pattern was upset by having to postpone the first lecture out of respect following the sudden death of New Zealand's premier, R S Seddon, aboard SS *Oswestry Grange* returning from a visit to Australia.[24] Bullen describes him as really the uncrowned king of New Zealand. In contrast to his engagements in Australia, which seem to have been restricted to Adelaide, Melbourne and Sydney, his tour embraced many more coastal locations in both the North and South islands of New Zealand, reached by a combination of steamship passages and rail journeys. At the majority of these locations the stay was brief, and only one or two lectures were delivered. From Auckland, Bullen took the coastal steamer *Tarawera* to anchor off Gisborne, on the east coast of North Island. There he encountered a former shipmate who was master of the steam tender by which he was taken ashore. This was a sheep town and Bullen was taken to tour the freezing establishment. Bullen's lectures there were attended by the students of the Maori Theological College, which he visited, and he attended the Maori Church of Te Aro. His stay in Gisborne meant parting company with *Tarawera*, and taking a later coastal vessel. It was a short run southwards in SS *Victoria* to Napier, where the ship berthed alongside. For this short call Bullen gives a very rare date, 21 June, midwinter day. Then it was onwards in *Victoria*, in preference to the rail connection, to Wellington at the southern tip of North Island, which became something of a hub for his travels. He now took a minor steamer, the *Pateena*, to Picton and Nelson across Cook Strait at the northern end of South Island. He gave a lecture at Nelson and returned to Wellington in the same ship, where he joined SS *Manuka* for the passage south to Dunedin via Lyttleton (the port for Christchurch, South Island, east coast).

With so many sea passages in a variety of ships, Bullen offers many more comments on shipping serving New Zealand, both from Britain and the frequent coastal services, with comments on the facilities New Zealand ports offered. He was only able to make a brief visit to Christchurch before *Manuka* carried him on to Port Chalmers/Dunedin. Clearly this visit was made with keen anticipation, being the scene of his essay into whaling and of his religious conversion. He was disappointed that Port Chalmers seemed almost deserted, as the channel up to Dunedin had been dredged, enabling international shipping to berth in that city. After his lectures in Dunedin, Bullen ventured further southwards to the inland town of Gore, and then set off by train northwards back to Christchurch and Lyttleton to catch SS *Mararoa* for the trip back to Wellington. He rounded off his New Zealand travels with a return rail trip northwards from Wellington to Palmerston and Wanganui. He left Wellington by steamer in time to catch SS *Omrah*, by then sailing for London on 28 August from Melbourne. *Omrah* reached the River Thames on 7 October. R S Smythe was widely reported in the Australian and New Zealand press as hailing Bullen's tour the most successful he had ever organised. However, from Bullen's standpoint, the tour was not a financial success and attendances were variable.[25] This was despite all his travel being sponsored by the respective shipping companies, Orient, Huddart Parker and Union Steamship, and New Zealand Government Railways. The causes, he argues, included the advent of the cinematograph (silent films), popular theatre performances either side of his lecture dates, the loss caused by the postponement owing to the death of the New Zealand premier, and poor supervision of the local administration of financial takings. Without openly stating it, Bullen points to the inefficiency of the tour agent. However, there was no doubting the enjoyment felt by the audiences, and their warm response to his presentations.

Bullen made a further overseas voyage in 1908, travelling in SS *Empress of Britain* from Liverpool, departing 14 July, to Montreal. He was accompanied by his wife. Nothing in his writing has so far been discovered about this visit, except that he may have been sponsored by the Canadian Northern Railroad System, as he wrote up his experiences of a rail journey in a booklet for the company published in 1910.[26] His final sea journey was from London to Madeira in SS *Norman* in January 1915, where he died and is buried.[27]

Running in parallel with his developing career as a public lecturer was Bullen's foray into writing short descriptive pieces drawing extensively on his seafaring experiences. The late Victorian blossoming of general interest part-works afforded numerous outlets in monthly, weekly or daily serial publications, particularly once a writer had become a familiar name. Some serials specialised in introducing new authors. Others actually hindered this process by accepting essays but omitting author credits. It seems likely that Bullen experienced this with his early pieces in the 1890s, accepted by the Edinburgh *Chamber's Journal*. The earliest of Bullen's essays that has been traced is a column in a Dundee newspaper of 1887 on the suitability of the Solander whaling ground off the south coast of New Zealand South Island, for the development of steam-powered whaling. He was similarly not named directly, but was introduced as the paper's New Zealand nautical correspondent. He complained that his fees for his early published pieces amounted to no more than £40 over a period of three years while he was still working at the Meteorological Office.[28] Elsewhere he credits the magazine *Young England* with first publishing his writing, though he found his first decided success with a series of essays in *Cornhill Magazine*, in 1897.[29]

A core topic in Bullen's written output while he was still at the Meteorological Office was whaling. Between 1887 and 1898 eleven out of forty-four articles address aspects of the South Seas whale fishery (as it was called), and that listing is certainly incomplete. In the early and mid 1890s he published one piece on whaling a year, but by 1898 his four essays on whaling were part of a very large annual output indeed. Of course, he was also writing his seminal book *Cruise of the Cachalot* in the late 1890s, apparently on his experiences of a round-the-world voyage in the whaler 'Cachalot' (sperm whale) from the US whaling port New Bedford. This was published at the end of November 1898 by Smith Elder, who had been promoting his writing in *Cornhill Magazine* since early in 1897. This was received with considerable acclaim in Britain and abroad, and rocketed Bullen to international literary fame. Publicity for much of Bullen's later writing and public speaking was prefixed with reference to this book. Praise for *Cachalot* was headed by Rudyard Kipling with a short letter following his reading of an advance copy: 'It is immense ... I congratulate you most heartily. It's a new world that you've opened the door to.' Most readers will have taken the book at its face value, but, as shown in Chapter 6, 'Cachalot' was really *Splendid*, which since coming under the New Zealand (British) flag, was never out of Pacific waters, and Bullen's text is a mix of fact and fiction.

With his improving success, and additions to his income, the invitation to join the staff of the London daily newspaper *Morning Leader* as maritime correspondent at the same wage as he was paid at the Meteorological Office was enough for him resign his clerkship, possibly from late summer 1899, and to make writing his means of earning a living. His contract with *Morning Leader* was to supply three columns each week on maritime topics of his choosing. Of these only 106 articles are known, but this is certainly an incomplete listing as it has not proved possible to view all Bullen's columns owing to the fragile state of some issues of the newspaper. In July 1899 Bullen was free to sail in HMS *Mars* as a special correspondent, reporting on the naval manoeuvres that summer. These became the subject for nineteen columns, including a set of four engravings based on photographs taken by Bullen. These were very quickly gathered together into a small paperback, *The Way They Have in the Navy*, becoming the fourth book he had published in barely twelve months.[30]

The appeal of collections of his short stories was realised with the publication of his second book early in 1899, and further such volumes would bring the total to seven. But certainly there were others of his books which drew heavily on his short form output: *Men of the Merchant Service, Creatures of the Sea, Our Heritage the*

171

Sea, Advance Australasia. Bullen expresses his religious adherence through *With Christ at Sea* and *The Apostles of the South East.*[31] The latter work, a novel, draws on his association with a free church religious grouping trying to establish itself, with his associates being the origins of its characters. There is thus a biographical element to be found in its pages, as there is in many of his magazine pieces. As already noted, whaling had a particular fascination for Bullen, with twenty or more short pieces and novels set in a whaling dimension, such as *A Whaleman's Wife* and *A Bounty Boy.* Fourteen of Bullen's thirty-seven books were novels mostly aimed at children. Their moralising and religious elements made them attractive as prizes in children's literary competitions and as Sunday School prizes. Many of his books ran to further editions or impressions, and some were issued in luxury bindings. Some remained in print for several years after his death, while his seminal works continue to be reissued. *Men of the Merchant Service* was for many years kept on the open reference shelves of the Public Record Office/National Archive.

It seems likely that Bullen's final years were increasingly marked by respiratory illness, forcing him to cut back on his public lecturing and reducing his written output. This may perhaps underlie the recommendation in 1911 that he be awarded a Civil List pension of £100 per annum.[32] Following his death in 1915, a Civil List pension was awarded to his wife, Amelia Bullen. Payment of that benefit would have been maintained until her death forty years later in 1945. Prior to his death, Bullen presumably made his wife an allowance, once they lived in separate households, he in Melbourn in Cambridgeshire, she in Camberwell, London. He rented the property in Melbourn for £40 annually, and satisfied a long-held desire, not necessarily unusual among merchant seafarers, to retire to the country and follow an interest in plants and animals. He asserts that the years there were his happiest ever.[33] When he made the move is uncertain, but his dedication in *The Call of the Deep*, dated June 1907, 'to my faithful helper M A T', is indicative of being by then well-established there. Martha Tappenden is listed as his housekeeper and secretary in his 1911 Census entry for the house. Some two or three years before Bullen expired, he moved to the somewhat milder climate of Bournemouth, naming the house in 52 Heathwood Road, 'Millfield', the name he had adopted for the house in Melbourn. Martha Tappenden moved with him, and was named as his executrix. She continued living in Millfield until about 1926, and then occupying 9 De Lisle Road, Bournemouth, as an 'apartment house proprietor' until at least 1939.[34] The introduction to his final book, *Recollections*, is dated Bournemouth, 17 December 1914. On 23 January 1915 he boarded SS *Norman* as a passenger, for the passage from London to Funchal, Madeira, presumably for a winter holiday, on a voyage from which there would be no returning. *Norman* would have reached Funchal on about 3 February. Bullen died on 26 February and is buried in the English cemetery.[35] His grave was unmarked until 1997 when descendants of Bullen's youngest daughter, Margaret Paul, had a headstone erected inscribed 'In Memory of Frank Thomas Bullen, Sailor, Whaler, Author, 1857–1915' with a note 'Erected 1997 by his descendants'.[36]

Appendix 1

Particulars of Merchant Ships in which Frank Thomas Bullen Served

(Updated from Alston Kennerley, 'Global Nautical Livelihoods in the Late Nineteenth Century', *International Journal of Maritime History*, vol 26, no 1 (February 2014), 3–24, Appendix 1)

Ships' Names	Official Number	Port of Registry	Tonnage GR	Rig/Str Type	Construction		Managing Owner
					Place	Year	
Caroline	908	London	385	Barque	London	1841	Henry Holmes
Investigator	23229	London	503	Barque	London	1848	J W Skelton
Potosi	Fr ship	Bordeaux	[Rescued crew of *Investigator*]	Barque	~~~	~~	~~~
Sea Gem	35472	St Andrews, NS	566	Barque	~~~	1864	J D de Wolf
Brinkburn	54835	Sunderland	540	Barque	Sunderland	1866	C C Dawson
Cuban SS ??	51424	Liverpool	1984	Steamer	Hebburn/Tyne	1865	WI & PSS, Lpl
Western Belle	48822	Greenock	1225	Ship	~~~	1866	Cuthbert
Pharos	US ship	Boston, US	1328	Ship	~~~	~~~	~~~
Wonga Wonga SS	31715	Sydney	682	Steamer	Glasgow	1868	ASN Co, Syd
Helen McGregor SS	56159	Sydney	252	Steamer	Glasgow	1866	C V Robinson
Wentworth SS	64433	Sydney	916	Steamer	Renfrew	1873	ASN Co, Syd
Harrowby	34892	London	515	Barque	~~~	~~~	C R Fenwick
Rangitiki	47395	London	1188	Ship	Hull	1863	NZS Co, NZ
Splendid	61018	Dunedin, NZ	359	Barque	Massachusetts	1835	W Elder, NZ
West York	74496	Liverpool	689	Barque	Sunderland	1876	Thomas Tompson
Dartmouth	27788	London	977	Barque	Dundee	1859	Merchant Ship Co
Columbus	60893	London	784	Ship	Govan	1863	G Lidgett
Bulwark	46115	London	1332	Ship	St John, NB	1862	J W Temple

Ships' Names	Official Number	Port of Registry	Tonnage GR	Rig/Str Type	Construction		Managing Owner
					Place	Year	
Day Dawn	46469	Adelaide	355	Barque	Fairhaven, US	1851	H Ward, SA
Schooner	Fr ship	Noumea, NC	[Indentured labour carrier]	Schooner	~~~	~~~	~~~
Day Dawn	46469	Adelaide	355	Barque	Fairhaven, US	1851	H Ward, SA
Harbinger	73711	London	1585	Ship	Greenock	1876	J Anderson
Herat	78737	Liverpool	1442	Ship	Hampshire	1879	E P Bates
Britannia	70985	Liverpool	1400	Ship	Sunderland	1875	Hamilton
Wanderer	61623	Country Hr, NS	249	Bgtn	Country Hr, NS	1877	Gallihar, NS
Keepsake	6995	Whitehaven	275	Snow	Sunderland	1846	Middleton
Daisy	71389	Parrsboro, NS	24	Sch	Parrsboro, NS	1877	J George
Migumooweesoo	64019	Digby, NS	31	Sch	Freeport, NS	1872	A S Bonyun
Campanero	72401	Greenock	360	Bqtn	Sunderland	1875	Foulds/Bone
Somerville	58119	London	264	Brig	N Hilton/Tees	1868	Porter, Ldn

Sources: 'Agreement & Account of Crew' at Maritime History Archive, Nfld, National Archive or National Maritime Museum, Greenwich. Data also drawn from *Lloyd's Register of Shipping*, and *Mercantile Navy List* via CLIP Ships Index. ~~~ Data not found.
Notes: NB = New Brunswick; NC = New Caledonia; NS = Nova Scotia; NZ = New Zealand; SA = South Australia.

Appendix 2

Frank Thomas Bullen's Experience in Merchant Ships, 1869–1882

(Updated from Alston Kennerley, 'Global Nautical
Livelihoods in the Late Nineteenth Century: The Sea Careers
of the Maritime Writers Frank T Bullen and Joseph Conrad,
1869–1994', *International Journal of Maritime History*,
vol 26, no 1 (Feb 2014), 3–24, Appendix 1)

Ships' Names		Last ship if named on AAC	Age	Capacity	Boarded/Engaged		Discharged/Left	
Actual	Bullen				Date	Place	Date	Place
Caroline	Arabella	Not been to sea	12	Boy	28/03/1870	London	13/09/1870	Sant' Ana, M
Investigator	Discoverer	~~~~	13	Boy	13/09/1870	Sant' Ana, M	27/09/1870	Cayo Arena, M
Potosi	Potosi [French rescue ship] ~~~		13	Boy	~~~~	Cayo Arena, M	12/10/1870	Havana, C
Sea Gem	Sea Gem	Investigator	14[13]	Boy	27/10/1870	Havana, C	13/02/1871	Liverpool
Brinkburn	Bonanza	Investigator	14	Boy	04/06/1871	London	01/08/1871	Falmouth, J
Schooner	[Br Falmouth, J]	~~~~	14	DBS		Falmouth, J	~~~~	Kingston, J
Cuban SS	[possibly the steamer in the text]		14	DBS	~~~~	Kingston, J	07/10/1871	Liverpool
Western Belle	Western Belle	Brinkburn	16[14]	Boy	13/11/1871	Liverpool	23/01/1872	London
Pharos	Pharos	~~~~	16	OS	26/01/1873	London	14/05/1873	Melbourne
Wonga Wonga SS	[stowaway]	~~~~	16	St'way	14/05/1973	Melbourne	16/05/1973	Sydney
Helen McGregor SS	Helen M'Gregor	~~~~	16	Lamps	~~~~	Sydney	~~~~	Sydney
Wentworth SS	Wentworth	~~~~	16	Lamps	~~~~	Sydney	~~~~	Melbourne
Harrowby	Harrowby	~~~~	16	AB	04/03/1874	Sydney	06/11/1874	London
Rangitiki	Rangitiki	~~~~	17	AB	17/12/1874	London	19/03/1875	Pt Chalmers, NZ
Splendid	Cachalot/Splendid	~~~~	18	AB	13/05/1875	Pt Chalmers, NZ	13/06/1876	Pt Chalmers, NZ
West York	West York	~~~~	19	AB	11/09/1876	Pt Chalmers, NZ	05/05/1877	Belfast
Dartmouth	Dartmouth	West York	20	AB	23/05/1877	London	01/03/1878	London
Columbus	Magellan	Dartmouth	20	AB	18/03/1878	London	06/08/1878	Lyttleton, NZ

Ships' Names		Last ship if named on AAC	Age	Capacity	Boarded/Engaged		Discharged/Left	
Actual	Bullen				Date	Place	Date	Place
Bulwark	*Bulwark*	~~~	21	2M	07/08/1878	Lyttleton, NZ	26/11/1878	Adelaide
Day Dawn	*Day Dawn*	~~~	21	2M	27/11/1878	Adelaide	~~~	Noumea, NC
Schooner	[Fr Noumea, NC]	~~~	21	1M	~~~	Noumea ?	~~~	Noumea ?
Day Dawn	*Day Dawn*	~~~	21	2M	~~~	Noumea ?	13/02/1879	Brisbane
Harbinger	*Harbinger*	*Day Dawn*	22[21]	2M	21/03/1879	Adelaide	09/08/1879	London
Herat	*Herat*	*Harbinger*	22	AB	30/08/1879	London	26/01/1880	Calcutta
Britannia	*Britannia*	*Herat*	23	2M	26/01/1880	Calcutta	06/07/1880	Dundee
Wanderer	*Wanderer*	~~~	23	1M	17/08/1880	London	18/09/1880	N Sydney, CB
Keepsake	*Amulet*	~~~	23	1M	20/09/1880	N Sydney, CB	03/12/1880	Parrsboro, NS
Daisy	*Daisy*	~~~	23	1M	~~~	Parrsboro, NS	~~~	St Johns, A
Migumoovesoo	*Migumoovesoo*	~~~	23	1M	~~~	St Johns, A	~~~	Barbados
Campanero	~~~	*Daisy*	24	1M	03/03/1881	Barbados	03/08/1881	Rotterdam
Somerville	~~~	*Campanello*	24[23]	1M	18/10/1881	London	30/09/1882	London

Sources: AAC = 'Agreement and Account of Crew' at Maritime History Archive, Nfld, National Archive, or National Maritime Museum, Greenwich. Some dates derive from press ship movement reports. ~~~ Firm data not available.

Bullen's voyage descriptions in *Log of a Sea Waif*, *With Christ at Sea* and *Cruise of the Cachalot*, where some ship names are falsified.

Notes: Bullen's service in all his ships is informed by his description of each voyage, where facts seem reasonably reliable.

Bullen's Certificate of Competency as Second Mate, No 04758, 13 March 1878; his certificate as First Mate, No 04758, 5 August 1880.

DBS=distressed British seaman; OS=ordinary seaman; St'way=stowaway; lamps=lamp trimmer; AB=able seaman; 2M=2nd mate; 1M=1st mate.

A=Antigua; C=Cuba; CB=Cape Breton; J=Jamaica; M=Mexico; NC=New Caledonia; NB=New Brunswick; NS=Nova Scotia; NZ=New Zealand.

The AAC for SS *Cuban* does not list Bullen, so must be considered a representative steamer for his passage from Kingston to Liverpool.

Appendix 3

Frank Thomas Bullen (1857–1915): Books

The arrangement is in chronological order of first edition. Bullen's more successful books ran to multiple impressions/editions, and were marketed in the United States, Australia, New Zealand, and Canada, as well as throughout the British Isles. Bullen's literary agent was A P Watt, a firm still in business in London.

The Cruise of the 'Cachalot' Round the World After Sperm Whales (London, Smith Elder, December 1898), 400pp

Idylls of the Sea and Other Marine Sketches (London, Grant Richards, March 1899), 284pp [short stories & essays]

Log of a Sea Waif: Being Recollections of the First Four Years of My Sea Life (London, Smith Elder, October 1899), 349pp

The Way They Have in the Navy: Being a Day to Day Record of a Cruise in HM Battleship 'Mars' During the Naval Manoeuvres of 1899 (London, Smith Elder, October 1899), 96pp [paperback, 18 essays from *Morning Leader*]

The Palace of Poor Jack (London, Nisbet, September 1900), 82pp [seamen's welfare establishment]

Men of the Merchant Service: Being the Polity of the Mercantile Marine for Longshore Readers (London, Smith Elder, October 1900), 366pp

With Christ at Sea: a Religious Autobiography (London, Hodder & Stoughton, December 1900), 322pp

With Christ in Sailortown: What the Seamen's Mission is Doing (London, Hodder & Stoughton, March 1901), 126pp

A Sack of Shakings (London, Pearson, March 1901), 398pp [short stories & essays]

Deep Sea Plunderings: a Collection of Stories of the Sea (London, Smith Elder, October 1901), 362pp

Apostles of the South East (London, Hodder & Stoughton, December 1901), 340pp [religious novel]

A Whaleman's Wife (London, Hodder & Stoughton, October 1902), 388pp

A Sailor Apostle (London, Religious Tract Society, May 1903), 60pp [novel]

Sea Wrack (London, Smith Elder, November 1903), 330pp [short stories & essays]

Sea Puritans (London, Hodder & Stoughton, September 1904), 374pp [historical novel]
Creatures of the Sea (London, Religious Tract Society, October 1904), 374pp [marine science essays]
Back to Sunny Seas (London, Smith Elder, September 1905), 302pp [travel experiences]
Sea Spray (London, Hodder & Stoughton, February 1906), 314pp [short stories & essays]
Our Heritage the Sea (London, Smith Elder, November 1906), 362pp [maritime essays]
Frank Brown, Sea Apprentice (London, Nisbet, 1906), 347pp [children's novel]
A Son of the Sea (London, Nisbet, March 1907), 360pp [children's novel]
Advance Australasia: a Day to Day Record of a Recent Visit to Australasia (London, Hodder & Stoughton, May 1907), 276pp [23 essays in *The Standard* under the collective title 'Australia Revisited']
A Bounty Boy (London, Marshall Brothers, October 1907), 362pp [novel]
The Call of the Deep: Being Further Adventures of Frank Brown (London, Nisbet, 1907), 382pp [children's novel]
Confessions of a Tradesman (London, Hodder & Stoughton, March 1908), 304pp [autobiography]
Young Nemesis or *The Pirate Hunter* (London, Nisbet, September 1908), 380pp
Seed of the Righteous (London, R Culley, September 1908), 292pp
Beyond (London, Chapman & Hall, May 1909), 318pp
The Bitter South (London, R Culley, September,1909), 294pp [children's novel]
Cut Off from the World (London, Unwin, September 1909), 294pp
Told in the Dog Watches (London, Smith Elder, May 1910), 342pp [short stories and essays]
Fighting the Icebergs (London, Nisbet, September 1910), 380pp
The Royal Road to Riches: as Viewed from the Canadian Northern Railway System (London, Waterlow, 1910), 130pp [travelogue]
A Compleat Sea Cook (London, Partridge, October 1911), 306pp [children's novel]
From Wheel to Lookout (London, T W Laurie, May 1913), 284pp [short stories]
The Salvage of a Sailor (London, Partridge, September, 1913), 304pp
Light Ho! Sir, and Other Sketches (London, Religious Tract Society, September 1913 [reissue]), 180pp [short stories]
Songs of Sea Labour [with W F Arnold] (London, Orpheus Musical Publishers, May 1914), xviii + 35pp

Recollections: the Reminiscences of the Busy Life of One Who Has Played the Varied Parts of Sailor, Author and Lecturer ... [with portrait] (London, Seeley (March 1915), 312pp
Stories of Deep Sea Fish (London, *Boy's Own Paper*, June 1922), 194pp
Stories of Whales and Other Sea Creatures (London, *Boy's Own Paper*, June 1922), 148pp

A note on Bullen's literary output

Almost all Bullen's non-fiction volumes draw heavily on his sizeable production of newspaper columns and essays in magazines. Further, seven volumes above comprise collections of magazine articles. At his peak, the scale of his short-form writing is indicated by the 106 columns he contributed to the London newspaper *Morning Leader* between 8 May 1899 and 23 February 1900, at the rate of about three per week. In the same period an incomplete listing of his magazine articles numbered at least thirty. These short pieces brought Bullen his national and international reputation as the apologist for the merchant seafarer.

Notes

Chapter 1: Infancy to Street Arab

1. Old Ordnance Survey Maps, *Paddington 1872* (Gateshead, Godfrey Maps), London sheet 60. Surveyed in the mid 1860s, this map is representative of the area of Bullen's early childhood. The map names streets mentioned in Frank T Bullen, *Recollections* (London, Seeley Service, 1915), pp19–30.
2. www.british-history.ac.uk/ British History on Line, Paddington, Public Services. The term Lock Hospital derives from late medieval isolation provision for leprosy sufferers, but by 1747 when this facility was established, it referred to isolation treatment for venereal disease sufferers. The hospital had moved from Westminster to this Harrow Road site in 1842, and its chapel survived into the 1950s.
3. General Register Office, Registration District Kensington, sub-district St Mary, Paddington, County of Middlesex, 'Certified Copy of an Entry of Birth', registered 16 May 1857, informant Margaret Bullen, mother.
4. 1861 Census entry for 15 Desborough Terrace.
5. Ordnance Survey map, Paddington parish, 1893–96 edition, XLVIII. *London Streetfinder* [atlas] (London, Nicholson, 1986), map 137 W2, names Torquay Street. Bullen, in *Recollections* (1914), p21, mistakenly gives Marlborough Street as the name at that date.
6. Holy Trinity Church, Paddington, Register of Baptisms, at Marylebone Record Office. The contemporary street directory names only four householders in Alfred Road and none in Desborough Terrace.
7. Frank T Bullen, *With Christ at Sea: a Religious Autobiography* (London, Hodder and Stoughton, 1900), pp1–12;

Frank T Bullen, *Recollections: the Reminiscences of the Busy Life of One Who Has Played the Varied Parts of Sailor, Author and Lecturer* (London, Seeley Service, 1915), pp19–30.
8. *Recollections*, pp20, 29.
9. Kensington, 1a p8.
10. Kensington, 1a p8.
11. *Recollections*, p21.
12. 1861 Census, 15 Desborough Terrace, Paddington.
13. 1841 Census, Dial House, Brislington, Keynsham Bristol, RG10/15/39/12.
14. S J Curtis, *History of Education in Great Britain* (London, UTP, 1948), p118; see also John Lawson & Harold Silver, *A Social History of Education in England* (London, Methuen, 1973).
15. Bullen, *Recollections*, pp22–4.
16. 1891 Census RG 12/53/139/19.
17. Dr Sieveking was a widely reported physician and medical lecturer in that period.
18. 1871 Census, RG 10/15/39/12.
19. *With Christ at Sea*, p12.
20. Frank T Bullen, *Confessions of a Tradesman* (London, Hodder & Stoughton, 1908), pp1–24.
21. *Confessions of a Tradesman*, pp15–19.
22. Census 1871, RG 10/875/108.

Chapter 2: First Voyage in Four Ships

1. Details about the ships Bullen served in are given in Appendix 1.
2. Frank T Bullen, *The Log of a Sea-Waif: Being the Recollections of the First Four Years of My Sea Life* (London, 1899), pp1–2. See also Frank T Bullen, *With Christ at Sea: a Religious Autobiography* (London, 1900), pp14–39.
3. Henry Mayhew, *Mayhew's London: being Selections from 'London Labour and London Poor' by Henry Mayhew* (London, 1851, 1969, ed Peter Quennell), p29.

4. Frank T Bullen, *The Confessions of a Tradesman* (London, 1908), pp38–49. According to the 1882 London directory the King's Head was at 49 Upper Thames Street.
5. For Bullen writing about crimps see 'Blue Book, c 9265: of Crimps, Bumboatmen, Sharks and Captains', *Morning Leader* (Monday, 5 June 1899), 6d. Bullen's articles in *Morning Leader* about seafarers and sailortown may be compared with the articles in the *Morning Chronicle* two decades earlier, part of the extensive series on 'Labour and the Poor'.
6. *Shipping and Mercantile Gazette* (2, 19 March 1870). From ten entries in *SMG* between 13 July 1869 for *Caroline*, p385, Gibbs, Millwall Dock, that ship was laid up for over six months before Bullen took over as master.
7. *The Log of a Sea Waif*, p2.
8. *The Mercantile Navy List 1864* (London, HMSO, 1864) alphabetical list of certificates of competency for masters and mates. The entry was coded: OC = ordinary master.
9. Maritime History Archive, St John's, Newfoundland, 'Agreement and Account of Crew', *Caroline*, ON 908, Voyage ending at Cork, 11 February 1871, p1; hereafter AAC *Caroline*.
10. AAC *Caroline*, Official Log, p2; unusually Captain Bullen records the dates crew members boarded the ship in West India Docks, the Blackwall Basin, prior to locking out into the River Thames, and at anchor off Gravesend. But Thomas Bullen's name is not among them.
11. *The Log of a Sea Waif*, p19.
12. Board of Trade/HMSO, *Notice of Examination of Masters and Mates under the Merchant Shipping Act of 1854 and of Engineers under the Merchant Shipping Act Amendment Act, 1862* (London 1863), p1.
13. *The Log of a Sea Waif*, pp27–31. Bullen uses 'chantey' but 'shanty' and other spelling variations are commonly found.
14. AAC *Caroline*. The official log contains certificates from the shipping master regarding the crew's refusal to work, their imprisonment, and the engagement of substitute seamen, thus confirming the essence of Bullen's description of events.
15. The precise location of Santa Ana is uncertain. The modern city of Campeche has a district of that name. Bullen names Tonala River, Tupilco, as well as Sant' Ana and Campeche in his writing. *The Log of a Sea Waif*, p45; *Christ at Sea*, p35; 'Alligators and Mahogany' in *A Sack of Shakings* (London, 1902), p101. AAC *Caroline*. Prior to being off Sant' Ana, Captain Bullen locates entries at Fontbeara (probably Frontera, Bay of Campeche), and Balwartie (not identified).
16. The sources consulted were the *Shipping and Mercantile Gazette* via the British Newspaper Archive for ships' movements; *Lloyd's Register of Shipping*, 1849 to 1870, for ship particulars; *The Mercantile Navy List*, 1860 and 1870, via the CLIP Ship's Index. See also *With Christ at Sea*, pp39–46. *Investigator* is named in connection with birds landing on ships in 'Country Life Aboard Ship', in Frank T Bullen, *A Sack of Shakings* (London, 1901), pp158–60.
17. AAC *Caroline*. After Sant' Ana *Caroline* went on to Galveston, Texas (about 6 November 1870), and to Nassau, New Providence island (Bahamas; about 7 December 1870), and finally to Queenstown/Cork, Ireland, for orders, where the voyage was terminated for the crew.
18. Cayo Arenas is marked on navigation charts in Lat 22° 07′ N, 91° 25′ W. *The Log of a Sea Waif*, pp53–60; see also Frank T Bullen, 'My First Shipwreck', *Cornhill Magazine*, vol 77 (February 1898), pp230–42.
19. MHA Newfoundland, AAC of *Investigator*, ON 23229, voyage terminated on 27 September 1870, by grounding. An entry in the official log of the previous voyage is a reprimand for being asleep on lookout and putting the man in irons for disobeying orders and abusive behaviour.
20. Bullen, 'A Waking Nightmare', in *Idylls of the Sea*, pp72–8.
21. *The Log of a Sea Waif*, pp62–75; see also Frank T Bullen, 'Havana in 1870', *Cornhill Magazine*, vol 78 (July 1898), pp53–65. See also *With Christ at Sea*, pp46–60.
22. *Morning Post* (19 December 1871) notes that a hurricane passed over Havana on 19 November 1870.

23. *The Log of a Sea Waif*, pp76–93; Maritime History Archive, St John's, Newfoundland, 'Agreement and Account of Crew', *Sea Gem*, ON 35472, voyage completed at Liverpool, 13 February 1871.
24. Handling a sailing ship at sea with reference to *Sea Gem* is discussed in 'The Way of a Ship' in Frank T Bullen, *A Sack of Shakings* (London 1901), pp173–5.

Chapter 3: A Voyage in Three Ships
1. *The Log of a Sea Waif*, pp94–100. See also *With Christ at Sea*, pp56–9.
2. So far 'Mr R' has not been identified.
3. See Alston Kennerley, 'Joseph Conrad at the London Sailors' Home', *The Conradian*, vol 33, no 1 (Spring 2008), pp69–102.
4. *The Log of a Sea Waif*, pp101–14.
5. Alston Kennerley, 'Ratings for the mercantile marine: the roles of charity, the state and industry in the pre–service education and training of ratings for the British Merchant Navy, 1879–1939', *History of Education*, vol 28, no 1 (1999), pp31–51.
6. *The Log of a Sea Waif*, pp115–27. MHA, Nfld, AAC and OL for *Brinkburn*, ON 54835, voyage ending 8 August 1871 at Falmouth Jamaica.
7. *The Log of a Sea Waif*, pp128–42.
8. MHA, Nfld, AAC and OL for SS *Cuban*, ON51424, voyage ending in Liverpool 7 October 1871.
9. *The Log of a Sea Waif*, p139.

Chapter 4: A Voyage without a Change of Vessel
1. *The Log of a Sea Waif*, pp143–59. See also *With Christ at Sea*, p60.
2. MHA, Agreement and Account of Crew of *Western Belle*, ON 48822, 1225 tons, voyage beginning 14 November 1871 in Liverpool and ending on 25 November 1872 in London. *The Log of a Sea Waif*, pp159–67.
3. *The Log of a Sea Waif*, pp168–77.
4. See also F T Bullen, 'The Passing of Peter', in *Idylls of the Sea* (London, Grant Richards, 1899), pp1–8.
5. *The Log of a Sea Waif*, pp178–88.
6. *The Log of a Sea Waif*, pp189–202.
7. *The Log of a Sea Waif*, pp192–3.

8. *The Log of a Sea Waif*, pp203–9.
9. 'Agreement and Account of Crew' of *Western Belle*, voyage ending 25 November 1872.
10. 'Country Life on Board Ship', in Frank T Bullen, *A Sack of Shakings* (London, 1901), pp113–28. This episode first appeared in Frank T Bullen, *The Cruise of the Cachalot* (London, 1898), pp186–8.
11. *The Log of a Sea Waif*, pp210–21.

Chapter 5: Sea Time in Coastal Steamers
1. *The Log of a Sea Waif*, pp222–32. See also *With Christ at Sea*, pp61–3.
2. http://freepages.rootsweb.com/, 'Cohasset's Deep Sea Mariners', *History of Cohassett*, p567.
3. https://mariners.records.nsw.gov.au/, Crew and passenger list of *Pharos*, arriving Sydney from Melbourne, 3 July 1873. This was the ship's passage after Bullen had deserted, along with a section of the then crew, at Melbourne.
4. *The Log of a Sea Waif*, pp233–45. See also *With Christ at Sea*, pp64–6.
5. *The Log of a Sea Waif*, p246. See also *With Christ at Sea*, p63.
6. https://mariners.records.nsw.gov.au/, Crew and Passenger List for *Wonga Wonga* arriving Sydney from Melbourne, 30 July 1869. Although Bullen's passage in *Wonga Wonga* was four years after this example, the crew was probably little different. The number of passengers would vary, of course, with demand.
7. https://mariners.records.nsw.gov.au/, Crew and Passenger list for *Helen McGregor* arriving Sydney from Melbourne, 6 April 1867.
8. *The Log of a Sea Waif*, pp259–71.
9. https://mariners.records.nsw.gov.au/, Crew and passenger list of SS *Wentworth* arriving Sydney from Melbourne on 10 February 1874.
10. *The Log of a Sea Waif*, pp272–82. See also *With Christ at Sea*, pp66–80.
11. https://mariners.records.nsw.gov.au/, Crew list of *Harrowby* arriving Sydney from Mauritius, 30 December 1873.
12. *The Log of a Sea Waif*, pp283–94.
13. *The Log of a Sea Waif*, pp295–308.
14. *The Log of a Sea Waif*, pp309–18.
15. *The Log of a Sea Waif*, pp319–32.
16. *The Log of a Sea Waif*, pp333–44.
17. *With Christ at Sea*, pp78–80.

Chapter 6: A Voyage in a Whaler

1. *The Log of a Sea Waif*, pp344–9; *With Christ at Sea*, pp81–4.
2. Alan Bott, *The Sailing Ships of The New Zealand Shipping Company, 1873–1900* (London, Batsford, 1972), pp17, 21, 26, 53–7, 79, 117–18.
3. *Otago Daily Times* (25 March 1875). In this period the New Zealand newspapers were using the spelling *Rangitikei* for the ship's name.
4. *Otago Daily Times* (5 April 1875).
5. National Maritime Museum, Mates' and Masters' qualifications filed under certificate No 04758. See Chapter 7 for a discussion of the licensing system.
6. 'From a New Zealand Nautical Correspondent', 'The Solander Whaling Ground', *Dundee Advertiser* (28 March 1887). This appears to be Bullen's first essay in print, and makes it clear he was there, though he does not name the ship. In 'A Day on the Solander Whaling-Ground', *Chamber's Journal* (24 March 1894), pp186–8, he is not named as author, but names *Splendid*; in F T Bullen, 'Humpbacking in the Friendly Isles', *Good Words* (1895), pp627–34, he names *Splendid* and the first mate, Mr Earle, later master, without concealment.
7. These are easily followed in the digitised newspapers using the Papers Past – New Zealand facility.
8. The data here is drawn partly from the CLIP Ships Index entries for *Splendid*, and New Zealand newspaper reports of about her movements: *Otago Daily Times* (3 February 1874, 9 May 1874, 15 October 1874, 27 October 1874, 1 April 1875, 24 April 1875).
9. *Otago Daily Times* (15 October 1874).
10. Rhys Richards, 'The Whaleship *Splendid* of Otago Confirmed as the Model for Frank Bullen's Fictitious *Cachalot*', *Turnbull Library Record*, vol 51 (July 2019), pp56–69. I am indebted to Rhys Richards for his transcriptions of parts of the Mackay diaries, including Mackay's lists of crew names, and for transcriptions of American and New Zealand newspaper reports about *The Cruise of the Cachalot*.
11. *Otago Daily Times* (2 March 1876, 6 March 1876).
12. Cited in an article in *Dominion* (Wellington, NZ) (17 March 1943), using material from a New York newspaper, *The Brooklyn Eagle*, of about 1902.
13. *Brooklyn Daily Eagle* (27 January 1901, 21 February 1901, 18 March 1901).
14. *Otago Daily Times* (29 February 1876).
15. *Otago Witness* [a weekly paper] (10 June 1876), p11, transcribed from a copy supplied by the Alexander Turnbull Library, National Library of New Zealand, Wellington. An identical block was previously published in the *Otago Daily Times* (6 June 1876), and a similar report appeared in *The Otago Guardian* (6 June 1876), supplied by the Hocken Library, University of Otago. The journalist uses the term 'Journal', but this reads like the master's voyage report to his owners, effectively an abstract from the ship's deck log of day-to-day activity aboard ship. There would also be an official log required by the Merchant Shipping Acts in which untoward events, like damage to the ship, illness, injury and death, running for shelter, etc, had to be recorded.
16. *Chambers's Journal* (24 March 1894), pp186–8; *Good Words* (1895), pp627–34.
17. G A Mawer, *Ahab's Trade: the Saga of South Seas Whaling* (New York, St Martin's Press, 1999), pp109–12.
18. *Evening Star*, (24 July 1876). See also *With Christ at Sea*, pp110–25.
19. *Otago Daily Times* (31 July 1876, 16 August 1876). The AAC for this *West York* voyage has not been discovered.
20. *With Christ at Sea*, pp123–71.

Chapter 7: Another Voyage in a Single Ship

1. *With Christ at Sea*, pp171–87.
2. *With Christ at Sea*, p177.
3. Frank T Bullen, 'Sailor's Pets', *A Sack of Shakings* (London, Pearson, 1901), pp 334–40.
4. *Lloyd's List* (8 September 1877).
5. Stephen Davis, *Strong to Save: Maritime Mission in Hong Kong from Whampoa Reach to the Mariners' Club* (Hong Kong, City University of Hong Kong Press, 2017).
6. Frank T Bullen, 'A Reminiscence of Manila', *National Review*, vol 31, no 186 (August 1898), pp856–67.
7. Bullen, 'A Reminiscence of Manila', p858.

8. *Lloyd's List* (5 January 1878; 2 March 1878).
9. Bullen, *The Men of the Merchant Service*, p124.
10. Board of Trade, *Notice of Examinations of Masters and Mates for Certificates of Competency under 'The Merchant Shipping Act', 1854, and of Engineers Under the Merchant Shipping Act Amendment Act, 1862* (London, HMSO, 1863). Successor updates were issued frequently with minor changes. Examples of textbooks include: J W Norie, *A Complete Epitome of Practical Navigation ... 21st ed* by Arthur B Martin (London, Charles Wilson, 1877); John Merrifield and Henry Evers, *Navigation and Nautical Astronomy for the Use of Students and Practical Men* (London, Longmans, 1873); for Bullen's summary of the syllabus see his *The Men of the Merchant Service*, pp122–3.

Chapter 8: Mixed Experiences in Five Vessels

1. *With Christ at Sea*, pp190–204.
2. Frank T Bullen, 'The Chums', *Deep Sea Plunderings* (London, Smith, Elder, 1901), pp183–92.
3. *Lloyd's List* (21 March 1878).
4. Frank T Bullen, *Men of the Merchant Service: Being the Polity of the Mercantile Marine for 'Longshore Readers* (London, Smith Elder, 1900), pp30–1.
5. *With Christ at Sea*, p197.
6. *Star* (NZ) (15 July 1878).
7. Bullen, *With Christ at Sea*, pp204–8; Bullen, *Men of the Merchant Service*, pp131–2.
8. *Globe* (NZ) (22 August 1878).
9. *Globe* (5 September 1878); *Evening Journal* (Adelaide) (7 October 1878).
10. *Evening Journal* (Adelaide) (1 November 1878); *Express and Telegraph* (Adelaide) (21 November 1878); Bulwark Lodge held a meeting in the Oddfellow's Hall.
11. *With Christ at Sea*, pp208–30.
12. Bullen, *Men of the Merchant Service*, p38.
13. Frank T Bullen, *Recollections: The Reminiscences of the Busy Life of One who has Played the Varied Parts of Sailor, Author and Lecturer* (London Seeley, Service, 1915), pp33–5.
14. *Morning Bulletin* (Rockhampton) (3, 10 December 1878, 27 February 1879); *The Week* (Brisbane) (7 December 1878); *Toowoomba Chronicle* (January 1879).
15. See for example *Sydney Daily Telegraph* (31 January 1880).
16. *Telegraph* (Brisbane) (10 February 1879); *Brisbane Courier* (11, 14, 15 February 1879); the incident was widely reported in the press.
17. *With Christ at Sea*, pp235–42.
18. Basil Lubbock, *The Colonial Clippers* (Glasgow, Brown, Son & Ferguson, 1921, 1948), pp232–6.
19. Harold A Underhill, *Sail Training and Cadet Ships* (Glasgow, Brown, Son and Ferguson, 1956), pp69–71.
20. Lubbock, *The Colonial Clippers*, p233.
21. Bullen, *Men of the Merchant Service*, pp146–7, 232.
22. Bullen, *Men of the Merchant Service*, p32.
23. Bullen, *Men of the Merchant Service*, p158.
24. Bullen, *With Christ at Sea*, pp243–4.

Chapter 9: A Voyage in Two Ships

1. Bullen, *With Christ at Sea*, pp245–59.
2. 1881 Census, RG1/735/43/47.
3. *Lloyd's List* (5 September 1879).
4. Bullen, *With Christ at Sea*, pp246–7.
5. Basil Lubbock, *The Last of the Windjammers Volume 1* (Glasgow, Brown Son & Ferguson, 1927), pp28, 240, 236); William L H Scarratt, *Lives and Work at Sea: Herbert Holdsworth, Colin Hannah, and the Ship Ladakh* (New York, Regatta, 2004), pp1–9. This book examines another Bates ship, its crew and a voyage, in detail.
6. *Lloyd's List* (1 January 1880, 11 June 1880).
7. *With Christ at Sea*, pp255–7.
8. In the writing about the development of the ministry to seafarers in Calcutta, there was mention of the surname Bullen: 'A Mr Bullen, a Merchant Navy officer' supporting the work there under the leadership of the Rev Charles Plomer Hopkins. However, that was in 1891, after FTB had left the sea and before he became a public figure in 1899, so that was probably a different Bullen; we cannot rule out, though, support through correspondence. R W H Miller, *Priest in Deep Water: Charles Plomer Hopkins and the 1911 Seamen's Strike* (Cambridge, Lutterworth, 2010), p87.

9. Bullen, *With Christ at Sea*, pp261–6.
10. *Shipping and Mercantile Gazette* (12 March 1880).
11. Frank T Bullen, *The Men of the Merchant Service* (London, Smith Elder, 1900), pp191–2. Bullen first used this experience in his discussions of ships' stewards in Chapter 21 of this book.
12. *Mercantile and Shipping Gazette* (7 July 1880).
13. Alston Kennerley, 'Joseph Conrad at the London Sailors' Home', *The Conradian*, vol 33, no 1 (Spring 2008), pp69–102.
14. Board of Trade, *Notice of Examinations of Masters and Mates under the Merchant Shipping Act, 1854, and of Engineers under the Merchant Shipping Act Amendment Act, 1862* (Form Exn 1, HMSO, 1863).
15. Bullen, *Men of the Merchant Service*, pp77–81.
16. Bullen, *Men of the Merchant Service*, pp123–30; Alston Kennerley, 'Early State Support of Vocational Education: the Department of Science and Art Navigation Schools, 1853–1863', *Journal of Vocational Education and Training*, vol 52, no 2 (2000), pp211–24.

Chapter 10: Two Voyages in Six Vessels
1. *Lloyd's List* (5 August 1880; 19 August 1880).
2. Frank T Bullen, *With Christ at Sea* (London, Hodder & Stoughton 1900), pp266–9.
3. Frank T Bullen, 'The Way of a Ship', *A Sack of Shakings* (London, Pearson, 1902), p171.
4. *Shipping and Mercantile Gazette* (5 October 1880).
5. See also Frank T Bullen, 'The Cook of the *Wanderer*', *Deep Sea Plunderings* (London, Smith Elder, 1901), pp288–97.
6. Bullen, *With Christ at Sea*, pp269–90; Bullen, 'The Skipper of the *Amulet*', *A Sack of Shakings*, pp60–70.
7. Maritime History Archive, Newfoundland, *Keepsake*, ON 6995, voyage ending at Little River 27 December 1880, General Register and Record Office of Shipping and Seamen, London, minutes and correspondence. See also Alston Kennerley, 'Alfred Holt's First Nautical Adviser: Captain Isaac Middleton, 1819–1878', *Liverpool*

Nautical Research Society Bulletin, vol 64, no1 (June 2020), pp34–41.
8. Bullen, *With Christ at Sea*, pp275–6.
9. *British Parliamentary Papers*, Report from the Select Committee on Shipwrecks of Timber Ships with the Minutes of Evidence, Appendix and Index, House of Commons, (18 June 1839).
10. Bullen, *With Christ at Sea*, pp287–8.
11. *Lloyd's List* (28 December 1880); *Shipping and Maritime Gazette* (29 December 1880). The reports describe the call at St John as 'for a harbour'.
12. *Lloyd's List* (30 December 1880). According to *Lloyd's List* (22 December 1880) Lloyd's [insurance] had received a confidential report concerning *Keepsake*.
13. *Bullen With Christ at Sea*, pp290–2. See also 'The Cruise of the *Daisy*' in Frank T Bullen, *Idylls of the Sea* (London, Grant Richards, 1899), pp25–31.
14. www.crewlist.org.uk, Crew list index project [CLIP] accessed October 2020. Bullen names *Daisy* as his last ship when signing on *Campanero*.
15. Bullen, *With Christ at Sea*, pp293–9.
16. Bullen, *With Christ at Sea*, pp300–1; Bullen, 'Country Live Aboard Ship', *A Sack of Shakings*, pp140–5.
17. Bullen, *With Christ at Sea*, pp301–11.
18. MHA, Newfoundland, AAC of *Campanero*, ON 72401, tonnage 360, Voyage ending 3 August 1881.
19. National Maritime Museum Cornwall, Bartlett Library, Fox Register of Vessel Arrivals in 1881.
20. Frank T Bullen, *Recollections: the Reminiscences of the Busy Life of One who has Played the Varied Parts of Sailor, Author and Lecturer* (London, Seeley, Service, 1915), p75.
21. Robin Ward, *The World of the Medieval Shipmaster: Law, Business and the Sea, c.1350–1450* (Woodbridge, Boydell and Brewer, 2009), pp192–4.
22. MHA, Newfoundland, 'Agreement and Account of Crew' for *Somerville*, ON 58119, for voyage ending 30 September 1882.
23. *Lloyd's List* (20 October 1881, 30 September 1882).
24. *Somerville* AAC contains a letter from Captain Wootton to the shipping office superintendent accounting for a missing consular endorsement, and

including the explanation that he was ill at the time.

25. Bullen, *Recollections*, p76.
26. F T Bullen, 'The Slaver', in *Idylls of the Sea and Other Marine Sketches* (London, Grant Richards, 1899), pp18–24.
27. Bullen, *Recollections*, pp35–6.
28. Alston Kennerley, 'Global Nautical Livelihoods: the Sea Careers of the Maritime Writers Frank T Bullen and Joseph Conrad', *International Journal of Maritime History*, vol 26, no 1 (February 2014), pp3–14, Appendix 1, 'Frank Thomas Bullen's Experience in Merchant Ships, 1869–82'. When this paper was written the real name of Bullen's first ship had not been discovered, and Bullen's cited year, 1869, was accepted.

Chapter 11: Struggles Making a Life Ashore in London

1. 1881 Census, RG1/735/43/47.
2. 1861 Census, RG 09/396/33/19.
3. Bullen, *Reminiscences*, p51.
4. I am indebted to Mark Beswick, Archive Information Officer, Met Office National Meteorological Archive, Exeter, for searching out this information from the Meteorological Council annual reports.
5. *Aberdeen Press and Journal* (28 January 1903). This contains a few column inches of Bullen's reply to an inquiry about his biography.
6. *British Imperial Calendar* 1891, Meteorological Office, 63 Victoria Street.
7. F T Bullen, 'The Working of the Weather Office', *Good Words* (July 1898), pp491–4.
8. Alston Kennerley, 'The Education of the Merchant Seaman in the Nineteenth Century (University of Exeter, unpublished MA thesis by research, 1978), Appendix 12, 'Training Ship Staff and Salaries, 1878', p227.
9. *Pall Mall Gazette* (21 January 1919). He was in a bus on his way to work.
10. See for example William Allingham, 'Board of Education Examinations in Navigation and Nautical Astronomy, in *Nautical Magazine*, vol 71 (1902), pp463–76; and 'Foreign Seamen in British Merchant Ships', in *Nautical Magazine*, vol 71 (1902), pp741–53.

11. Frank T Bullen, *Confessions of a Tradesman* (London Hodder & Stoughton, 1908), p62 onwards.
12. 'Arthur Twidle' by Robert J Kirkpatrick, bearalley.blogspot.com/2018/arthur-twidle.html.
13. *Recollections*, pp51–6.
14. Frank T Bullen, *The Apostles of the South East* (London, Hodder & Stoughton, 1901).
15. *Recollections*, 'Preface'.
16. Data sourced from transcriptions of birth and death registrations. *Hull Daily Mail* (18 May 1908), Steamer *Hazelmoor* arrived at the River Tyne on 16 May 1908 when her master reported the death of Bullen's eldest son at Ancona (Italy, Adriatic coast, about 120 nautical miles south of Venice), in March in a cliff fall.
17. *Confessions of a Tradesman*, pp210–11.
18. *London Gazette*, no 26607 (15 March 1895), p1576; no 26688 (19 March 1895), p1742; no 27132 (2 November 1899), p6656; no 27146 (22 December 1899), p8593.
19. 'Literary Gossip, 1898', *The Globe* (31 December 1898), p6.

Chapter 12: Success in Self Employment as Lecturer and Writer

1. *London Daily News* (22 May 1901); *London Evening Standard* (16 December 1901); *Manchester Courier* (18 April 1902); *London Daily News* (7 March 1903).
2. *The Times* (18 May 1901); *The Queen* (27 December 1902); *London Evening Standard* (7 November 1904); *The Times* (19 September 1907); *Kentish Mercury* (29 April 1910).
3. *The Times* (30 November 1898); *London Daily News* (28 February 1908).
4. *Sheffield Daily Telegraph* (6 July 1899), advertisement.
5. *Dundee Evening Post* (21 October 1901), interview report. Breathing problems are mentioned in *Recollections*, p257.
6. *Westminster Gazette* (2 January 1901).
7. *Recollections*, pp125–6. *Western Morning News* (12 March 1902), lecture advertisement.
8. Not to be confused with Devonport's Mechanics' Institute, which was in a separate borough. Alston Kennerley, *The Making of the University of Plymouth* (Plymouth, University

of Plymouth, 2000), pp9–11.
Advertisement in the *Western Morning News* (6 March 1902) for the lecture on 12 March 1902.

9. *Western Evening Herald* (13 March 1902).
10. *Recollections*, pp222–4.
11. *Pall Mall Gazette* (22 January 1898).
12. *Surrey Comet* (7 March 1903).
13. *Cambridge Daily News* (30 August 1901).
14. Outward Passenger List SS *Tagus* departing from Southampton on 13 April 1904, cabin passengers. SS *Tagus*, 3056 tons net, 5545 tons gross, 1100hp, built 1899. The other ships Bullen travelled in on this round voyage were SS *Eden*, 1374 tons net, 2145 tons gross, 350hp, built 1882, and SS *Orinoco*, 2451 tons net, 4572 tons gross, 870hp, built 1886. Sources: Clip Ships Index: *Mercantile Navy Lists*.
15. Frank T Bullen, *Back to Sunny Seas* (London, Smith, Elder, 1905).
16. *Table Talk* [Melbourne] (12 April 1906).
17. 'Australia Revisited', *The Standard* [London] (3 December 1906 to 31 December 1906), thirteen articles; 'Australia Revisited', *The Standard* [London] (2 January 1907 to 23 January 1907), ten articles. [Twenty-three articles published at three per week (M,W, F); edited versions published as *Advance Australasia* (1907)].
18. Outward Passenger List SS *Omrah* from London departing 8 March 1906. His age was entered erroneously as forty-one, instead of forty-nine. SS *Omrah*, built 1898, 4419 tons net, 8130 tons gross, 1350hp, Orient Steam Navigation Coy.
19. Frank T Bullen, *Advance Australasia: a Day-to-Day Record of a Recent Visit to Australasia* (London, Hodder & Stoughton, 1907, pp14–17.
20. *Advance Australasia*, p53.
21. *Sydney Morning Herald* (26 May 1906); *Advance Australasia*, p85. SS *Ortona* built 1899, 4115 tons net, 7945 tons gross, 1750hp, Pacific Steam Navigation Company.
22. *Advance Australasia*, pp119–22. See also John Ramsland, 'Life Aboard the Nautical School Ship, *Sobraon*, 1891–1911, *The Great Circle*, vol 3, no 1 (April 1981), pp29–45.

23. SS *Zealandia*, built 1899, 1736 tons net, 2771 tons gross, 437hp, Huddart Parker.
24. *Advance Australasia*, pp151–6. SS *Oswestry Grange*, built 1902, 4742 tons net, 7368 tons gross, 860hp, owned by Houlder Brothers.
25. *Recollections*, pp227–37.
26. Frank T Bullen, *The Royal Road to Riches: The Canadian Northern Railroad System* (London, Waterlow, 1910).
27. British Consulate, Madeira, Death Certificate dated 21 July 1997, registered 27 February 1915; death occurring 26 February 1915 at Funchal, Madeira. Burial at the English Cemetery, Funchal.
28. *Aberdeen Press & Journal* (28 January 1903).
29. *Sketch* (11 July 1900).
30. Frank T Bullen, *The Way They Have in the Navy: being a day-to-day record of a cruise in HM battleship 'Mars' during the naval manoeuvres of 1899* (London, Smith, Elder, 1899), 96pp. The discussion of Bullen's literary output is informed by Alston Kennerley, 'Frank Thomas Bullen, 1857–1915: Whaling and Nonfiction Maritime Writing', *The American Neptune*, vol 56, no 4 (Fall, 1996), pp353–70.
31. See Alston Kennerley, 'Frank Thomas Bullen: Christian Maritime Author', *Maritime Mission Studies*, no 2 (Autumn, 1995), pp49–54.
32. *British Parliamentary Papers*, 1912–1913 (167), Civil list pensions. List of all pensions granted during the year ended 31 March 1912, and payable under the provisions of section 9 (1) of the Civil List Act, 1910: '13 July 1911, Mr Frank Thomas Bullen, £100, In consideration of the literary merits of his writings.'
33. *Recollections*, pp44–7.
34. Registers of electors for Melbourn, Cambridgeshire, and Bournemouth, Hampshire; 1939 Census return for Martha Tappenden.
35. *Recollections*, 'Publisher's Note', 4 March 1915; Register of Death, British Consulate Madeira, 27 February 1915. English Cemetery Funchal burial register, grave no 396. In the 1990s North American Bullen descendants paid for a headstone to be erected.
36. E-mail message, Diana Peters (great-granddaughter, née Culbard) to Alston Kennerley, 22 October 1997.

Sources and Bibliography

Primary sources
Frank T Bullen books are listed in Appendix 3

Digital archives
British History Online, www.british-history/ac/uk
British Newspaper Archive, britishnewspaperarchive.co.uk
Brooklyn Daily Eagle, www.nypl.org/.../brooklyn-daily-eagle-online-1841-1902
Crew List Index Project [CLIP], https://www.crewlist.org.uk
Crew lists entering Australian ports, https://mariners.records.nsw.gov.au
Find My Past, findmypast.co.uk for census, b, d and m data, register of electors, passenger
    lists, etc
Lloyds Register of Shipping [annual], hec.lrfoundation.org.uk/archive.library/lloyds-
    register-of-ships-online
Mercantile Navy List [annual] via CLIP
Papers Past [New Zealand newspapers], paperspast.natlib.govt.nz/newspapers
The Spectator, archive.spectator.co.uk
Trove [Australian newspapers], trove.nla.gov.au/search/advanced/category/newspapers
http://freepages.rootsweb.com

Archives
Maritime History Archive (MUN, St John's, Newfoundland, Canada), 'Agreements and List
    of Crew'
Marylebone Record Office [London]
The National Archives (UK), BT 'Agreements and List of Crew' and Official Log Books
National Maritime Museum (UK), 'Agreements & List of Crew', Certificates of Competency
National Maritime Museum Cornwall, Bartlett Library, Fox Register of Vessel Arrivals in
    1881

Contemporary publications
Board of Trade/HMSO, *Notice of Examination of Masters and Mates under the Merchant
    Shipping Act of 1854 and of Engineers under the Merchant Shipping Act Amendment Act,
    1862* (London, HMSO 1863).
British Imperial Calendar (London, 1891)
British Parliamentary Papers, Report from the Select Committee on Shipwrecks of Timber
    Ships with the Minutes of Evidence, Appendix and Index, House of Commons (18 June
    1839).
British Parliamentary Papers, 1912–1913 (167), Civil list pensions. List of all pensions
    granted during the year ended 31 March 1912, and payable under the provisions of section
    9 (1) of the Civil List Act, 1910
London Gazette, no 26607, 26688, 27132, 27146 (1895–1899)
Mackay, Robert Percy, deck apprentice, whaler *Splendid* c1874–1877, Diary courtesy of Rhys
    Richards (ed), 'Robert Percival Mackay: Carpenter's Boy on the *Splendid*, 1875–1877' (nd)
Mayhew, Henry, *Mayhew's London: being Selections from 'London Labour and London Poor'
    by Henry Mayhew* (London, 1851, 1969, ed Peter Quennell).
——, 'London Labour and London Poor', letters published in *Morning Chronicle* (January to
    May 1850), on London merchant shipping, merchant seafarers, seamen's lodging houses,
    seafaring charities.

SOURCES AND BIBLIOGRAPHY

Merrifield, John, and Henry Evers, *Navigation and Nautical Astronomy for the Use of Students and Practical Men* (London, Longmans, 1873)
Norie, J W, *A Complete Epitome of Practical Navigation* ... 21st, ed Arthur B Martin (London, Charles Wilson, 1877)
Stansfeld-Hicks, C, *Our Boys and What to do with Them: the Merchant Service, What it is and How to Enter It* (London, Sampson Low, Marston, Searle, & Rivington, 1886)

Secondary sources
Allingham, William, 'Board of Education Examinations in Navigation and Nautical Astronomy, *Nautical Magazine*, vol 71 (1902), 463–76
——, 'Foreign Seamen in British Merchant Ships', *Nautical Magazine*, vol 71 (1902), 741–53
Bott, Alan, *The Sailing Ships of The New Zealand Shipping Company, 1873–1900* (London, Batsford, 1972)
'Cohasset's Deep Sea Mariners', http://freepages.rootsweb.com/
Curtis, S J, *History of Education in Great Britain* (London, UTP, 1948)
Davis, Stephen, *Strong to Save: Maritime Mission in Hong Kong from Whampoa Reach to the Mariners' Club*, (Hong Kong, City University of Hong Kong Press, 2017)
Innes, Hammond, 'Introduction', Frank T Bullen, *The Cruise of the Cachalot The Log of a Sea-Waif* (London, Collins, 1953), 9–12
Kennerley, Alston, 'The Education of the Merchant Seaman in the Nineteenth Century (University of Exeter, unpublished MA thesis by research, 1978)
——, 'Bullen, Frank Thomas, 1857–1915', *Dictionary of National Biography: Missing Persons* (Oxford, OUP, 1993), 100–1
——, 'Frank Thomas Bullen: Christian Maritime Author', *Maritime Mission Studies*, No 2 (Autumn 1995), 49–54.
——, 'Frank Thomas Bullen: Whaling and Non-Fiction Maritime Literature', *American Neptune*, vol 56, no 4 (Fall 1996), 353–70 [published 1997]
——, 'Ratings for the mercantile marine: the roles of charity, the state and industry in the pre-service education and training of ratings for the British Merchant Navy, 1879–1939', *History of Education*, vol 28, no 1 (1999), 31–51
——, 'Early State Support of Vocational Education: the Department of Science and Art Navigation Schools, 1853–1863', *Journal of Vocational Education and Training*, vol 52, no 2 (2000), 211–24
——, *The Making of the University of Plymouth* (Plymouth, University of Plymouth, 2000)
——, 'Bullen, Frank Thomas, 1857–1915', *Oxford Dictionary of National Biography* (Oxford, OUP, 2004)
——, 'Joseph Conrad at the London Sailors' Home', *The Conradian*, vol 33, no 1 (Spring 2008), 69–102
——, 'Global Nautical Livelihoods in the Late Nineteenth Century: the Sea Careers of the Maritime Writers Frank T Bullen and Joseph Conrad, 1869–1994', *International Journal of Maritime History*, vol 26, no 1 (February 2014), 3–24.
——, 'Alfred Holt's First Nautical Adviser: Captain Isaac Middleton, 1819–1878', *Liverpool Nautical Research Society Bulletin*, vol 64, no 1 (June 2020), 34–41
Kirkpatrick, Robert J, 'Arthur Twidle', bearalley.blogspot.com/2018/arthur-twidle.html
Lawson, John, and Harold Silver, *A Social History of Education in England* (London, Methuen 1973)
Lubbock, Basil, *The Colonial Clippers* (Glasgow, Brown, Son & Ferguson, 1921, 1948)
——, *The Last of the Windjammers Volume 1* (Glasgow, Brown, Son & Ferguson, 1927)
Mawer, G A, *Ahab's Trade: the Saga of South Seas Whaling* (New York, St Martin's Press, 1999)
Miller, R W H, *Priest in Deep Water: Charles Plomer Hopkins and the 1911 Seamen's Strike* (Cambridge, Lutterworth, 2010)
Ramsland, John, 'Life Aboard the Nautical School Ship, *Sobraon*, 1891–1911', *The Great Circle*, vol 3, no 1 (April 1981), 29–45
Richards, Rhys, 'The Whaleship *Splendid* of Otago Confirmed as the Model for Frank Bullen's Fictitious *Cachalot*', *Turnbull Library Record*, vol 51 (July 2019), 56–69.
Scarratt, William L H, *Lives and Work at Sea: Herbert Holdsworth, Colin Hannah, and the Ship Ladakh* (New York, Regatta, 2004), 1–9
Underhill, Harold A, *Sail Training and Cadet Ships* (Glasgow, Brown, Son and Ferguson, 1956)
Ward, Robin, *The World of the Medieval Shipmaster: Law, Business and the Sea, c1350–1450* (Woodbridge, Boydell and Brewer, 2009)

195

Index

Note: Invented ship names are in quotation marks, eg 'Discoverer'; actual ship names are in italics, eg *Caroline*.

Freepost Plus RTKE-RGRJ-KTTX
Pen & Sword Books Ltd
47 Church Street
BARNSLEY
S70 2AS

DISCOVER MORE ABOUT MARITIME AND NAVAL HISTORY

Seaforth PUBLISHING is the country's leading maritime book publisher, producing the very best reference books, narrative histories, ship monographs and modelling books, all reflecting the latest research and designed and printed to the highest standards.

Can we stay in touch? From time to time we'd like to send you our latest catalogues, promotions and special offers by post. If you would prefer not to receive these, please tick this box. ☐

We also think you'd enjoy some of the latest products and offers by post from our trusted partners: companies operating in the clothing, collectables, food & wine, gardening, gadgets & entertainment, health & beauty, household goods, and home interiors categories. If you would like to receive these by post, please tick this box. ☐

We respect your privacy. We use personal information you provide us with to send you information about our products, maintain records and for marketing purposes. For more information explaining how we use your information please see our privacy policy at www.pen-and-sword.co.uk/privacy. You can opt out of our mailing list at any time via our website or by calling 01226 734222.

Mr/Mrs/Ms ....

Address...

Postcode...................................... Email address...

Website: www.seaforthpublishing.com – Email: enquiries@seaforthpublishing.com
Telephone: 01226 734555

Sunda Straits, East Indies, 94
Sunday school, 5,
Superintendent, Shipping Office, 16
Surrey Commercial Dock, 131
Sydney, NSW, 61, 67

Tales of Unrest, 156
tallying, 144
Tamatave, Madagascar, 144, 145
Taylor, Miss, 165
teachers of navigation, 98–102
teetotal crew, 108
temporary employment, 31
Thames Street, Tower Hamlets, 11, 32
tidal rise and fall, 133
tiers, ship mooring, 11
Times, The, 157
Tobago, 165
Tonga, island group, 85
Tonola River, Mexico, 142
Torres Strait, 67
towage, 47
Tower of London, 12
training schools for seamen, 32–3
training ship, 49
Transmission of Wages scheme, 118
travel to lectures, 160–1
Trinidad, 165
Trinity House pilot, 56
Tupilco, Mexico, 21
Turk, James, 90
Twidle, Arthur, 151

Union Steamship line, 169
United States, 78–83, 139, 145, 164
unloading coal, 94
unmooring, 24
Uppingham School, 161

Venezuela, 165
visiting preacher, 160
visual aids, 153
voyage (definition), viii, 16

wages payment, 144
watch selection, 48
water collection, 50
Watt, A P, 158
Way They Have in the Navy, The, 171
Wellington, NZ, 168
West Australian, 167
West India Dock, 13, 14, 19, 131
West India Dock Road, London, 32, 57
West Indies, 145
West Indies & Pacific SS Co, 38
Westbourne Grove, 9
Westbourne Park railway station, 5, 8
Western Evening Herald, 161
Westminster Abbey, 92
Whaleman's Wife, A, 164, 172
whaling, 77–88, 170–1
Whampoa, Canton, 95
Wickham Court, Bromley, 10
Willesden, London, 92
Williamstown, Melbourne, 60
Windward Islands, 165
With Christ at Sea, vii, viii, 5, 164, 172
workhouses, 1, 7
Writ of Capias, 138

Yarmouth Harbour, NS, 139
yellow fever, 26, 41, 42
York Cottage, 159
Young England magazine, 170
Young Men's Christian Association, 161
Yukatan peninsula, 21, 24, 142

Zanzibar, 143, 144

The Author

Alston Kennerley was born into a seafaring family and his own early experience at sea included ten months' service as a cadet aboard the German four-masted barque *Passat*. Later, after reading History at the University of Wales, Lampeter, he went into teaching and became Principal Lecturer in the Institute of Marine Studies at the University of Plymouth. He retired in 2000, since when he has maintained an active research portfolio in maritime social history.